UNITY IN HARDY'S NOVELS

UNITY IN
HARDY'S NOVELS

'Repetitive Symmetries'

Peter J. Casagrande

The Regents Press of Kansas
Lawrence

First published in the UK 1982 by
THE MACMILLAN PRESS LTD

First published in the USA 1982 by
THE REGENTS PRESS OF KANSAS
Lawrence, Kansas 66045

ISBN 0 7006 0209 7

Printed in Hong Kong

To my parents and brothers
to my children
to my wife, Pamela

In broad detail certain general states of nature recur, and . . . our very natures have adapted themselves to such repetitions. But there is a complementary fact which is equally true and equally obvious:– Nothing ever really recurs in exact detail. No two days are identical, no two winters. What has gone has gone forever.

Alfred North Whitehead, *Science and the Modern World* (1925)

Contents

Acknowledgements   ix
Note on the Texts   x

Introduction   1

1 **Hardy's Deterioristic Mode of Regard**   12
   The Break with Higher Bockhampton   14
   The Failure of Love and Marriage   27
   The Failure of a Redemptive Faith   41
   The Futility of Architectural Restoration and the
      Poetics of Futility   52

2 **'Thinking o' Perfection': the Novels and Poems
      to 1875**   61
   Hope Unblooms: the Poems of the 1860s   63
   'The Poor Man and the Lady'   69
   Desperate Remedies (1871)   74
   'Man's Goodnesse': *Under the Greenwood Tree* as
      Comedy of Forgiveness   81
   A Pair of Blue Eyes (1873)   85
   Gabriel Oak and the 'Art Which Does Mend Nature'   95
   Oak as Agent of Rational Nature   105

3 **'Nothing Backward Climbs': the Futility of
      Return in *The Return of the Native*, *The
      Woodlanders* and *The Well-Beloved***   115
   The Hand of Ethelberta (1876)   118
   Son and Lover: the Dilemma of Clym Yeobright   126
   Another Version of the Same: *The Woodlanders* (1887)   143
   The 'Native of Natives': Jocelyn Pierston of *The Well-
      Beloved*   153
   The 'Poems of 1912–13': Hardy's Poetic Narrative of
      Return   160

4 **'Twice-Over Cannot Be': the Futility of Restoration in *The Mayor of Casterbridge*, *Tess of the d'Urbervilles* and *Jude the Obscure*** 170

Three 'Architectural' Novels: *A Laodicean*, *The Trumpet-Major* and *Two on a Tower* 175

The Architectural Matrix of *The Mayor of Casterbridge* 183

Tess versus *Jude* 199

Conclusion: 'One Man's Literary Purpose' 219

Notes 224
Select Bibliography 240
Index 244

Acknowledgements

My thanks go first to those scholars and critics of Hardy whose work has been a constant guide and inspiration, in particular Dale Kramer, J. Hillis Miller, Michael Millgate, Harold Orel, Frank Pinion, Robert Schweik and Robert Gittings. Gittings's *Young Thomas Hardy* and *Thomas Hardy's Later Years*, both of which appeared during the course of my preparation and writing, unlocked many doors for me. For many fruitful conversations about Hardy and things Hardian I am grateful to Marlene Springer and particularly to my distinguished colleague Harold Orel, as well as to the students and faculty of English 998 in the autumns of 1977 and 1978. Two teachers, Edna Imhof and Irvin Ehrenpreis, set standards of expression and scholarship that I continue to try to meet. Part of chapter 3 is based on an earlier study which I completed in 1971 and which appeared in *English Literary History*, vol. xxxviii, and I should like to thank the Johns Hopkins University Press for permission to reproduce this material. Financial support from the University of Kansas General Research Fund and from the National Endowment for the Humanities freed me from other duties and enabled me to study in England in 1973–4. Much of my time there was spent in the Dorset County Museum, and I am indebted, like so many other students of Thomas Hardy, to Mr Roger Peers, Museum Curator, for his unfailingly kind assistance. Finally, to those generous and hospitable natives of Dorset who opened their homes to my family and me during our visit I tender a very special thanks.

Note on the Texts

References to Hardy's fiction (except *An Indiscretion in the Life of an Heiress*) are from the Wessex Edition, titled *The Works of Thomas Hardy in Prose and Verse* (London: Macmillan, 1912–31). The following works of fiction are cited in this study. Each is preceded by the initials used throughout to identify it and is followed by the date of its first publication in book form.

DR	*Desperate Remedies* (1871)	
UGT	*Under the Greenwood Tree* (1872)	
PBE	*A Pair of Blue Eyes* (1873)	
FMC	*Far from the Madding Crowd* (1874)	
HE	*The Hand of Ethelberta* (1876)	
RN	*The Return of the Native* (1878)	
TM	*The Trumpet-Major* (1880)	
L	*A Laodicean* (1881)	
TT	*Two on a Tower* (1882)	
MC	*The Mayor of Casterbridge* (1886)	
W	*The Woodlanders* (1887)	
TD	*Tess of the d'Urbervilles* (1891)	
JO	*Jude the Obscure* (1895)	
WB	*The Well-Beloved* (1897)	

Other works by Hardy are cited from the following editions:

ILH	*An Indiscretion in the Life of an Heiress* (1878), ed. Carl J. Weber (Baltimore, Md.: Johns Hopkins University Press, 1935)
CP	*The Complete Poems of Thomas Hardy*, ed. James Gibson (London: Macmillan, 1976)
PW	*Thomas Hardy's Personal Writings*, ed. Harold Orel (Lawrence, Kansas: University of Kansas Press, 1966)

Life   Florence Emily Hardy, *The Life of Thomas Hardy 1840–1928* (London: Macmillan, 1962).

The *Life* was first published in two volumes, *The Early Life of Thomas Hardy* (1928) and *The Later Years of Thomas Hardy* (1930). Though the name of the second Mrs Hardy appears on the title-page, the *Life* is Hardy's own work. All references are from the one-volume edition.

Introduction

This study is organized, as its title suggests, around the premise that there is a pattern and a unity in Hardy's novels, and that by describing this pattern we can discern a unity, that is, a number of structural and thematic kinships and concerns that can help us to view the novels as parts of a single process and as expressions of a particular temperament. This approach to Hardy's fiction began some years ago as an attempt to describe the motif of return, or homecoming, in *Under the Greenwood Tree*, *The Return of the Native* and *The Woodlanders* (*English Literary History*, xxxviii [1971]). My purpose then, as now, was to do two things: to plot a new way of grouping Hardy's novels for reading and teaching them; and, on the basis of this, to reinterpret them with reference chiefly to their internal kinships. Hardy's use of the same story in a comic novel of 1872, a tragic novel of 1878, and a tragi-comic novel of 1887 seemed to me then, as it does now, more than the result of the pressures of serial publication. His treatment in different modes of the story of a native's return suggests that what he himself liked to call his 'tentativist' or 'impressionist' way of thinking may have shaped his fiction even more than critics have realized.

To the reader who may fear that such an approach to the novels cannot help but oversimplify them, I would point out that no less a contemporary of Hardy's than Marcel Proust recognized 'the repetitive symmetries of Hardy's work as a whole' and placed Hardy among those writers who create the same work over and over again in their lives: 'the great writers have never written more than a single work, or rather have refracted across diverse milieux that unique beauty which they bring into the world'.[1] D. H. Lawrence, so admiring of Hardy in other ways, was not so sympathetic as Proust with the repetitions he found in Hardy's novels: he almost snorted in disgust at finding *Jude*, in his terse phrase, 'only *Tess* turned round about'.[2] Closer comparison of *Tess* and *Jude* might have shown Lawrence that there is indeed a turnabout between the two – an exhibition of the regenerative power of tragedy in *Tess*, a total rejection of tragic values in *Jude*. A similar tentativism is at work between *The Mayor of Casterbridge* and the three novels that immediately precede it, *The Trumpet-Major, A Laodicean* and *Two on a Tower*, though in this group the dominant motif is not return, as in *Greenwood Tree, The Return* and *The Woodlanders*, but the analogous, cognate one of restoration, the attempt to retrieve a lost innocence and its attendant glory. My approach is that of the practical critic seeking to explore and illuminate what the novels in their kinships invite. If I seem to simplify Hardy, it is only that I might display certain strongly recurrent patterns and themes in the novels. I do not wish to minimize the differences between Hardy's novels, but to suggest a context in which these differences might be usefully explored. It is important to my argument, and to any understanding of Hardy's genius, that the richness and variety within the apparent simplicity be seen.

Thus two basic patterns can be seen in the fiction. There are the major novels of return (*Under the Greenwood Tree, The Return of the Native, The Woodlanders*) and the major novels of restoration (*Far from the Madding Crowd, The Mayor of Casterbridge, Tess of the d'Urbervilles* and *Jude the Obscure*), and all have their antecedents or rehearsals in early or in minor novels: e.g. *Madding Crowd* and *Tess* in *A Pair of Blue Eyes; The Return* in *A Laodicean; The Mayor* in the three novels that immediately preceded it. In the novels of return Hardy depicted the attempt – always painful – to return to one's native place after long absence. In the novels of restoration he exhibited the struggle – always futile – to atone for error or mend defect. The theme in both is the same – there is no return, no restoration. The minor novels, most of which Hardy himself described as romances, fantasies or novels of ingenuity, are those in which he set aside his stern belief in the unregenerateness of things to entertain various means of regeneration or remedy. It is an obvious and striking fact that in all the novels (and in many of the stories and poems[3]) Hardy's subject is the desire – almost always hopeless – to alter or retrieve things past.

A working definition of some key terms – return, restoration, redemption, remedy and regeneration – is here in order. The last, 'regeneration', I use as inclusive of the first four, as the general term for Hardy's persistent concern to depict the difficulties of getting back to first things and of trying to undo the ravages of time. By 'return' I mean homecoming, as in Clym Yeobright's return to Egdon Heath and his birthplace at Bloom's End. 'Restoration' takes on two distinct but often analogous meanings in the novels, one architectural and one moral: the attempt to reinstate an ancient edifice to its former condition, as in Stephen Smith's efforts with Endelstow Church in *A Pair of Blue Eyes*; or the attempt to recover an earlier and purer moment of life, as in Henry Knight's attempt, in the same novel, to recover a lost childhood simplicity through love of Elfride. The illusoriness of architectural restoration is used frequently to comment on the difficulty, if not the impossibility, of moral restoration. By 'redemption' is meant the traditional Christian belief in regeneration through a supernatural agency, a belief that Hardy himself knew and abandoned but continued to scrutinize closely, almost wistfully, throughout his career. By 'remedy' I mean the secular or purely human substitute for supernatural renewal, as in Cytherea Graye's forgiving Miss Aldclyffe or Abel Whittle's loyalty to Michael Henchard at the end of *The Mayor*. These four terms – return, restoration, redemption, remedy – convey Hardy's varying but at the same time constant concern for the plight of uprooted or grievously flawed men and women, for those who long to return to their origins and those who yearn for a lost innocence.

The fundamental unity of form and content suggested by these considerations is confirmed when we consider them together with the actual sequence in which the novels appeared (see the table on p. 4). The first thing to be said about this division of the novels is that it is somewhat illusory, for the two motifs are almost never used in total isolation from one another. Because they are vehicles for the same emotion and idea – the sad irreparability of things – the story of return and the story of restoration constantly dissolve into one another. The beginnings of the narrative of return, fully dominant for the first time in *Greenwood Tree*, are in the social dilemmas of *déracinés* such as Will Strong of 'The Poor Man' and Edward Springrove of *Desperate Remedies*; and, in the novels of restoration, return or homecoming always figures in an important way. For example, the awkward homecoming of Stephen Smith in *A Pair of Blue Eyes* amplifies the failure of restoration in the same novel; the successful return of Bob Loveday in *The Trumpet-Major* enlarges and enhances the happily illusive restoration of things past that occurs there. And Michael Henchard, Tess Durbeyfield and Jude Fawley all, in the course of their unregenerate lives, return to settings of an innocence to which they cannot be restored (Henchard to Weydon-Priors, Tess to Marlott, Jude to Marygreen). In these novels,

Novels of restoration	*Novels of return*

1. 'The Poor Man and the Lady' (1867)
2. *Desperate Remedies* (1871)

3. *Under the Greenwood Tree* (1872)

4. *A Pair of Blue Eyes* (1873)
5. *Far from the Madding Crowd* (1874)

6. *The Hand of Ethelberta* (1876)
7. *The Return of the Native* (1878)
   − −[*An Indiscretion in the Life of an Heiress* (1878)]

8. *The Trumpet-Major* (1880)
9. *A Laodicean* (1881)
10. *Two on a Tower* (1882)
11. *The Mayor of Casterbridge* (1886)

12. *The Woodlanders* (1887)

13. *Tess of the d'Urbervilles* (1891)

14. *The Well-Beloved* (1892, 1897)

15. *Jude the Obscure* (1895)

thwarted homecoming or thwarted return is a symbol of thwarted regeneration.

Conversely, the question of restoration, especially as it emerges through Hardy's concern with guilt and forgiveness, arises in all the novels of return. Parson Maybold's struggle to forgive Fancy Day her wayward affections, Ethelberta's regret for having deserted her Wessex home, Clym's remorse over his mother's and wife's deaths, George Melbury's wish to atone to Giles Winterborne's father by making an offering of Grace to Giles, Jocelyn Pierston's guilty fear lest he betray Aphrodite by loving her human incarnations – all this guilt and sorrow, usually unrelieved, is the equivalent in moral terms of the social disruption that accompanies the homecomings. The questions of return and restoration were cognate questions for Hardy, and this probably accounts for his recurring use, in both groups of novels, of strikingly similar character-types, the most important one being the 'nostalgic idealists', figures such as Henry Knight, Clym Yeobright, Angel Clare, Sue Bridehead and Jocelyn Pierston, men and women whose troubled sexuality almost always profoundly affects the destinies of their flawed mates. Knight cannot forgive Elfride's having loved another; Clym cannot put off his devotion to his mother; Clare cannot forgive Tess's ruin; Sue clings desperately to her virginity at the same time that she coquettes; Pierston pursues an ideal love from mother, to daughter, to granddaughter and beyond.

A second point, hardly visible on the chart, is that the novels of return are, in different ways, novels set in nature (a forest, a heath, a granite isle). In contrast, in the novels of restoration nature is either displaced by or joined with architecture as the dominant element of the setting. The meaning of this is discussed more fully in Chapter 4, but it can be noted here that after 1880 the ruinous or rotting edifice – Stancy Castle, Ring's Hill Speer, the houses and inns of Casterbridge, the d'Urberville tomb, the colleges of Christminster – comes to the centre of Hardy's fiction as a symbol of the decadence and unregenerateness he saw in humanity and its institutions.

A third point, and one important to any understanding of Hardy's development as a novelist, is that the narratives of return were, by and large, products of the 1870s, when Hardy first gained literary success, then married and found it necessary to break almost completely with his family and his rural background. Not only were *Greenwood Tree*, *Ethelberta* and *The Return* written in these years, but it is certain that *The Woodlanders* was conceived and outlined in the mid 1870s and highly likely that *The Well-Beloved* was conceived, perhaps even sketched, then as well.[4] Thus the novels of return, in conception if not always in composition, precede the novels of restoration, *Greenwood Tree* coming before *Blue Eyes* and *Madding Crowd*, *Ethelberta* and *The Return* before *The Mayor* and its three predecessors of the 1880s, *The Woodlanders* before *Tess*, *The Well-Beloved* (in its serial form) before *Jude*. This is more than a mere statement of the obvious. The story of return was a deeply personal one for Hardy. After all, he began his career as a novelist only upon his return to Higher Bockhampton in 1867 after five years in London; and his first five novels were written in Dorset. Similarly, his return to Dorchester in 1881, after living elsewhere for nearly a decade, marked the beginning of his period of greatest productivity.[5] Homecoming, the return to beginnings, whether in fact or in fiction, nurtured and stimulated Hardy's creative genius. He simply did not write well when away from his native place, and contemplation of the problem of separation from beginnings fed and informed his greatest narratives. The story of return was not, of course, unique to him. In different ways and to different ends, Homer, Plato, Virgil, Dante, Goethe and Wordsworth all told the same story. Though Hardy knew his great predecessors, his narratives of homecoming, as well as his novels of restoration that proceed out of them, are highly personal in origin and manner. The fundamental assertion of *The Mayor*, of *Tess* and of *Jude* – that regeneration is either impossible or horribly painful – grew out of the cognate discovery, distressingly personal, in *The Return* and *The Woodlanders*, that going home again is a difficult and, finally, an insoluble problem. Hardy is a *homely* writer in a root sense of the word, an exhibitor of the beauty of men's hopeless yearning for what Søren Kierkegaard has called 'the first existence'.[6]

Finally, running through both the novels of return and the novels of restoration is a similar modal pattern. The movement from pastoral romance and comedy in *Greenwood Tree*, to tragedy in *The Return of the Native*, to tragi-comedy in *The Woodlanders* has its counterpart in the movement from pastoral romance and comedy in *Madding Crowd* and *The Trumpet-Major*, along an ascending scale of realism to near-tragedy in *Two on a Tower*, tragedy in *The Mayor* and *Tess*, and anti-tragedy or irony in *Jude* (a novel that defies categorization). The movement resembles what Northrop Frye has described as the shift in Western fiction from a mythic, to a high mimetic, to a low mimetic or ironic mode. This shift reflects, according to Frye, a sense that 'the hero's power of action' is in decline from 'godlike heroism' to 'all-too-human irony'.[7] The tendency in Hardy's novels, both in the stories of return and the stories of restoration, is from a romantic or comic mode marked by pastoral conventions to a low mimetic or ironic mode marked by tragic ones. Thus from the imperfect but humanly amendable worlds of Fancy Day and Gabriel Oak we move toward the imperfect, irremediable and hostile worlds of Sue Bridehead and Giles Winterborne.

As these last remarks may suggest, a study of the pattern of Hardy's fiction soon becomes an inquiry into the view of things inherent in the cognate stories that make the pattern. Return and restoration were for Hardy metaphors of what for him and his age was a larger issue, aptly described by Lionel Trilling in a famous essay as a concern for salvation.[8] Hardy's version of this concern, given his religious upbringing and his nostalgic temperament, took the form of a quest for regeneration through the return to or restoration of things past. Having lost at an early age all his trust in the definitively Christian teaching that fallen man can be delivered from the bondage of sin only by a supernatural agency, Hardy fell back, his scepticism unimpaired, on the secular myth of regeneration through return and that myth's psychological analogue, the story of moral restoration through human agencies. From Hardy's highly sceptical treatment of all these myths it seems clear that, though he shared his age's concern with salvation, he distrusted and rejected its belief in human means of remedy and amelioration. He opposed this prevailing belief in progress with his view of time as decay and change as irrecoverable loss. Hardy is well described, I think, as a highly self-critical and highly reluctant primitivist, a believer by temperament in the absolute superiority of first things who was always tormented by the intellectual certainty that first things are beyond recovery.

The roots of this view – which can be called deteriorism – are traceable to four encounters with irretrievable loss that shook Hardy between 1840 and 1880. The first was personal and social – his separation by education, by work and by marriage from his beloved family, his natal spot, and from an almost ghostly 'simpler self' that for him always resided at Higher Bockhampton. Hardy's desire to bridge the gap between his early and later years was, I believe, the chief motive for his return to Dorset in 1867 and 1881 and the seminal impulse behind his stories of thwarted homecoming. The same motive probably played a part in his courting and marrying the childlike, sequestered Emma Gifford, though he would discover that for him conjugal love could not replace the love he had known as a child at Bockhampton, a love he was coming to regard as ideal. The failure of his marriage would constitute his second experience of the irretrievable. His third encounter with the irretrievable had already occurred, as I have noted. It was theological – his rejection of Christian supernaturalism, in particular his childhood faith's promise of spiritual renewal and everlasting life. Hardy's loss of faith has usually been thought of as complete by 1865, but his views on the Resurrection and the Redemption seem never to have been settled. They surface in *Tess* and *Jude*, in *The Dynasts*, and in poems and memoranda to the end of his life. Hardy's fourth experience of the irreparable came in architecture, in his gradual realization by 1872 that his work as a restorer of crumbling Gothic churches was false and destructive.

No return, no Redemption, no restoration – Hardy's departure from Higher Bockhampton, his loss of faith, his unhappy marriage and his work in architecture combined to teach him to view time, history and consciousness as aspects of a process of irreversible decline. From the very beginning of his career as a writer he embraced this deterioristic view of things as an accurate account of 'Nature's defects'. At the same time, as he went on to remark in a note of 1876, he sought through 'the *art* of poetry and novel-writing' to make 'these defects the basis of a hitherto unperceived beauty, by irradiating them with "the light that never was" on their surface, but is seen to be latent in them by the spiritual eye' (*Life*, p. 114). Hardy's novelistic art took the form of variations on the twin stories of return and restoration, with the result several interpretations of the same phenomenon, that is, of the defect in nature that inexorably drives men and women from their early felicity, or makes them nearly helpless victims of their characters and circumstances. The result of this play of intellect and imagination is an aesthetic and multiple rather than a metaphysical and integrated rendering of nature's defects. Hardy saw in nature's misworkings a beauty that he wished to convey to his readers. Perception of this beauty-in-ugliness was what for him could ultimately redeem defective nature in the eyes of suffering humanity. Though he believed there was nothing men and women could do to alter nature's misworking, he did not think them utterly helpless if they could learn to look on things with an eye to the beauty of the truth, however ugly, that nature does not exist to comfort man.

Deterioration or degeneration was not, of course, the whole story for Hardy. And critics such as Roy Morrell have shown convincingly that Hardy often allows for the successful working of intelligence, will and affection.[9] But to make too strong a case for human means of amendment in Hardy's world is to ignore not just the frequency with which human means fail in that world, but, more important, the beauty with which Hardy endowed the human failures. Why, for example, did Hardy find the original conclusion to *The Return of the Native*, which would have left Thomasin and Diggory unmarried, superior to the second, the happy, one? Because the original, in which Diggory was 'to have retained his isolated and weird character to the last, and to have disappeared mysteriously from the heath, nobody knowing whither – Thomasin remaining a widow', was more 'consistent' and more 'true'; but also, and equally important, more expressive of that unorthodox beauty, suggested by the words 'isolated', 'weird' and 'mysteriously', that the novel was designed to exhibit. 'Haggard Egdon', we are told in the first chapter of the novel, 'appealed to a subtler and scarcer instinct, to a more recently learnt emotion, than that which responds to the sort of beauty called charming and fair'. A happy ending smacks of Heidelberg, Baden, the Alps – of an 'orthodox' scenic beauty unacquainted with tragic reality. Why, to take a second example, is the appeal of such a wretchedly imperfect man as Michael Henchard of *The Mayor* made so much greater for us than that of the resourceful, successful and humane Donald Farfrae? And why does Hardy lend so powerful a dignity and pathos to Henchard's last moments of life through the simple and eloquent words of Abel Whittle? We might ask the same about Marty South's role in *The Woodlanders*. Why is her appeal made so much greater than that of the sensible, realistic and forgiving Grace Melbury, the heroine of the novel? It could not have been mere pastoral sentiment that led Hardy to give Marty the novel's magnificent last sentences, probably the finest he ever wrote:

> 'Now, my own, own love,' she whispered, 'you are mine, and only mine; for she has forgot 'ee at last, although for her you died! But I – whenever I get up I'll think of 'ee, and whenever I lie down I'll think of 'ee again. Whenever I plant the young larches I'll think that none can plant as you planted; and whenever I split a gad, and whenever I turn the cider wring, I'll say none could do it like you. If ever I forget your name let me forget home and heaven! . . . But no, no, my love, I never can forget 'ee; for you was a good man, and did good things.   (ch. 48)

These words seem designed to convey more than the superiority of a rustic to a civilized sensibility, and indeed they do. They convey the beauty of the irremediable suffering and the irreparable loss that occasioned them, the beauty of Marty's wholly futile struggle against the deathward tendency of things. To make too much of Hardy as either a covert or misinterpreted champion of human possibility or of man's freedom to 'strive against the *natural* flow of things'[10] is to diminish something of great importance – the beauty he shows us in the process of decay he depicts as life, the human

value of what he called in *Tess* 'a negative beauty of tragic tone' (ch.
45). After all, the question is not only whether life is as grim as
Hardy says it is, but also how Hardy endows the grim spectacle he
exhibits. There was for him, and there can be for Hardy's reader, a
beauty in it, a beauty born of the sad truth of the irreparability of
things. *Sunt lacrimae rerum.*

This seems to have been Hardy's point in the note of 1876 quoted
above. He would make the same point, but even more compellingly,
in chapter 12 of *Tess*, where he gives us Tess, a 'maiden no more',
upon her return to her native Vale of Blakemore after her fall.
Several weeks have passed since the night in the Chase with Alec,
and the ruined maid, filled with loathing for her seducer and for
herself, has returned to the place of her innocence. But she knows
her innocence is beyond recovery.

> The incline was the same down which d'Urberville had driven
> with her so wildly on that day in June. Tess went up the
> remainder of its length without stopping, and on reaching the
> edge of the escarpment gazed over the familiar green world
> beyond, now half-veiled in mist. It was always beautiful from
> here; *it was terribly beautiful to Tess to-day*, for since her eyes last fell
> upon it she had learnt that the serpent hisses where the sweet
> birds sing, and her views of life had been fatally changed for her
> by the lesson. Verily another girl than the simple one she had
> been at home was she who, bowed by thought, stood still there,
> and turned to look behind her. She could not bear to look forward
> into the Vale. (emphasis added)

We shall have occasion later, in chapter 4 of this study, to look more
closely at this particular episode. Here it may simply be noted that
the phrase 'terribly beautiful' describes not only Tess's hard-won
knowledge that life is a baffling mixture of good and evil but also
Hardy's sense that there is a peculiar beauty in loss. One is reminded
perhaps of the 'terrible beauty' born to Yeats in the wake of death in
'Easter, 1916', and of Keats's remark in one of his letters that the
intensity of art, of a play such as *King Lear*, for example, makes 'all
disagreeables evaporate, from their being in close relationship with
Beauty and Truth'. Life is a mixture of good and evil terrible in its
beauty; and it was Hardy's endeavour, as he declared in 1876, to
irradiate this sense of life with 'the light that never was'. He
borrowed this phrase, interestingly enough, from Wordsworth's

'Elegiac Stanzas', where it describes Wordsworth's optimism before the death of a brother destroyed his belief in nature and the imagination. Hardy's choice of the phrase suggests what both the pattern of his life and the pattern of his novels suggest, that he worked at the urging of a powerful nostalgia, an irresistible need to reach back in an act of natural piety to defeat change and restore things past. But he made this retrospective effort more in sadness than in hope, for his sense of the irretrievable was stronger than his belief in the possibility of regeneration through any agency – human, natural or divine. This sadness, compassionate rather than melancholy, is the great humanizing emotion of the novels. It produced Wessex, that half-real, half-dream world through which Hardy found it paradoxically possible to show the inevitable passing of those very things he was in the act of preserving in his memoried narratives of return and restoration.

I have arranged the four parts of my study so as to show both the important structural kinships among the novels and the shifting treatment of the motifs of return and restoration throughout them. In chapter 1 I discuss some of the biographical circumstances surrounding Hardy's deterioristic view of things. In chapter 2, I describe Hardy's handling of return and restoration in the novels and poems he wrote between 1867 and 1875. The major novels of return and restoration can be seen to have their formal origins in these early works: the novels of return, my subject in chapter 3, in *Under the Greenwood Tree*; the novels of restoration, the subject of chapter 4, in *A Pair of Blue Eyes* and *Far from the Madding Crowd*.

1 Hardy's Deterioristic Mode of Regard

> I have wanted to know him ever since I found out how much
> his experiences had dictated his statuary . . . .   (*WB*, ii, ch. 2)

The young lady's remark in *The Well-Beloved* about the sure connection between Pierston's romantic experiences and his art raises one of the most interesting of all literary questions: how does the experience of an author dictate or shape his art? It is a question made almost impossibly difficult by the word 'experience', by which can only be meant the totality of an author's perceptions. There must be, we know, as many answers as there are authors and possible combinations of experiences. For Hardy, the question was, as he asserted repeatedly, the crucial one. 'A writer who is not a mere imitator', he wrote in 'The Profitable Reading of Fiction' (1888), 'looks upon the world with his personal eyes, and in his particular moods; thence grows up his style, in the full sense of the term.' My discussion of the novels will suggest that Hardy's moods and personality led him to view the world as would a man distressed by the process of irremediable decay he saw inexorably at work there, and that his style – in the broad sense of the word – is essentially repetitive, taking the form of a series of fictional variations on a single theme, the theme of regeneration. The seminal experience of leaving home and family and returning to them is explored and re-explored throughout the novels of return at the same time that a cognate story, the story of moral restoration, is explored and re-explored in the novels of restoration. But why should this be so? How did Thomas Hardy come to look upon the world as a spectacle of thwarted efforts of regeneration?

Four events in Hardy's life, all different in appearance but alike for him in tendency and form, shaped his deterioristic way of seeing things and exposed his temperament, an essentially nostalgic one. These were his departure from and return to his native Dorset in

1862–7 and again in 1874–81, his loss of religious faith between about 1859 and 1865, his disillusionment with his work as a restorer of Gothic churches by about 1872, and his disappointment with love and marriage by 1879, if not before. Hardy's first forty-three years, more than half of his life, take the form of an odyssey. The Dorset boy, deeply attached to his family, his birthplace and his early religious experience, moving by age nine in a rhythm of departure and return that was to shape his life for the next thirty-four years, and marked by a 'lateness of development in virility' (*Life*, p. 32), returned to his native place as a successful novelist at age forty-three. This homecoming in the 1880s repeated the homecoming of 1867, when, after five transformative years in London, Hardy had returned to live restlessly at home at Higher Bockhampton and to write his first five novels. Nearness to that dear place was necessary to his writing, and yet he could not live there comfortably, so great were the changes brought on him by work and study in London.

The other three events that occurred between 1856 and 1883 anticipated or repeated certain elements of this initial uprooting. In the late fifties, at the same time as he was reading the *Essays and Reviews* and *Origin of Species*, his involvement in a prolonged debate on the question of infant baptism weakened radically his attachment to a theology based, in the words of the baptismal rite in the Book of Common Prayer, on the belief that 'the old Adam in this Child may be so buried, that the new man may be raised up in him'. For a time between 1870 and 1879, during his courtship of and then his marriage to a 'girl of grace', Hardy must have felt that he had recovered the lost joy he identified with the days of his childhood. But by January 1879, perhaps even earlier, the marriage seems to have been in serious difficulty. Finally, by the early 1880s, when, after a decade of growing disenchantment with his work as a restorer of Gothic architecture, Hardy joined the Society for the Protection of Ancient Buildings, he seemed to have realized that architectural restoration was destructive and deceiving. Thus his early discovery that there was no supernatural redemption was strongly confirmed, not just by the discovery that there was for him no going home again, but also – and ever so much more palpably – by the lessons that there was not to be through marriage a recovery of the glory and gleam of youth, nor through architectural restoration a recovery of an earlier style and order. This strong sense of decline in things probably explains in part the emergence by 1874, in *Far from the Madding Crowd*, of the mythic Wessex, a place both fictive and

real whose people, buildings and ways Hardy could both preserve
and elegize.

The point is that the futility of redemptive and remedial ideas
and actions was brought home to Hardy repeatedly and forcefully
by his social, religious, romantic and architectural experiences
between 1856 and 1886. Or, to put it another way, Hardy's
powerfully nostalgic temperament shaped his perceptions of society,
of religion, of love and of architecture in strongly similar ways.
Though his deteriorism was undoubtedly challenged by his reading
of Mill, Spencer and Comte, and by the general belief in progress at
that time, his deeply learned lessons of experience, reinforced by the
vein of nostalgia in his make-up, prevailed. From his break with
home, through his doubts about a redemptive theology, from his
distaste for architectural restoration, and in his profound disappointment with marriage, Hardy learned and relearned the same
truth – that the past and the ideal that for him was intimated by
memories from the past are irretrievable. This sad truth and its
attendant beauty was, as I shall try to show, Hardy's recurring
concern throughout the novels.

THE BREAK WITH HIGHER BOCKHAMPTON

A view of Hardy as one whose life and art were shaped by his need to
explore and re-explore an inner conflict between a strong impulse to
reinstate things past and an even stronger impulse to show the
irremediable working of decay is invited by Hardy himself in the
first few pages of the *Life*, where he used the poem 'Domicilium' to
counter his melancholy sense of the obliteration of things of 'his
child-time':

> The lifeholds [at Higher Bockhampton] fell into hand, and the
> quaint residences with their trees, clipped hedges, orchards,
> white gatepost-balls, the naval officer's masts and weather-cocks,
> have now perished every one, and have been replaced by
> labourers' brick cottages and other new farm-buildings, a
> convenient pump occupying the site of the mossy well and
> bucket. The Hardy homestead, too, is weather-worn and
> reduced, having comprised, in addition to the house, two gardens
> (one of them part orchard), a horse-paddock, and sand-and-
> gravel pits, afterwards exhausted and overgrown: also stabling

and like buildings since removed; while the leaves and mould washed down by rains from the plantation have risen high against the back wall of the house, that was formerly covered with ivy. The wide, brilliantly white chimney-corner, in his child-time such a feature of the sitting-room, is also gone.   (p. 3)

'Fell into hand', 'have now perished', 'have been replaced', 'weather-worn and reduced', 'exhausted and overgrown', 'since removed', 'also gone' – the sense of decay denoted by these phrases is countered by the precise enumeration of remembered objects: 'quaint residences with their trees, clipped hedges, orchards, white gatepost-balls, the naval officer's masts and weather-cocks', 'the mossy well and bucket', the 'wide, brilliantly white chimney-corner'. Verbs and nouns are in an odd state of tension in a passage such as this one, for the action conveyed by the verbs condemns at the same time as it conveys the life of the nouns. Perhaps this is why the memoirist interrupted his elegy to his birthplace with a poem, 'some Wordsworthian lines – the earliest discoverable of young Hardy's attempts in verse – [that] give with obvious and naive fidelity the appearance of the paternal homestead at a date nearly half a century before the birth of their writer, when his grandparents settled there, after his great-grandfather had built for their residence the first house in the valley' (*Life*, p. 4).

In 'Domicilium' Hardy contemplates his birthplace and recalls a moment, perhaps in 1850, when he had asked his grandmother to recall this lonely, silent spot between heath and wood as it had been before his birth and before its cultivation. He learned from her that gardens and orchards throve where brambles and thorn trees once ruled, that roads had replaced fern- and tree-shrouded paths, that cows, pigs and horses had ousted snakes, efts, bats and wild ponies. The Hardys' house had been the *first* house in the wild valley, and the nearness of his ancestors to that primitive and primal moment seems to have appealed to the childless septuagenarian – the last of his line – and to have caused him to place at the beginning of his memoirs a poem (his earliest) about a moment in his childhood when he had gained an intimation of his Dorset beginnings. Through this three-layered look into the past – through the eyes of the memoirist of the 1900s, of the poet of the late 1850s, and the boy of the 1840s – he managed to stem the flow of time, though not for long, for at the urging of his need to show the constant working of decay he turned quickly to an account of his family's decline. At his birth on 2 June 1840, he tells us, his father's people were already an exhausted line, and his mother's, if more prolific, none the better for it. One of her ancestors had been sent into exile for his part in the Monmouth uprising; her mother had been left penniless after an imprudent marriage; she herself had been a charity girl, then a cook. And she had conceived him out of wedlock.[1] Hardy thought of himself as having 'the characteristics of an old family of spent social energies' and of his family as a part of a traditional rural culture rapidly nearing its end (*Life*, p. 5). Yet so attached was he to his past that he could not bring himself to look away from it to the future for fulfilment or for happiness. For Hardy, as for Marcel Proust, the true paradise was in the past. And this was so for both social and temperamental reasons.

Perhaps because he underwent so dramatic a change in social station between 1840 and 1867, and because by 1875 he was almost completely cut off from his family by his marriage to a 'better' woman, Hardy viewed his childhood at Higher Bockhampton as a lost paradisiacal time with which his only connection could be his memories of it. Possibly the intense pleasure he found in remembering the forties was connected with his privileged position in the family. He was, after all, the first child, the eldest son, and the one deputed to carry on the family's name. Thought to be dead at birth, he was for several years frail and therefore probably much fretted over and indulged even after he began school at the rather ripe age of eight. He enjoyed the maternal attentions not just of his mother, Jemima, but also of grandmother Hardy and of an aunt, Mary Head, who lived with the family until 1847. After the birth of Mary Hardy in 1841, he must soon have learned to enjoy – like Wordsworth and Browning, like Rasselas in one of his favourite books in boyhood – the attention of a devoted younger sister.[2] His keen and cherished sense of being 'the midmost' of this childhood world may well have derived from the prominence in it of ministering women – not just mother, grandmother, aunt and sister, but possibly the Sparks women from nearby Puddleton and, after 1847, Lady Augusta Martin, of whom more later.

For this precocious, highly-sensitive boy – his earliest memories were of dancing ecstatically to his father's fiddle and gazing into the intense glow of a Venetian red staircase infused with the rays of the setting sun – the first eight years of life seem to have been so filled with pleasing sensation and emotion that growing up and departing was an expulsion rather than a liberation. The *Life* preserves a remarkable instance of this reluctance to leave childhood behind:

One event of this date [1848–9] or a little later stood
out . . . more distinctly than any. He was lying on his back in the
sun, thinking how useless he was, and covered his face with his
straw hat. The sun's rays streamed through the interstices of the
straw, the lining having disappeared. Reflecting on his experience of the world as far as he had got, he came to the
conclusion that he did not wish to grow up. Other boys were
always talking of when they would be men; he did not want at all
to be a man, or to possess things, but to remain as he was, in the
same spot, and to know no more people than he already
knew . . . .   (*Life*, pp. 15–16)

The poem 'Childhood among the Ferns' (*CP*, p. 864) suggests the
precise appeal for Hardy of this early environment. As in
'Domicilium', it is the lush vegetal surroundings that the imaginative boy makes over into a friendly, sheltering world all of his own. A
clump of ferns becomes a protective house during rain, then a source
of 'sweet breath' when sunshine ends the shower and pierces the
'green rafters' of the make-believe house. Compared to the sweet,
silent warmth of this world of 'green ways', manhood and the noisy
bustle of its world have little appeal. A similar episode in *Jude the
Obscure* (I, ch. 4) reveals something else – that such dreaming is
doomed to violent interruption. Jude's dream of learning, like his
dreams of love and of religion, is shattered by his appetites, by the
manoeuvrings of Arabella, and by the prejudices of his society.
Hardy's own wish not to grow up was ended by Jemima Hardy's
ambition for him, by education, by work and marriage, and by a
literary fame that removed him forever from moments such as those
preserved in 'Domicilium', 'Childhood among the Ferns' and 'The
Self-Unseeing'. In this last poem he relishes an earlier, happier time,
with mother, father and hearth forming the circumference of a
glowing circle whose midmost is himself, a joyous, dancing child:

> She sat here in her chair,
> Smiling into the fire;
> He who played stood there,
> Bowing it higher and higher.
>
> Childlike, I danced in a dream;
> Blessings emblazoned that day;
> Everything glowed with a gleam;
> Yet we were looking away.

(*CP*, pp. 166–7)

The memory of his father's music, of his mother's smiling approval, and of the warm, bright hearth recreates the complete security of the family circle and makes possible the re-enactment (in the last stanza) of a precious moment of childhood. The circle was broken not just by the death of his father in 1892 or by his own departure from Higher Bockhampton for work in the world of architecture and literature, but by the failure of the family itself to savour that moment for all its dearness and uniqueness. All were instead 'looking away' – perhaps to the prospects lying before the talented child.[3] The language of the last stanza – 'dream', 'blessings', 'glowed', 'gleam' – echoes Wordsworth's 'Ode: Intimations of Immortality from Recollections of Early Childhood', Hardy's frequent touchstone in the novels for deciding the meaning and value of such treasured moments from the past.[4] Hardy's intimations, however, are of mortality. The 'ancient floor / Footworn and hollowed and thin' and the poem that contains this image and the memories associated with it are all that survive that holy day.

The wish of the precocious boy of eight or nine 'to remain as he was, in the same spot' was probably challenged by three books given to him by his mother at this time, Dryden's *Virgil*, Johnson's *Rasselas* and Bernardin de St Pierre's *Paul and Virginia*. As stories, all probably sharpened Hardy's sense of the perils of leaving home, childhood and innocence for life in the great world. On the other hand, all – especially Virgil, his great favourite – exhibit in powerful and beautiful terms the inevitability of growing, of changing, of leaving beginnings behind. Perhaps Jemima, a shrewd and literate woman whose own favourite book was *The Divine Comedy*, was seeking to curb an excessive home-attachment she perceived in her son when she set him to reading the account of Aeneas's sublimely sad discovery of his destiny to depart Troy and found a great empire, the philosophic tale of the Prince of Abyssinia's escape to and return from Egypt, and the romantic tale of Paul and Virginia's discovery of the folly of trying to avoid the world and its ways. This is speculation, but it is consistent with Jemima's apparent fear, at this same time (1848–9), that her impressionable eldest son might form too close an attachment to Lady Augusta Martin, the childless, middle-aged patroness of his first school who had a strong, almost maternal, affection for the boy. Perhaps this is why Jemima took young Thomas with her at this time to live for a month with relatives in Hertfordshire, then, upon return, transferred him from Lady

Martin's school in Stinsford to a Dorchester day-school, much to the annoyance of Lady Martin and of the young Hardy as well. For he eagerly returned her affection: 'His feeling for her was almost that of a lover', and he 'secretly mourned the loss' of her (*Life*, p. 19).

It is worth digressing briefly here to note that Hardy's devotion to Lady Martin lasted well into the sixties, when he visited her in London (in 1862) and found to his great disappointment that, though her butler 'looked little altered', the great lady of his boyhood had withered and faded:

> The lady of his dreams – alas! To her, too, the meeting must have been no less painful than pleasant: she too was plainly embarrassed at having in her presence a young man of over twenty-two, who was very much of a handful in comparison with the rosy-cheeked, innocent little boy she had almost expected 'Tommy' to remain. (*Life*, p. 41)

A letter from her in the autumn of 1874 recalled to him a letter from her in 1863 'which [had] revived throbs of tender feeling in him, and brought back to his memory the thrilling "frou-frou" of her four grey silk flounces when she had used to bend over him, and when they brushed against the font as she entered church on Sunday [at Stinsford in the 1840s]' (*Life*, p. 102). In the typescript of the *Early Years*, this passage continued as follows:

> Thus though their eyes never met again after his call on her in London [in 1862], nor their lips from the time when she had held him in her arms [in the 1840s], who can say what both occurrences might not have brought in the order of things, if he had developed their reacquaintance earlier [in 1863], now that she was in her widowhood, with nothing to hinder her mind from rolling back the past.[5]

One is reminded by this suppressed passage of Swithin St Cleeve's reunion with a faded Lady Constantine at the end of *Two on a Tower*, and of Jocelyn Pierston's reunion with Marcia Bencomb at the end of *The Well-Beloved*, as well as of the haunting poem titled 'The Revisitation', in which a man returns after twenty years to reunite with his beloved Agnette, only to find 'crease where curve was, where was raven, grizzle – / Pits, where peonies once did dwell' (*CP*, p. 194). Hardy never tired, it seems, of tracing the spectacle of decay in women.

Hints of a tense family drama emerge from the cautious early pages of the *Life*: the struggle of an ambitious and forceful mother to extricate her gifted son from a dreamy tendency that would lead him to follow in the footsteps of his somewhat happy-go-lucky father, or to bask in the affectionate patronage of the Lady of the Manor, or to dangle from her (Jemima's) apron strings. If she could not persuade her husband to move to a 'more convenient centre' for the sake of the family business (*Life*, p. 21), she could urge her children to hard study, to exemplary conduct, and to careers above their lower-middle beginnings. We even find her insisting on one occasion – over her husband's objections – that young Thomas accompany his father on the fiddle at weddings, 'possibly from a feeling that [such experiences] would help to teach him what life was' (*Life*, p. 23).[6] When, in 1853–4, Hardy found himself following his Dorchester schoolmaster, Isaac Last, to a new school in Dorchester, it must have been clear to him that his mother, whom he called 'a "progressive" woman', was successfully ejecting him from the warm, green world of Higher Bockhampton (*Life*, p. 23). Her efforts almost surely met with his resistance, resistance that she appears to have countered ruthlessly. For example, when he informed her, in 1848–9, that he did not wish to grow up, she completely rejected his view of himself: 'To his great surprise she was very much hurt, which was natural enough considering she had been near death's door in bringing him forth. And she never forgot what he had said, a source of much regret to him in after years' (*Life*, pp. 15–16). The opprobrium and even violence directed at ambitious or domineering parents such as Mrs Yeobright of *The Return of the Native* or George Melbury of *The Woodlanders* may well reflect Hardy's resentment of his mother's success in thwarting his nostalgic clinging. She was the first object of his love, the first embodiment for him of the elusive well-beloved,[7] and yet she had pushed him out of the happy world whose centre he had been. Though Jemima upheld her gifted son with the authority of 'matchless . . . might' and 'measureless scope', she was apparently determined not to let *him* live and die where he was born.[8] If Hardy's nostalgia derived from a father who 'had not the tradesman's soul' and liked in the hot days of summer to lie 'on a bank of thyme or camomile with the grasshoppers leaping over him' (*Life*, p. 21), his scorn for the results of nostalgia – so strong an element in his censorious view of Henry Knight, Clym Yeobright, Angel Clare and Sue Bridehead – probably derived from his 'progressive' mother.

Yet so attached was he to persons and places of his early experience that with puberty and the first signs of sexual awakening, in the 1850s, came an almost fearful detachment from others, a trait that was to characterize him for much of his career. Only a few years before, he had enjoyed and returned the affectionate embraces of Lady Martin. Now, perhaps as a result of an increasingly ambiguous regard for his mother, there began a series of sudden and in some ways 'negative' fascinations with strange girls.[9] For example, the *Life* records an incident of 1854 when he fell head over heels in love with a girl who passed him on horseback near the South Walk in Dorchester:

> She was a total stranger. Next day he saw her with an old gentleman, probably her father. He wandered about miserably, looking for her through several days, and caught sight of her once again. Then she disappeared forever. He told other boys in confidence, who sympathized, but could do nothing, though some boarders watched for her on his behalf. He was more than a week getting over this desperate attachment. (*Life*, p. 25)

After this dreamlike encounter he saw another girl to whom 'he lost his head for a few days . . . just after he had been reading Ainsworth's *Windsor Castle*'; and another, a gamekeeper's daughter whom he recalled in 'Lizbie Browne' as being as forward in sexual development as he was backward in it. He was, he said, 'a child until he was sixteen, a youth till he was five-and-twenty, and a young man till he was nearly fifty'.

> His immaturity . . . was greater than is common for his years, and it may be mentioned here that a clue to much of his character and action throughout his life is afforded by his lateness of development in virility, while mentally precocious. . . . Whether this was intrinsic, or owed anything to his having lived in a remote spot in early life, is an open question. (*Life*, p. 32)

After Lizbie Browne, there was Louisa Harding, whose appeal to Hardy was long-lasting. He wrote the endearing 'Louisa in the Lane' a few months before his death in 1928, and in 'Louie', dated July 1913, he raised her ghost – almost defiantly – between memories of Emma, only seven months dead, in 'When Oats are Reaped' and 'She Opened the Door'.[10] And it was in the middle fifties, as Robert Gittings has shown, that Hardy's attempt to make advances on his cousin Rebecca Sparks was violently rejected, with lasting sexual trauma a possible result for him. He was, it seems, caught up in an emotional fantasy in which he was transferring his love for his mother successively to Rebecca, to Martha Mary and to Tryphena Sparks, maternal first cousins who greatly resembled Jemima Hardy. This peculiar fascination with women did not end with his marriage in 1874. Hardy seems to have conceived a fascination for Helen Paterson, the illustrator of *Far from the Madding Crowd*. Later he formed attachments to Agnes Grove and Florence Henniker.[11] He would marry Florence Dugdale fifteen months after Emma's death in November 1912.

Robert Gittings is probably correct in suggesting that 'a delayed or imperfect physical development' was the source of Hardy's 'sexual curiosity', his 'continual speculation about almost every woman he meets, and his habit of passing from one to another without conscious volition'.[12] But to assert that *The Well-Beloved* is 'a sketch of his own temperament in very realistic detail',[13] and to say no more, is to ignore that novel's position, as shall be seen, as but the last in a series of self-sketches, and the position of its hero, Pierston, as the last of a long line of characters who struggle to recover a lost ideal through the love of a pure woman. Henry Knight, Clym Yeobright, Angel Clare, Jocelyn Pierston, even Edred Fitzpiers – the similarities among the surnames are suggestive – are all partial self-sketches, varied expressions of what Hardy called his 'lateness of development in virility' as well as of what is referred to in the *Life* as his constitutional tendency to care for 'life as an emotion rather than . . . as a science of climbing' (p. 53). What he meant by 'life as an emotion' is suggested by several events that occurred during the critical years between his return to his mother's house at Higher Bockhampton in July 1867, and his first meeting with Emma Gifford in March 1870.

Hardy blamed incessant study and the stench of the Thames at low tide for the poor state of health that brought him home in the summer of 1867, after five years in London. But the language of the *Life* suggests another cause – his sense that he has been spiritually defiled by leaving the purity of Dorset for the corruption of London. His was 'a constitution that had grown up in a pure country atmosphere'. After several years in London, he had come to feel that 'he would rather go into the country altogether. He constitutionally shrank from the business of social advancement, caring for life as an emotion rather than as a science of climbing' (*Life*, p. 53; cf. pp. 87, 104). On 2 June 1865, his twenty-fifth birthday, he felt that he 'had lived a long time and done very little' (*Life*, p. 50). In August of the same year, smarting from his failure to publish the poems he was then writing, and thinking of the effect of his failure on his family (probably his worshipful sister Mary in particular), he wrote, 'The anguish of a defeat is most severely felt when we look upon the weak ones who have believed us invincible, and have made preparations for our victory' (*Life*, p. 50). In the spring of 1866 he recorded the sensations of 'a certain man' who knows the defects in the 'ends', though not in the 'means', of the efforts of other people (*Life*, p. 55). Pained by the imperfections of general knowledge, this man, a man of 'capacious mind', seeks knowledge of particulars. Looking about himself at London society, perhaps from the unique perspective of an architect's assistant who was courting a lady's maid,[14] he remarked, 'The defects of a class are more perceptible to the class immediately below-it than to itself' (*Life*, p. 55). As shall be seen, a similar sense of futility, of failure, and of radical defect in things pervades the poems and novels of the 1860s; and this vision 'ghast and grim' is frequently connected with loss of innocence or with estrangement from an earlier, happier, simpler time. Hardy's oft-repeated desire to care for, or to live, life as 'an emotion' rather than as 'a scientific game' has the same root.

What Hardy meant by life as a 'scientific game' is clear: 'the business of social advancement', carrying on novel-writing or architecture as a 'regular trade'; going about 'to dinners and clubs and crushes as a business' (*Life*, pp. 53, 104). What he meant by 'carry[ing] on his life . . . as an emotion' was living his life, both through poetry and through fiction, in as intimate as possible a relation with the fleeting, difficult-to-capture beauty glimpsed in his early years then lost to time and experience. It is in part what Gittings has called Hardy's 'intense familial sense', but it is more than the strong tribal loyalty that phrase suggests; it is also a devotion to a certain quality of feeling that Hardy associated with an ideal truth and beauty.[15] An episode of June 1867 illustrates the point.

Before returning from London to Dorset in July, Hardy per-

formed a revealing and typical act of nostalgia. He returned to a
cherished spot he had not visited for many years. He went to
Hatfield, Hertfordshire, the town that he had visited with his
mother eighteen years earlier, when he was a boy of nine. It was a
spot he could associate not just with his own mother-centred
boyhood but also with the penumbra of another poetic idealist, his
beloved Shelley (*Life*, pp. 17, 55). He found, as might be expected,
that Hatfield had changed lamentably. 'A youth [he met there]
thought the altered highway had always run as it did. Pied rabbits
in the Park, descendants of those I knew. The once children are
quite old inhabitants. I regretted that the beautiful sunset did not
occur in a place of no reminiscences, that I might have enjoyed it
without their tinge' (*Life*, p. 55). Change and the ignorance of youth
to change, generation of new lives, regret that a beautiful evening
should be marred by memory of a joyous moment forever lost –
these are the melancholy reflections of a man of twenty-seven on a
place he had visited as a boy of nine with a still-attractive, youthful
mother who shared his 'innocent glee' on this as on other occasions
(*Life*, p. 21). During those exciting weeks eighteen years before, the
sole companion of his mother, young Thomas had attended a
private school, endured the hazing of strange boys, proved himself
their intellectual superior and, perhaps best of all, stayed with
Jemima at the Cross-Keys Inn, St John Street, Clerkenwell –
possibly, he liked to think, in the same room occupied some forty
years earlier by Shelley and Mary Godwin. The room he and
Jemima occupied 'was *unaltered* from its state during the lovers'
romantic experiences there – the oval stone stair case, the skylight
and the hotel entrance being *untouched*' (*Life*, p. 17; emphasis
added). Here, in the cautious pages of the *Life*, Hardy's persistent
desire for the unchanging and pure thing of dream informs, in apt
association with the author of 'Hymn to Intellectual Beauty',
'Epipsychidion' and *Laon and Cythna*, the revival of a precious
moment of childhood, a moment much tarnished in 1867 by the
realities of growth and change. 'Had the teachings of experience
grown cumulatively with the age of the world', he had written in
April, only two months earlier, 'we should have been ere now as
great as God' (*Life*, p. 55). Wisdom, in this view, derives not from
experience, but from a source within, a source easily fouled or lost.
And so, less than a month later, in July 1867, Hardy returned to
Dorset, the place of his earliest sensations and experiences.

The effect on his health of going home was almost miraculous: 'A few weeks in the country – where he returned to his former custom of walking to the Dorchester architect's office from his mother's house every day – completely restored him' (*Life*, p. 56). Re-enactment in 1867 of a routine he had followed in 1856 – 62 was a tonic, though only a temporary one, for, though he fell gratefully into old habits, after five years 'superadded of experience as a young man at large in London, it was with very different ideas of things' (*Life*, p. 56). This view of experience in July 1867 sharply contradicts that of the previous April, when, full of the need to get back to his beginnings, experience had seemed worthless to him. Once home again, the value of the London experiences could be held up against the values of the traditional rural order and all its traces of things past. In July 1868 he was reading the seventh book of *The Aeneid*, where he must have found Aeneas's joy at discovering his ancestral homeland after long wandering an apt analogue to his own homecoming. Perhaps this is why he paid Virgil's poem the rare tribute of calling it a work 'of which he never wearied' (*Life*, p. 59). But if Italy was for Aeneas a second Troy, a place to at once realize his destiny and recapture a lost glory, Higher Bockhampton was no such place for Hardy. If Hardy had an 'Italy', it was Jersey, where his paternal ancestors, the le Hardys, had lived for centuries. Though 'he often thought he would like to restore the "le" to his name, and call himself "Thomas le Hardy"'', he never, so far as is known, considered returning to Jersey (*Life*, p. 50). In sum, though homecoming was a tonic, the years between 1867 and 1870 were marked not by repose but by restless movement between Dorset and London. The homecomer soon discovered that if his heart was in Dorset his intellectual props were in London, the place where he might fulfil his dream of literary accomplishment, a dream he now associated with that of the Swinburnean youth 'of whom it may be said . . . that "save his own soul he hath no star"'' (*Life*, p. 56).[16]

In April 1869, after several weeks in London, Hardy returned once more to Dorset and to country architecture, though this time as an assistant to G. R. Crickmay, an architect of Weymouth who had taken over John Hicks's Dorchester office after Hicks's death in February. Hardy's sojourn in London must have brought on another bout of poor health, for we are told now of a second magical restoration of health, this one as the result of swimming in the bay at Weymouth, the resort town just a few miles south of Dorchester:

Being – like Swinburne – a swimmer, he would lie for a long time on his back on the surface of the waves, rising and falling with the tide in the warmth of the morning sun. He used to tell that, after the enervation of London, this tonic existence by the sea seemed ideal, and that physically he went back ten years in his age almost as by the touch of an enchanter's wand. (*Life*, p. 64)

Hardy thought of himself as a 'young man' between twenty-five and fifty. To lose ten years at twenty-nine was (for him) virtually to regain childhood, for he liked to say that he was a child until he was sixteen (*Life*, p. 32). One cannot help but wonder if this sketch of himself floating blissfully in watery warmth does not screen an unconscious desire to retreat even further into the past – to the warmth of the parent-encircled hearth depicted in 'The Self-Unseeing', to the damp security of the fern-house in 'Childhood among the Ferns', even to the wet warmth of the womb. If this seems mere speculation, it is not contradicted by the fact that in February 1870 Hardy suddenly left the pleasures of Weymouth to return to 'the seclusion of his mother's house' because he found offensive a dancing class 'where a good deal of flirtation went on, the so-called "class" being in fact, a gay gathering for dances and lovemaking by adepts of both sexes' (*Life*, p. 64). He himself may have formed a disillusioning attachment to one of these 'adepts', for the poem 'At Waking', subtitled 'Weymouth, 1869', expresses bitter disenchantment with a woman. A man wakens at dawn, perhaps in bed beside his lover, and suspects, then detects, an unstated but clearly unflattering truth about her. Perhaps he discovers that she is not an innocent, for her charm is suddenly lost to him and she becomes 'but one / Of the common crowd', a fact he would like to 'unrecognize'. He cannot, of course, and he is shattered, in much the way that Henry Knight and Angel Clare are shattered upon discovering imperfection in their chosen ones: 'O vision appalling / When the one believed-in thing / Is seen falling, falling / With all to which hope can cling' (*CP*, p. 224).

If Hardy turned back to the house he liked to refer to as 'his mother's' in order to escape a corrupt world and its deceiving women, he did not find there the harmony of former times. In his Bible he jotted the date '1868–71' beside Job 12:4 ('I am as one mocked of his neighbour'). He must have felt himself an outsider at home. The poem 'Welcome Home' (*CP*, p. 593) conveys the disappointment, even the bitterness, of a man 'keen . . . to dwell in amity' with his race, only to find that his old friends have forgotten him. He hails them from their beds, tells them his name, his plans and the reasons for his return. He seeks warm welcome but gets instead this drowsy reply:

> 'Did you? . . . Ah, 'tis true,'
> Said they, 'back a long time,
> Here had spent his young time,
> Some man such as you . . .
> Good-night.' The casement closed again,
> And I was left alone in the frosty lane.[17]

The discovery that he was something of a stranger at home was probably one thing that moved him to break with a local girl (and first cousin) such as Tryphena Sparks shortly after meeting, in March 1870, the daughter of a solicitor, sister-in-law of an Anglican clergyman, and niece of the Canon of Worcester. Like Virgil, Hardy was not so much putting the past behind him as seeking it in the future. Hardy sought in Emma Gifford's love the emotional support he could no longer find in his family, his relatives, or the society whose tastes and values rubbed against his recently acquired ones. With Emma, a childlike woman who had led a secluded but genteel life, it might be possible to live life as an emotion. But it was not to be. Hardy demanded of Emma and of marriage what he demanded of his work in architecture, of his religious faith, and of his literary art – that they appease or at least minister to his nostalgia, that they satisfy his yearning for a lost felicity. Like his religion and his architecture, his marriage and wife would fail him in this. Only his art would answer the cry of his irrepressible nostalgia.

THE FAILURE OF LOVE AND MARRIAGE

Far from the Madding Crowd (1874) did not just make Hardy famous; it enabled him to do what his own Egbert Mayne of *An Indiscretion in the Life of an Heiress* (1867/78) and Stephen Smith of *A Pair of Blue Eyes* (1873) had been denied the pleasure of doing. It enabled him to marry a lady – on 17 September 1874, 'at St. Peter's, Elgin Avenue, Paddington', in a ceremony conducted by the lady's uncle, 'Dr. E. Hamilton Gifford, Canon of Worcester and afterwards Archdeacon of London [a relative for whom the bride had a great affection. Dr. Gifford himself had married as his second wife a sister of Sir Francis Jeune, afterwards Lord St. Helier, and the family connection thus formed was a source of much social intercourse to the Hardys in after years]'.[18] We cannot be sure why the passage in brackets was not printed in the *Early Life* – possibly because it is somewhat flattering to Emma Gifford, of whom the second Mrs Hardy, who edited and published the *Early Life* and *Later Years*, was reputedly jealous.[19] Restored, it illustrates Hardy's wish, as late as 1917 or 1918, to show the world that by marriage to Emma Gifford he had raised himself far above the circle at Higher Bockhampton, where he had, somewhat ironically, completed *Far from the Madding Crowd* only a few months before the marriage. This thirty-four year old son of a stonemason and a servant suddenly found himself welcome in the house of Leslie Stephen, editor of the prestigious *Cornhill* and one of the leading men of letters of the time. There he met Mrs Stephen, daughter of William Makepeace Thackeray, her lively sister Anne, and notables such as G. Murray Smith, the publisher, Mrs Procter, and Helen Paterson, the illustrator of *Far from the Madding Crowd*.

The break with Higher Bockhampton, in process since 1862, was now, at least in social terms, complete. A passage in a letter of May 1873 from Horace Moule to Hardy suggests the precariousness of Hardy's social standing in his family at this time: 'I trust I address you rightly on the envelope', wrote Hardy's old friend and mentor. 'I conjectured that you would prefer the absence of the "Esq" at Upper Bockhampton.'[20] If Moule's remark suggests an uneasiness in the Hardy family with its eldest's rise, a letter from Hardy in London to his brother Henry in Dorset, a letter dated 18 September 1874, the day after the wedding in Paddington, suggests a partial break in communication with his family: 'There were only Emma and I, her uncle who married us, and her brother, and my landlady's daughter signed the book as one witness. I am going to Paris for materials for my next story [*The Hand of Ethelberta*]. Shall return the beginning of October – and shall call at 4 Celbridge Place [Hardy's London address] to see if there is any letter.'[21] Henry Hardy had not filled the traditional role of groomsman; Mary, Thomas Hardy's favourite sister and confidante, had not attended the ceremony; the newly-weds had not found it convenient to go to France via Dorchester and Weymouth. It seems altogether probable, as Gittings has suggested, that at the time of the marriage the bride knew little of the groom's humble origins. And he was probably not eager to enlighten her. For whatever Hardy's essential loyalties to home and family, by the autumn of 1874, the people and places of Dorset were being seen through the quizzing eye of the creator of Wessex. They were becoming quaint and picturesque to his London-trained eye. The cidermaking in which Hardy had joined his father in the autumn of 1873 would find its way into *The Woodlanders*, which he began the next year. Characteristics of the old fiddler who talked interminably to Hardy in 1873 had already appeared in the figure of the Tranter in *Under the Greenwood Tree* (1872). In a letter of October 1873, to Leslie Stephen, Hardy had expressed hope that in the illustrations for *Madding Crowd* 'the rustics, although *quaint*, may be made to appear intelligent, and not boorish at all'. He found it a great advantage, he said, in another letter to Stephen, 'to be actually among the people described at the time of describing them' (*Life*, pp. 96–9). Like Ethelberta Petherwin, the heroine of the story he had mentioned in the business-like note to his brother, Hardy found it impossible to follow the advice he had placed in the mouth of Ethelberta's humble and shrewd father:

> Much lies in minding this, that your best plan for lightness of heart is to raise yourself a little higher than your old mates, but not so high as to be quite out of their reach. All human beings enjoy themselves from the outside, and so getting on a *little* has this good in it, you still keep in your old class where your feelings are, and are thoughtfully treated by this class: while by getting on *too much* you are sneered at by your new acquaintance, who don't know the skill of your rise, and you are parted from and forgot by the old ones who do. (*HE*, ch. 7)

Literary success and marriage to a woman of the middle class had indeed raised Hardy out of the reach of his old mates and out of the matrix of his earliest feelings. For a man of his deep loyalties to home, to mother and to rural ways, this break could only be excruciatingly painful. Joy of a new wife and pride of literary fame may have blotted out for a time his memories of a lost joy associated with the people and ways of Higher Bockhampton. But his hard-won success was soon 'sneered at' and disturbed. Quizzing personal criticism of *Far from the Madding Crowd* which urged that its author might be a house-decorator jarred on his sense of social inferiority and turned him away from the writing of pastoral romance, a mode

congenial to both his experience and his temperament. An aversion
to women, manifested in *Under the Greenwood Tree*, *A Pair of Blue Eyes*,
and especially *Far from the Madding Crowd*, may have been
connected with the deterioration of his marriage, which, after a
happy beginning, seems to have been in difficulty by January 1879,
and perhaps earlier.[22] In the novels up to 1878, Hardy's men and
women typically seek salvation through the love of another person:
Geraldine through Egbert in *An Indiscretion in the Life of an Heiress*,
Miss Aldclyffe and Aeneas Manston through Cytherea Graye in
Desperate Remedies, Henry Knight through Elfride Swancourt in *A
Pair of Blue Eyes*, Boldwood through Bathsheba Everdene in *Far from
the Madding Crowd*. These novels have in common the movement of
two or three men about a central female figure. In them, as J. Hillis
Miller has said, the beloved becomes 'a center of the world', the
chief source of happiness, and 'the only guiltless escape from the
poverty of detachment'.[23] For at least a time Hardy must have
found something similar in his love for Emma. But love and
marriage, as well as life among the London literati – the stuff of his
second dream – failed to provide the yearned-for thing; and so in the
1870s we find Hardy again contemplating his first dream, the
childhood idyll the vehicle for whose recovery, the story of the
return of a native, had been one of his earliest narrative strategies.
But now success and marriage had removed him from the primal
place. And so, in *The Hand of Ethelberta*, in *The Return of the Native*, in
The Woodlanders, as earlier in *Under the Greenwood Tree*, Hardy
brought his own dilemma, the dilemma of the uprooted native, to
centre stage. His treatment of the problem would vary – social
comedy in *Ethelberta* and *Greenwood Tree*, tragedy in *The Return*,
tragi-comedy in *The Woodlanders* – but his conclusion would be the
same, that reinstatement is difficult or impossible. What had been
lost to growing up and to getting on in the world and could not be
retrieved in the love of a woman, was not to be recovered by going
home again.

The even more unhappy truth that must have bored into Hardy
soon after his marriage to a woman he could not easily bring home
was that all his novels up to 1874 had been written at home. He had
found it difficult if not impossible to write fiction when he was away
from Higher Bockhampton and its environs. 'The Poor Man and the
Lady', *Desperate Remedies* and *Under the Greenwood Tree* were written
there. In September 1872, unable to get on with *A Pair of Blue Eyes* in
London, he 'went down to the seclusion of Dorset to set about it

more thoroughly' (*Life*, p. 91). *Far from the Madding Crowd*, whose success made possible his marriage to a 'better' woman, was written in the house often referred to in the *Life* as 'his mother's'. It is no surprise then to find Hardy and his new wife, in May 1875, 'in Dorset house-hunting' (at Shaftesbury, Blandford, Wimborne, and finally at Swanage, where they went into lodgings and where he wrote *Ethelberta* in the winter of 1875). For Hardy, living life as an emotion meant living it as a writer whose subject was 'the substance of life' and not 'social and fashionable life' (*Life*, p. 104). When forced in March 1879 by 'the practical side of his vocation of novelist' to move from Sturminster Newton (Dorset) to London, he did so with great reluctance because, he said, 'the nature of his writing' made it unwise (*Life*, p. 118). In order to write about life's substance Hardy needed to live in or near the places of his earliest sensations and memories. He was not merely in need of local colour, though local effects were of great importance to his fiction; he needed, rather, to live amongst the palpable traces of the deep split between his personal past and present. The strange combination of feelings this brewed in him is revealed in the poem 'Concerning his Old Home' (*CP*, pp. 859–60), in which he almost bluntly announces the chaos of feelings (nostalgia, contempt for the past, guilt for having deserted the ways of the past, love for those left behind) that lie behind the novels of return:

> *Mood I*
> I wish to see it never –
> That dismal place
> With cracks in the floor –
> I would forget it ever!
>
> *Mood II*
> To see it once, that sad
> And memoried place
> Yes, just once more –
> I should be fairly glad.
>
> *Mood III*
> To see it often again
> That friendly place
> With its low green door
> I'm willing anywhen!

Mood IV
I'll haunt it night and day
That loveable place
With its flowers' rich store
That drives regret away!

What role had Emma – the emblem of his new status, the
supplanter of his mother – in the real-life drama of return Hardy
was playing out between 1874 and 1883, when he would return to
live in Dorchester and build Max Gate? The only answer is that it
was a difficult if not an impossible role, for Emma had married a
man who lived along a radius the centre of which was Dorset,
in particular the cottage at Higher Bockhampton – a man who
wanted desperately to rise in the world, yet at the same time
believed deeply that to rise was to betray one's self and kin. This
explains Hardy's circling, probing movements around Dorchester
and Higher Bockhampton between 1874 and 1883. After leaving home to marry in September 1874, Hardy did not visit
Bockhampton with Emma (judging mainly from the record he left
in the *Life*) until Christmas of 1876, when he was living in Yeovil,
Somerset, a town about twenty miles north of Bockhampton. He
had completed *The Hand of Ethelberta* seven months before, and he
may have used the Christmas visit in 1876 to gather materials for
The Return of the Native, whose hero returns to his native heath and
his imperious mother on a Christmas Eve. The next visit recorded in
the *Life* occurred in February 1879, shortly after the serial
publication of *The Return of the Native* and only one month after the
marital crisis depicted in the poem 'A January Night, 1879'. At this
time, Hardy came from London for two weeks, alone it seems, and
probably because Jemima Hardy was ill. In August 1879, some six
months later, he visited Higher Bockhampton again, and again
alone. Emma did not arrive until a week later, and then they took
lodgings in Weymouth, some half-dozen miles from Higher
Bockhampton. The *Life* records that Jemima visited them there.
Though the record provided in the *Life* is probably not complete, it
seems altogether possible that after an initial meeting between
Emma and the family in 1876 it took Hardy three years to bring his
wife and his mother together again. We cannot be certain. It seems
probable that there would have been other visits, especially while
the newly-weds were living at Sturminster Newton.[24] And yet, it is
important to remember that the plot of *The Return of the Native*,
begun as early as the winter of 1876,[25] and centred on the tragedy of

Clym Yeobright's failure to reconcile love for his mother and native place with love for a wife who longs to live elsewhere, turns on Mrs Yeobright's abortive visit to the newly-married Clym and Eustacia at the cottage at Alderworth. Through a freakish sequence of events, Mrs Yeobright is turned away from her son's door to perish, full of bitter resentment, on the torrid heath in the company of an uncomprehending child named Johnny Nunsuch.

Did Jemima Hardy journey to Sturminster, to the small house called Riverside Villa, or to London, or to one of her son's other residences between 1874 and 1879, only to be rebuffed in some way, with a long estrangement between the two houses the result? We shall probably never know. What does seem clear, however, is that between September 1874 and midsummer 1883, when the Hardys moved to Shirehall Lane, Dorchester, Hardy was searching – like Clym Yeobright – for a suitable distance and relationship to home, that alternately 'dismal', 'memoried', 'friendly', and 'loveable' place that 'drives regret away'. The Hardys' many moves during these years suggest as much: from September 1874 to August 1875 they lived in London; in Swanage until the spring of 1876; in Yeovil to midsummer 1876; at Sturminster Newton until March 1878; then in London until the midsummer of 1881. In 1881 the Hardys moved to Dorset (Wimborne Minster) until midsummer 1883, when they moved to Shirehall Lane, Dorchester. There they stayed until midsummer 1885, when they took occupancy at Max Gate, their last home – built, it is worth noting, on a line between Dorchester and Higher Bockhampton. Once installed at Max Gate, the Hardys seem to have improved relations with Higher Bockhampton. Although Emma had opposed the choice of Dorchester as a permanent home (she much preferred her native Devon), in their first few years at Max Gate she accompanied her husband on weekly visits to the old folks. Later, for reasons we do not know, she refused to go.[26] But the native had returned; his wife's wishes were as nothing beside the demands of his nostalgia and the art it nurtured. Hardy's 1874–85 odyssey repeated his 1862–7 odyssey; even the illness that sent him home in 1867 was repeated in the serious illness of 1880–1. More important, the artistic outpouring of 1867–74 was repeated and exceeded in the deluge that began with *The Mayor of Casterbridge* (1886) and ended with *Winter Words* (1928). With the exception of *The Return of the Native*, his great inquiry into the difficulty of going home again, Hardy's greatest novels were written in the immediate locale of his lost paradise.

It is worth digressing here to remark that several of Hardy's notes

from the 1870s reveal an increasingly deterioristic view of things
that seems to crystallize around his disappointment in love and
marriage. In June 1876, for example, we find him assimilating
human evolution to the view that time and history are processes of
decline:

> If it is possible to compress into a sentence all that a man learns
> between 20 and 40, it is that all things merge into one another –
> good into evil, generosity into justice, religion into politics, the
> year into the ages, the world into the universe. With this view in
> mind the evolution of species seems but a minute and obvious
> process in the same movement.   (*Life*, p. 111)

Men and their greatest achievements – morality, religion, government and science – are but unimportant parts of a cosmic process
whose tendency is downward. Though he uses the neutral verb
'merge' to describe change, his examples – 'good into evil, generosity into justice, religion into politics, the year into the ages, the
world into the universe' – suggest decline or dissolution. In a note of
July 1876 he dismissed one of his mentors of the 1860s, the gloomy
though ultimately hopeful Preacher of Ecclesiastes, as something of
an optimist, suggesting thereby how uncongenial for him had
become the comic vision of novels of the seventies such as *Under the
Greenwood Tree*, *Far from the Madding Crowd* and *The Hand of
Ethelberta*:

> 'All is Vanity,' saith the Preacher. But if all were only Vanity,
> who would mind? Alas, it is too often worse than vanity; agony,
> darkness, death also. A man would never laugh were he not to
> forget his situation, or were he not one who never has learnt it.
> After risibility from comedy, how often does the thoughtful mind
> reproach itself for forgetting the truth? Laughter always means
> blindness – either from defect, choice or accident.   (*Life*, p. 112)

Laughter provoked by comedy is irresponsible, then, even false to
reality, because the truth is too often 'agony, darkness, death'; not as
temporary or remediable states but rather as normal conditions
directing all of life. So words such as 'time', 'history', 'consciousness'
become ironic metaphors for deterioration, decline and decay. This
is the defect in nature that Hardy at this time proclaimed it the duty
of the artist to apprehend and to transcribe:

There is enough poetry in what is left [in life] after all the false romance has been abstracted, to make a sweet pattern: e.g., the poem by H. Coleridge: 'She is not fair to outward view.' So, then, if Nature's defects must be looked in the face and transcribed, whence arises the art in poetry and novel-writing? I think the art lies in making these defects the basis of a hitherto unperceived beauty, by irradiating them with 'the light that never was'[27] on their surface, but is seen to be latent in them by the spiritual eye. (*Life*, p. 114)

Hardy's pointed use here of Hartley Coleridge's 'She is Not Fair' to illustrate 'Nature's defects' suggests perhaps the role his foundering marriage played in the shaping of his deterioristic view of things.

Coleridge's poem describes a maid whose beauty is not in her face but in in her eye, which is 'a well of love, a spring of light'. But as years pass, even her eye grows 'coy and cold', though her faithful lover finds 'her frowns fairer . . . / Than smiles of other maidens'. It is difficult not to associate Hardy's allusion to Hartley Coleridge's fading maiden with his thoughts of Emma Hardy in 1877. The door of romance that Emma had opened for Hardy seven years before was swinging shut, and he was, in all likelihood, trying to make the most of things, trying to make a 'sweet pattern' of the reality he now perceived. Whether that reality was a case of mild madness, or mere eccentricity, or sexual incompatibility is uncertain.[28] But one thing is sure. The two happy years at Sturminster Newton had come to a sour end:

> Lost: such beginning was all;
> Nothing came after: romance straight forsook
>   Quickly somehow
> Life when we sped from our nook,
> Primed for new scenes with designs smart and tall . . .
> A preface without any book,
> A trumpet uplipped, but no call
>   That seems it now.

('A Two-Years Idyll', *CP*, pp. 628–9)

The joys of parenthood denied them, mutual difficulties of temperament now painfully apparent to them, the Sturminster Newton idyll, their 'happiest time', soon ended (*Life*, p. 118).

Hardy's 'New Year's Thought' for 1879 was that of a frustrated idealist: 'A perception of the FAILURE OF THINGS to be what they are meant to be, lends them, in place of the intended interest, a new and greater interest of an unintended kind.' He then remarked that the poem 'A January Night, 1879' derived from an incident that occurred at the house in Tooting where 'their troubles began'. In January 1879, they 'seemed to begin to feel that "there had passed away a glory from the earth"' (*Life*, p. 124). The phrase from Wordsworth's 'Intimations Ode', taken with the one from his 'Elegiac Stanzas' that Hardy used in the note of June 1877 (see note 27), suggests that Hardy, in making 'Nature's defects' the basis of a hitherto unperceived beauty', in seeking new worth in things that had failed, was trying to achieve a sense of compensation and gain like that achieved by Wordsworth in the great ode. Only three years before, Hardy had found it possible to depict just such a power (possibly with stanza ten of the Ode in mind) in Gabriel Oak of *Far from the Madding Crowd*. At the loss of his flock, for him a complete social and economic disaster, Oak is sadder but wiser:

> Gabriel was paler now. His eyes were more meditative, and his expression was more sad. He had passed through an ordeal of wretchedness which had given more than it had taken away. He had sunk from his modest elevation as pastoral king into the very slime-pits of Siddim; but there was left to him a dignified calm he had never known before, and that indifference to fate which, though it often makes a villain of a man, is the basis of his sublimity when it does not. And thus the abasement had been exaltation, and the loss gain.   (ch. 6)

But Hardy's personal situation, fortified by his determination to make nature's defects the basis of a new beauty, was less like Oak's than it was like the grieving Wordsworth's in 'Elegiac Stanzas', where sorrow at the death of a beloved brother leads to rejection of the idea of a beneficent nature and to a declaration of new sympathy for man based not on love of nature but on pity for men:

> So once it would have been, – 'its so no more;
> I have submitted to a new control:
> A power is gone, which nothing can restore;
> A deep distress hath humanized my Soul.

Not for a moment could I now behold
A smiling sea, and be what I have been:
The feeling of my loss will ne'er be old;
This, which I know, I speak with mind serene.[29]

Like Wordsworth, Hardy was chastened by loss, which he
ascribed to a 'defect in Nature', to 'the FAILURE OF THINGS to be what
they are meant to be'. And like Wordsworth at a similar juncture,
Hardy rejected the idea that nature is a beneficent, regenerative
power:

The rain smites more and more
The east wind snarls and sneezes;
Through the joints of the quivering door
    The water wheezes.

The tip of each ivy-shoot
Writhes on its neighbour's face;
There is some hid dread afoot
    That we cannot trace.

('A January Night, 1879', *CP*, p. 466)

But unlike Wordsworth, Hardy did not gain 'new control' and
broader human sympathy from experience of defect and treachery
in nature. Ironic, self-admonishing poems such as 'Overlooking the
River Stour', 'The Musical Box', and 'On Sturminster Footbridge'
suggest instead a failure of love and intelligence at this time.[30] In the
first, the poet laments his failure to turn from the eye-filling beauties
of a June day to see 'the more behind [his] back' – that is, the loving,
perhaps emotionally troubled, wife who watches him set out from
their home. The splendours of the day, though infinitely less than
the person behind him, had claimed his attention (*CP*, p. 482). 'The
Musical Box' (*CP*, pp. 482–3) is based on another irony, the poet's
failure to see that the two happy years at Sturminster Newton could
not continue 'lifelong'. As the poet of 'Overlooking the River Stour'
fails to see 'the more' from which he turns away, the poet of 'The
Musical Box' fails to see or hear the shadowy spirit speaking,
through the 'thin mechanic' voice of a music box, of the wisdom of
'mak[ing] the most of what is nigh'. He fails because of a 'dull soul-
swoon', a melancholy whose only relief is the severe one of a tragic

art, a precise depiction – as in 'On Sturminster Footbridge' – of life
and light at play inconclusively in a world of darkness:

> Reticulations creep upon the slack stream's face
>   When the wind skims irritably past,
> The current clucks smartly into each hollow place
> That years of flood have scrabbled in the pier's sodden base;
>   The floating-lily leaves rot fast.
>
> On a roof stand the swallows ranged in wistful waiting rows
>   Till they arrow off and drop like stones
> Among the eyot-withies at whose foot the river flows:
> And beneath the roof is she who in the dark world shows
>   As a lattice-gleam when midnight moans.

(CP, p. 484)

In these lines we find, even more clearly rendered than in the other
two poems, an example of what Hardy meant by an art to be
cultivated in the face of 'nature's defects'. Such an art must infuse
darkness and disorder with a light and a harmony that make the
darkness 'the basis of a hitherto unperceived beauty'. Thus the
importance of the 'white-muslined' form standing in the gloom ('she
who in the dark world shows / As a lattice-gleam when midnight
moans') in both 'Musical Box' and 'On Sturminster Footbridge'. It
is from this darkness-defying light that the poet of 'Overlooking the
River Stour' has foolishly and selfishly turned away, in order to gaze
on the surface lights and superficial beauties ('river gleam',
'shavings of crystal spray', 'stream-shine', 'golden and honeybee'd'
day) of a Dorset June.

This contemplation of light-amidst-darkness is connected with
the new idea of beauty Hardy announced in the early pages of *The
Return of the Native* and in some notes of April 1878. The idea consists
of the 'infusing [of] emotion into the baldest external objects either
by the presence of a human figure among them, or by mark of some
human connection with them' to produce a 'beauty of association
[that] is entirely superior to the beauty of aspect, and [makes] a
beloved relative's old battered tankard [superior] to the finest Greek
vase. Paradoxically put, it is to see the beauty in ugliness' (*Life*, p.
120). This is, of course, an extension of his determination to make
nature's defects 'the basis of a hitherto unperceived beauty'. In *The*

Return of the Native, the novel on which Hardy was at work during the very year (1877) depicted in the three Sturminster Newton poems, this aesthetic paradox is refocused and used to illustrate a deterioristic view of history. By 'refocused' it is meant that the idea of light-in-darkness associated with Emma in the poems is attached to Mrs Yeobright in the novel, a fact that suggests the similar and competing role the two women played in Hardy's emotional and imaginative life. Even Hardy's example in the note of 1878 – 'a beloved relative's old battered tankard' – is associable with Mrs Yeobright, who on the crucial journey to Alderworth brings an antique cup as a gift for Clym and Eustacia. Mrs Yeobright lives at Bloom's End, a house set off from dark Egdon Heath by a fence with white pales. She is described on her first appearance as follows: 'Her face, encompassed by the blackness of the receding heath, showed whitely, and without half-lights, like a cameo' (*RN*, 1, ch. 3). Eustacia, repeatedly associated with figures from classical mythology, recalls 'the finest Greek vase' of Hardy's notes. At one point in the story, Mrs Yeobright and Clym quarrel because Clym has given Eustacia a recently exhumed burial urn. The sexual significance of the tankard, the cup, and vase, and the urn seems obvious. Assuming the late poems to be an accurate record of Hardy's mixed feelings about his wife in 1877, it can be seen how the shift from wife to mother between the poems and the novel might be accompanied in the novel by a deterioristic view of history and a new idea of beauty:

Fair prospects wed happily with fair times; but alas, if times be not fair! Men have oftener suffered from the mockery of a place too smiling for their reason than from the oppression of surroundings over-sadly tinged. Haggard Egdon appealed to a subtler and scarcer instinct, to a more recently learnt emotion, than that which responds to the sort of beauty called charming and fair.

Indeed, it is a question if the exclusive reign of this orthodox beauty is not approaching its last quarter. The new Vale of Tempe may be a gaunt waste in Thule: human souls may find themselves in closer and closer harmony with external things wearing a sombreness distasteful to our race when it was young. The time seems near, if it has not actually arrived, when the chastened sublimity of a moor, a sea, or a mountain will be all of nature that is absolutely in keeping with the moods of the more thinking among mankind. (*RN*, 1, ch. 1)

This primitivist yearning for the youth of the race – balanced, to be sure, by recognition of the race's tragic old age – suggests the importance of an episode like the one that occurred in London in the summer of 1878.

The Hardys had not been long in their house on Arundel Terrace, Upper Tooting, when Emma looked out of the window and saw her husband dashing hatless down Trinity Road. When he returned, he explained that he had heard 'a street barrel-organ playing somewhere near at hand the very quadrille over which the jaunty young man who had reached the end of his time at Hicks's [in Dorchester, in 1856] had spread such a bewitching halo more than twenty years earlier by describing the glories of dancing around to its beats on the Cremorne platform or at the Argyle Rooms, and which Hardy had never been able to identify'.

> He had thrown down his pen, and, as she had beheld, flown out and approached the organ-grinder with such speed that the latter, looking frightened, began to shuffle off. . . . [Hardy] had till then never heard it since his smart senior had whistled it; he never heard it again, and never ascertained its name. It was possibly one of Jullien's – then gone out of vogue – set off rather by the youthful imagination of Hardy at sixteen than by any virtue of the music itself. (*Life*, p. 123)

Such excitement in a man of Hardy's reticence and reserve suggests something of the power certain of his early experiences held over him. The same nostalgia would cause him to seek – in London, in May 1889 – a copy of the old song 'How oft Louisa', because he remembered that he had promised a copy to Louisa Harding of Stinsford more than a quarter-century before (*Life*, p. 219). The same passion to recover things past would lead him, during a visit to the Continent with Emma in September 1896, to 'put up for association's sake at the same hotel they had patronized twenty years before', during the happiest days of their marriage. This was quite probably an attempt, during some of the unhappiest days of their marriage, to revive old sympathies. But there was no revival: they found that the hotel 'had altered for the worse since those bright days' (*Life*, p. 284).

The marriage that began on 'a perfect September day' (in a phrase from Emma's *Recollections*) had also altered for the worse, and with it Hardy's second dream of felicity. Emma has frequently been viewed as a foolish or mildly deranged woman who made life nearly unbearable for her husband. But, as Robert Gittings has suggested, and as these remarks on the working of Hardy's nostalgia should also suggest, Hardy probably brought to his marriage expectations and limitations beyond Emma's, perhaps anyone's, power to satisfy or overcome.[31] By 1870, Hardy was a lacerated idealist, a man looking desperately for 'the one believed-in thing', for the truth, the beauty, the joy he had known as a child, then lost. And by 1874, judging from the portrait of Elfride in *A Pair of Blue Eyes* and of Bathsheba in *Far from the Madding Crowd*, his thinking about women, always central to his fiction, had taken a turn toward misogyny. By 1885, against the wishes of his wife, he was back in the environs of his lost paradise. Emma deserves to be judged more leniently than she has been, and perhaps that will be made easier when it is seen that Hardy's religious and architectural views – at the urging of his virulent nostalgia – took the same kind of disillusioning turn as his marriage.

THE FAILURE OF A REDEMPTIVE FAITH

The story of Hardy's troubled attachment to the Church of England has been told too well by others to be repeated here.[32] It is worth noting, however, that at its fullest Hardy's faith was the complex devotion of one who knew and loved not just the teachings, but also the music, the literature and the architecture of Anglican Christianity. Even more important, many of his fondest memories of his early days were connected with the church at Stinsford, with his lingering ambition to be a clergyman (something his mother and father seem to have encouraged), and with his father's, uncle's and grandfather's connections with the Stinsford Church choir, connections he fondly commemorated in *Under the Greenwood Tree*. Poems such as 'Afternoon Service at Mellstock (c. 1850)', 'The Oxen' and 'Yuletide in a Younger World' reveal a longing well into his late years for a lost time of simple devotion, visioned piety and untroubled belief:

We heard still small voices then
And, in the dim serene
Of Christmas Eve
Caught the far-time tones of fire-filled prophets
Long on earth unseen.

(*CP*, p. 861)

It comes as no surprise to find then, that, even after Hardy rejected the Church's doctrines, he continued to revere her music, visit her cathedrals, work at the restoration of her aging buildings, read and quote her liturgy, and, of course, keep her observances. As William James has wisely said, 'the most violent revolutions in an individual's beliefs leave most of his old order standing'.[33] This is not to say that Hardy was a covert Christian, but rather to suggest that certain patterns of his thought and feeling – e.g. his concern with questions of guilt, sin and forgiveness – learned in a High Church home from an exacting mother remained intact and responsive to other, often contradictory, ideas and values. These things are well known, as has been pointed out. What deserves to be noted, however, is that Hardy's strong temperamental sense of irreparable loss, his sense that growth is decay, made Christian belief difficult, even treacherous, for him in its central and definitive teaching – the mystery of the Resurrection and the hope of redemption that flows from it.

There is a suggestion of precisely this in an odd incident involving the Eucharist that occurred in Westminster Abbey in July 1865 (possibly earlier).[34] But even if we knew nothing of that incident (to be discussed a little later), we might infer from some events in Dorchester in the 1850s that a chief cause of Hardy's unbelief was his distrust of the idea of a supernatural deliverance from the burden of sin. In a letter to Lord Morley in November 1885, for example, he would lament the neglect shown by religious writers for 'the religious wants . . . of thoughtful people who have ceased to believe in supernatural theology' and would describe his 'dream that the church, instead of being disendowed, could be made to modulate by degrees . . . into an undogmatic, nontheological establishment for the promotion of that virtuous living on which all honest men are agreed'.[35] This hope in a secularized faith probably originated in his reading of *Essays and Reviews* under the guidance of Horace Moule in the late 1850s; for the authors of that heterodox volume, especially Rowland Williams, C. J. Bunsen and Benjamin Jowett, sought to translate Christian supernaturalism into moral and psychological

terms.[36] Hardy would seek to effect a similar translation in a number
of the novels.

In *Under the Greenwood Tree*, for example, communal values of a
secular kind are seen as replacing traditional religious values
represented by the defunct Mellstock Quire. In *A Laodicean* Hardy
holds up with something like scorn the beliefs of the Baptist
preacher, Reverend Woodwell, who seeks to rebaptize the Anglican
heroine, Paula Power. In *Two on a Tower* he satirizes Viviette
Constantine's confusion of romantic with religious feeling when she
urges Confirmation on the agnostic Swithin St Cleeve. In *Tess of the
d'Urbervilles* he depicts with bitter indignation his heroine's need to
baptize her dying infant, to play saviour and redeemer to her needy
family, then to offer herself as a living sacrifice to a Christian
society's laws on the pagan altar at Stonehenge. In the same novel,
Angel Clare, the agnostic son of a Low Church clergyman, decides
against a career in the Church because he cannot accept its
'untenable redemptive theolatry'. That is, Angel cannot subscribe
to Article IV ('Of the Resurrection of Christ') of the Thirty-Nine
Articles of Religion, which reads as follows: 'Christ did truly rise
again from death, and took again his body, with flesh, bones, and all
things appertaining to the perfection of man's nature; wherewith he
ascended into Heaven, and there sitteth, until he return to judge all
Men at the last day'.[37] From the death and resurrection of Christ
flow the distinctive features of Christian theology and moral
teaching. That Hardy was deeply imprinted with a redemptive
theology and its counsel of forgiveness is clear not only from his
writings but also from his markings in his Book of Common
Prayer, his hymnal, his Bibles and his copy of Keble's *Christian
Year*.

For example, in one of his Bibles, signed 'Thos. Hardy, 1861',
against Nathan's assurance to David that David's sin with
Bathsheba has been forgiven (2 Sam 12:13), Hardy drew up a list of
passages that treat sin and forgiveness ('[2 Sam] 24:10; Job 7:20; Ps
32:5; Ps 51:4; Pvbs 28:13'). By way of contrast to the promise of
forgiveness and redemption in these passages, he marked passages
such as this one in Job: 'As the cloud is consumed and vanisheth
away: so he that goeth down to the grave shall come up no more. He
shall return no more to his house, neither shall his place know him
any more' (7: 9–10). Chapter 14 of Job, Job's moving plea for
redemption in the face of irrecoverable loss, Hardy marked beside
fifteen of its twenty-two verses, among them the following: 'He
[man] cometh forth like a flower and is cut down: he fleeth also as a

shadow, and continueth not. . . . Who can bring a clean thing out of an unclean? not one. . . . If a man die, shall he live again? All the days of my appointed time will I wait, till my change come.' The whole of Psalm 24, an exhortation to receive God as King of all creation, he marked and dated '4.6.63'. Against verses 7 and 8 of Psalm 49, a plea that faith in the Resurrection be built on God rather than on things of the world, Hardy marked 'Matt. 16; Job 36: 18–19', passages which juxtapose nicely the just God of Elihu's vision and the redeeming Christ, son of the living God, of Matthew's. In David's prayer for remission of his sins in Psalm 51, Hardy marked verse 10 ('Create in me a clean spirit, O God; and renew a right spirit within me') and noted the similar thought in 'Acts 15:9, Eph 2:10'.[38]

Sincere Christianity was for Hardy synonymous with charity, forgiveness and loving-kindness, though like many nineteenth-century sceptics he wanted to preserve a Christian morality free of Christian supernaturalism. And Hardy's Anglican rearing would have been enough to implant deep within him a belief in a 'redemptive theolatry'. But his Anglican training – and this is the chief point here – was but one element of his view of redemption; for between 1856 and about 1861 Hardy was deeply affected by an even more dramatic and personal view of redemption when he fell in with some Baptists of Dorchester whose ardent belief in adult baptism drove him to doubt the authority for the Anglican form of the rite, and probably the efficacy of the rite itself.

One of Hardy's colleagues at the office of John Hicks was Henry Robert Bastow, a shadowy figure in Hardy's early life whose influence on the young Hardy, at least for a time, was probably as strong as Horace Moule's. Bastow was an ardent Baptist who in 1856, the year Hardy arrived at Hicks's, became 'very doctrinal' and was baptized. Hardy was so impressed by his senior colleague's action and by 'the necessity of doing likewise' that 'he almost felt that he ought to be baptized again as an adult' (*Life*, p. 20). However, being a staunch churchman, he first sought the advice of the vicar of Stinsford and then of a curate from another parish. Neither, however, could convince him of the unassailable authority of the Anglican practice of infant baptism. Disappointed and probably embarrassed before the zealous and argumentative Bastow, he studied as many books and pamphlets on paedobaptism as he could find, only to be 'appalled at the feebleness of the arguments for infant christening' (*Life*, p. 20). But he 'incontinently determined to "stick to his side", as he considered the Church to be, at some costs to his conscience' (*Life*, p. 20). The debate did not end here – with Hardy retreating behind a bastion of Anglican orthodoxy. Two sons of a Dorchester Baptist minister named Perkins (the original for Pastor Woodwell in *A Laodicean*) joined Bastow against Hardy. To hold his own against them, since they read the New Testament in the Greek of the original, Hardy bought Griesbach's Greek Testament and taught himself to read it. For he was convinced, at least for a time, that Bastow and the Perkins brothers were right; though 'his convictions on the necessity of adult baptism gradually wore out of him' (*Life*, p. 30).

Though the episode undoubtedly threatened some of Hardy's deepest beliefs and loyalties at a most impressionable time of his life, his account of it in the *Life* is brief and, as some unpublished letters from Bastow to Hardy suggest, scarcely descriptive of the depth and intimacy of his involvement with Bastow on religious questions.[39] The letters strongly suggest that Hardy was more actively involved with Bastow and other members of this militantly redemptivist group than either the *Life* or later accounts have shown. In the *Life* Bastow is portrayed as a strong but passing influence on the young Hardy; in the letters that survive Bastow emerges as an aggressive spiritual adviser to a passive disciple. In a letter dated 22 January 1861, for example, we find Bastow (writing from Tasmania) urging Hardy to hold Christ above all else:

And now dear Tom about more important things. Don't let study or business or anything else take the place the precious Saviour ought to have in your heart. You are going to see Him some day, and don't go to see him as a stranger. Cultivate acquaintance with Him now – day by day, and let all your activities be in the full consciousness that he is with you – and you can enter upon this without in the least desiring his absence or dishonouring Him.

By May 1862 Hardy may have begun to shun correspondence with the zealous Bastow, for the latter complained bitterly in a letter of that date of Hardy's failure to write to him. In the same letter he recommended for Hardy's study a book or pamphlet by 'Bonar' titled *The Person of Christ*, then cautioned him, with almost fulsome intimacy, to avoid the appeal of Rome:

Dear Old Tom, don't you let your eye off Jesus. I did hear a whisper that *you* had begun to think that *works may do something* in the way of salvation – but dear fellow if you think so – don't oh don't for a moment let it prevent you leaning for *all your* salvation on 'Him'.

Bastow's fear lest Hardy value 'works' over faith as a means of salvation suggests that Hardy, possibly at the encouragement of Horace Moule, was already moved by the example of Newman.[40] The picture that emerges of a youthful Hardy being pulled in one direction by 'his ardent Baptist-senior' (*Life*, p. 31) and in quite another by the urbane and eclectic Moule is a most interesting one; for Hardy was much under the influence of Horace Moule by 1862, and was reading with his guidance the heterodox pages of *Origin of Species*, *Essays and Reviews* and the *Saturday Review*. Under these influences he must have found Bastow's emphatically Christocentric views increasingly quaint and uncongenial. Another letter from Bastow, dated 23 December 1863, reveals Bastow's concerns lest Hardy's intellectual and architectural ambitions overshadow his religious beliefs. Referring possibly to some of Hardy's early poems, or to the prize-winning architectural essay Hardy wrote earlier in the year, Bastow scolds, 'I really did not know that you considered the pen as one of the weapons of your *struggle for life*.' The last phrase suggests that Bastow might have heard 'a whisper' of Hardy's regard for Darwin's *Origin of Species*. He then reminded Hardy, and his tone suggests strongly that he regarded Hardy as a subordinate and even as a disciple, of his duty to be loyal to his earlier beliefs:

I can't stop however without asking you if you have forgotten altogether all the glorious things we have so often talked about. I do trust my dear old Tom, that while you are diligent in business – and remembering that by so doing you are pleasing your earthly master – you do not forget too that you are not only or mainly serving him, but the Lord Jesus. If you have not now the deep abiding sense of a present and gracious God and Father ever near you – and ordering all for good. . . .[41] And at the beginning say – God be merciful to me a sinner. And as a sinner go to him who will in no wise cast out. *You know as well as I that you once professed to love a crucified saviour and to know him as yours.* Oh cling to him – be faithful. Let not business or pleasure, ambition or money-making draw you from Him.   (emphasis added)

Bastow's letters strongly imply that Hardy, between the ages of sixteen and twenty, professed a redemptivist faith above and beyond that learned in an Anglican home, where there was a healthy regard for the demands of the 'earthly master'. 'Don't you dear Brother forget', Bastow wrote in February 1861, 'our little meetings together at our place of assignation, and oh do let Jesus have the very best of all your times and thoughts, and indeed let Him be your all in all. Cultivate a closer acquaintance with Him by ever walking as in His sight, and entering into no engagements without you can be sure of His companionship and blessing.'[42]

This glance into Hardy's religious life in the late 1850s sheds light perhaps on that other moment of religious decision, mentioned above, that occurred in London in July 1863 (see note 34), at which time we find him reading Newman's *Apologia* at the urging of Moule and pondering 'a highly visionary scheme' of 'combining poetry and the church':

> [He] wrote to a friend in Cambridge [probably Charles Moule] for particulars as to matriculation at that University, which with his late classical reading would have been easy for him. He knew that what money he could not muster himself for keeping terms his father would lend him for a few years, his idea being that of a curacy in a country village. This fell through less because of its difficulty than from a conscientious feeling, after some theological study, that he could hardly take the step with honour while holding the views which on examination he found himself to hold. And so he allowed the curious scheme to drift out of sight, *though not till after he had begun to practise orthodoxy*. For example: July 5. Sunday. To Westminster Abbey morning service. Stayed to the Sacrament. A very odd experience, amid a crowd of strangers. (*Life*, p. 50; emphasis added)

This note is one of the most puzzling in the somewhat puzzling entirety of the *Life*. It seems that in 1863, in spite of the doubts that had grown up since 1858–9, Hardy still seriously entertained the possibility of becoming a clergyman. Architecture demanded social activity of a kind he detested, and his poems were being rejected by the magazines. His plan was to take a degree from Cambridge, Horace as well as Charles Moule's University. But upon examination of his religious views he felt he could not go on with it. Poems of this time such as 'Hap', 'Dream of a City Shopwoman', 'At a Bridal', 'Discouragement' and 'Heiress and Architect' suggest why he could not. He was discarding his belief in a beneficent God and nature, the belief he had shared for a time with Bastow.

All this seems clear enough. But then comes his concluding remark that he did *not* discard his clerical scheme until 'he had begun to practise orthodoxy'. This is perplexing, because it is natural to assume that anyone seriously considering a career in the Church would have been practising orthodoxy. But this apparently was not the case. Only 'after he had begun to practise orthodoxy' did he allow 'the curious scheme [of combining poetry and the church] to drift out of sight'. He illustrates this decision with a description of his attendance at Holy Communion in Westminster Abbey. He called this 'a very odd experience', perhaps because he was among strangers, perhaps because he had not received the Sacrament for a long time, but more probably because the trust in supernatural powers of regeneration exhibited there by the faithful would seem 'very odd' indeed to a man thoroughly imbued with a deteriorist view of things. The poem 'The Impercipient (at a Cathedral Service)' comes to mind, for in it the poet contemplates the strangeness and the mystery of his alienation from a 'bright believing band['s]' devotion to a God who 'breathes All's Well' to them but not to him (*CP*, pp. 67–8). In this episode at Westminster Abbey and in the poem, Hardy, like Paula Power and George Somerset in *A Laodicean*, like Swithin St Cleeve in *Two on a Tower*, like Angel Clare in *Tess*, balked at the Church's redemptive theology, embodied not just in the Sacrament of the Eucharist but also in its first sacrament, Baptism, whose authority Hardy had come to question just a few years before with the help of both the anabaptist Bastow and Horace Moule and the 'Seven against Christ'. If Hardy could not be a clergyman, he could, in spite of his doubts, receive the Sacrament that renews the purifying effect of Baptism and thus participate in the Church's central teaching that sin and defect are amendable. But, as might be expected, for the author of poems such as 'Hap' and 'Heiress and Architect', for one temperamentally convinced of the absolute pastness of the past, this involved terrible difficulties.

What the Redemption provides, whether through the Sacraments, through prayer, or through life in a Christian community, is deliverance from sin and from mortality. It also in a sense promises renewal: that is, restoration to an earlier, purer state of spiritual

being. Time, history, the relentless movement of the individual
toward death can be undone; the clock can be turned back. Thus
the Redemption offered Hardy the spiritual equivalent of
homecoming. And in fact Eden and Bockhampton had certain
affinities, probably because uncritical belief in the former had been
a part of an untroubled early life in the latter. The boy who recited
Dr Watt's 'And now another day is gone' when the evening sun
shone into the red staircase at Higher Bockhampton would also 'on
wet Sunday mornings . . . wrap himself in a tablecloth, and read
the Morning Prayer standing in a chair, his cousin playing the clerk
with loud Amens, and his grandmother representing the
congregation' (*Life*, p. 15). But as Hardy's critical view of Christ
(Bastow's 'crucified saviour') in a number of the poems makes quite
clear, the Redemption, like the return to Bockhampton in 1867, like
the marriage to a 'girl of grace' in 1874, was contradicted and
thwarted by a universal law of decay. Decay is king ('A Sign-
Seeker', *CP*, pp. 49–50), and so life is 'sad past saying / Its greens
forever graying / Its faith to dust decaying' ('To Sincerity', *CP*, pp.
278–9). This vision removed Hardy not only from the band of the
faithful at Westminster but from the circle at Higher Bockhampton,
as is suggested in 'Night in the Old Home' (*CP*, pp. 269–70), in
which the poet imagines himself upbraided not by strangers but by
spectral kinsmen for being a thinker 'on that which consigns men to
night after showing the day / To them'. Hardy's Christ is a great but
a wholly mortal ethical teacher, not a man–god and maker of
miracles. Though Christ's teachings can be the basis of an ethical
idealism, his alleged resurrection cannot undo the sins of men and
confer eternal life on them. For Hardy, the Crucifixion was simply
one, much celebrated, example of self-sacrifice; as he notes with
some asperity in the poem 'Unkept Good Fridays', there were many
'Christs of unwrit names', many martyrs to virtue and self-denial
(*CP*, pp. 842–3). He insisted, as in the bitter words of 'A Drizzling
Easter Morning', that the Resurrection had not altered the lot of a
toiling, aching humanity:

> And is he risen? Well, be it so . . .
> And still the pensive lands complain,
> And dead men wait as long ago,
> As if, much doubting, they would know
> What they are ransomed from, before
> They pass again their sheltering door.

> (*CP*, pp. 658–9)

Hardy's disenchantment with the redemptive centre of Christian teaching went hand-in-hand with his rejection of the romantic view of nature as a benignly creative and regenerative force. After reading Darwin, Hardy could no longer view nature as either inherently moral or progressive. Its compelling, unconscious aspect seemed to him its defining one, and its tendency, even after his excursion into evolutionary meliorism in *The Dynasts* (1903–8), seemed to be downward into greater and greater disorder. More particularly for him after 1865, nature was no longer a setting in which renewal or restoration of the human spirit could occur. The idea of nature as a place of 'peace', or of 'ease' and 'soft release', was lost to him; he found 'no grace' taught him by trees ('In a Wood', *CP*, pp. 64–5).[43] In fact, he personified Mother Nature as one who had changed for the worse. Her pure intentionality had been defiled by 'her unfaithful lord' ('Discouragement', *CP*, p. 829); she had declined after a fair beginning, 'as of an angel fallen from grace' ('The Lacking Sense', *CP*, p. 116); she had wrought, then slumbered, and her creatures suffer the dire consequences ('The Sleep-Worker', *CP*, pp. 121–2). She herself mourns because mankind holds 'in doubt and disdain' her 'ancient high fame of perfection', a view of her that she has come to regret:

> . . . 'My species are dwindling,
>   My forests grow barren,
> My popinjays fail from their tappings,
>   My larks from their strain.
>
> 'My leopardine beauties are rarer,
>   My tusky ones vanish,
> My children have aped mine own slaughters
>   To quicken my wane.
>
> 'Let me grow, then, but mildews and mandrakes
>   And slimy distortions,
> Let nevermore things good and lovely
>   To me appertain.'
>
> ('The Mother Mourns', *CP*, pp. 111–13)

In the poignantly ironic 'To Outer Nature', the poet joins the mourning Mother in lament, but he laments not her loss of good fame but his loss of his earlier view of her as a divinely wrought expounder of 'glad things that men treasure'. Only reluctantly has he become one of those unruly reasoners who heartlessly proclaim her defects:

> O for but a moment
> Of that old endowment –
>   Light to gaily
>   See thy daily
> Iris-hued embowment!
>
> But such re-adorning
> Time forbids with scorning –
>   Makes me see things
>   Cease to be things
> That were in my morning.

This death for him of nature-as-manifestation-of-God's-plan was one cause of his sense that he had lost forever a primal felicity:

> Fad'st thou, glow-forsaken,
> Darkness-overtaken!
>   Thy first sweetness
>   Radiance, meetness,
> None shall re-awaken.
>
> Why not sempiternal
> Thou and I? Our vernal
>   Brightness keeping,
>   Time outleaping;
> Passed the hodiernal.
>
> (*CP*, pp. 61–2)

'Why not sempiternal?' Because the author of 'To Outer Nature' is a man blind to something he once could see, and irremediably the worse for his blindness. And as is so often the case in Hardy, the touchstone for the experience of loss is the language of the Intimations Ode: a 'radiance' and a 'brightness' have been lost. His rejection of the romantic view of nature, like his abandonment of belief in the Redemption, was a rejection of supernatural possibilities for regeneration.[44]

THE FUTILITY OF ARCHITECTURAL RESTORATION AND THE POETICS OF FUTILITY

No return to things past, no redemption through an agent of the supernatural or through love of a fellow human being, no renewal through sympathetic identification with nature. By about 1883 these negations were integral parts of Hardy's view of things, and were checked only by his belief, itself steadily fading, in human powers of amendment or remedy, as embodied in comedic novels such as *Under the Greenwood Tree*, *Far from the Madding Crowd* and *The Trumpet-Major*. In addition, since about 1872, as suggested by his symbolic use of architecture in *A Pair of Blue Eyes*, Hardy had found yet another example of his sense of the irretrievable pastness of the past – the strongly insistent example provided him by his work as a restorer of Gothic. He had come to believe that architectural restoration was futile. Hardy gave up architecture as a livelihood in 1872, but his interest in it never diminished. It may be said that his experience of architecture, like his experience of childhood, religion and love, entered his imagination only when it was behind and beyond him. Not only would he use architectural settings and ideas throughout the novels, but in 1899, after he had given up fiction for poetry, he would find it 'obvious that he carried into his verse . . . the Gothic art-principle in which he had been trained – the principle of spontaneity' (*Life*, p. 301). And shortly before his death, thinking of the 1850s and of Bastow, Hicks and old Dorchester, he would remark 'that if he had his life over again he would prefer to be a small architect in a country town, like Mr Hicks of Dorchester, to whom he was articled' (*Life*, p. 443).

But such fondness had not always been the case. In the early 1880s, when he joined the Society for the Protection of Ancient Buildings, he had learned to deplore the destructive results of architectural restoration. He turned from architecture not just because it required that he live his life as a 'science' rather than an 'emotion', but also because he found hopeless all attempts to restore Gothic churches. He had learned that restoration was but another word for desecration and obliteration. For example, in the case of St Juliot's Church, in Cornwall, whose restoration he directed and

then turned to fictional use in *A Pair of Blue Eyes*, the tower, the
north aisle and the transept were pulled down; a north door, much
like a Saxon one, was destroyed; and seat-ends and other details
were removed. He deplored the loss of these 'original' features of the
Church and was happy that 'the old south aisle was kept intact, with
its arcade, the aisle . . . being adapted for a nave' (*Life*, p. 79).
Hardy fully agreed with Ruskin, whose *Seven Lamps of Architecture*
had appeared in 1848, that restoration was 'a lie from beginning to
end' and therefore 'the most total destruction which a building can
suffer'. 'It is *impossible*', Ruskin had written, 'as impossible as to raise
the dead, to restore anything that has ever been great or beautiful in
architecture. . . . The life of the whole, that spirit which is given
only by the hand and eye of the workman, can never be recalled.'
Hardy agreed and, again like Ruskin, sought to preserve what he
could not resurrect. He made drawings of the Saxon door and the
highly ornate bench-ends of St Juliot. He also used materials from
the old church to build the new one, and not just for thrift's sake.
The integration of old with new materials was a means of preserving
some of the old, and for Hardy, as for Ruskin, preservation was no
merely sentimental gesture: it was one, perhaps the only, practical
way to counter decay and total obliteration. Old buildings had to
come down; but if their histories, by which Hardy meant their
designs, their materials, *and* their human associations, could be
retained in some way, the loss would not be total. In sum, as an
active participant from 1856 to 1872 in a national movement to
revive a medieval style of architecture, Hardy faced almost daily an
issue that, though perhaps purely an architectural one for Hicks,
Blomfield and Crickmay, was for him an urgently philosophical and
personal one. The question of restoration was for him another form
of the question of return and the question of redemption; and his
negative reply to it was even less ambiguous than his negative
replies to the other two. A man might go home again, as Hardy did
in the 1860s and again in the 1880s; a man might please himself with
human substitutes for divine love; but no man could recall, as
Ruskin put it, 'the life of the whole, that spirit which is given [to a
building] by the hand and eye of the workman', a workman long
dead. Return, redemption and restoration posed for Hardy the same
dilemma—how to counter the working of the law of decay?—in
progressively more difficult terms. He was even more sceptical about
the possibility of restoring a crumbling Gothic church than he was
about the possibility of regaining 'the splendour in the grass', of

redeeming a lost soul, or of finding grace among trees.

Two important elements of Hardy's view of his artistry – his rejection of realism (as copying) and his concept of an 'idiosyncratic mode of regard' – are connected with his sense that time, history and consciousness are made up of a series of unique, unreturning and irretrievable events. Two remarks of the late 1880s, both of them the result of his study of the water-colours of J. M. W. Turner, strongly suggest the connection:

> After looking at the landscape ascribed to Bonington in our drawing room I feel that Nature is played out as a Beauty, but not as a Mystery. *I don't want to see landscapes, i.e., scenic paintings of them, because I don't want to see the original realities – as optical effects, that is, I want to see the deeper reality underlying the scenic, the expression of what are sometimes called abstract imaginings.* The 'simply natural' is interesting no longer. The much decried, mad, late-Turner rendering is now necessary to create my interest. The exact truth as to material fact ceases to be of importance in art – it is a student's style – the style of a period when the mind is serene and unawakened to the tragical mysteries of life; when it does not bring anything to the object that coalesces with and translates the qualities that are already there – half-hidden, it may be – and the two united are depicted as the All. (*Life*, p. 185; emphasis added)

> Turner's water-colours: each is a landscape *plus* a man's soul [Hardy's emphasis]. . . . What he paints chiefly is light as modified by objects. *He first recognizes the impossibility of really reproducing on canvas all that is in a landscape; then gives for that which cannot be reproduced a something else which shall have upon the spectator an approximative effect to that of the real* [emphasis added]. He said, in his maddest and greatest days: 'What pictorial drug can I dose man with, which shall affect his eyes somewhat in the manner of this strange reality which I cannot carry to him?' – and set to make such strange mixtures as he was tending towards in 'Rain, Steam, and Speed', 'The Burial of Wilkie', 'Agrippina Landing with the Ashes of Germanicus', 'Approach to Venice', 'Snowstorm and a Steamboat', etc. Hence, one may say, Art is the secret of how to produce by a false thing the effect of a true. . . . (*Life*, p. 216)

Because like Turner he recognized the unique and unreproducible nature of the moments and particles that make up reality, Hardy sought to approximate fleeting reality by substituting illusion for that which he could not reproduce. Through that illusion he might exhibit the beauty of a reality underlying the surface or scenic reality; for by 'illuding' he would translate the merely optical perception of physical reality into the imaginative perception or vision of an abiding reality and thereby preserve what otherwise might be irretrievably lost. This 'deeper reality' resembles closely the 'beauty of association', the 'beauty in ugliness', the 'hitherto unperceived beauty' he sought to exhibit in *The Return of the Native*.

But the choice of illusion depended wholly for Hardy on the personality and the peculiar experiences of the artist:

> Art is a changing of the actual proportions and order of things, so as to bring out more forcibly than might otherwise be done that feature in them which appeals most strongly to the idiosyncrasy of the artist. The changing, or distortion, may be of two kinds: (1) the kind which increases the sense of vraisemblance: (2) that which diminishes it. (1) is high art: (2) is low art. . . .
>
> Art is a disproportioning – (i.e., distorting, throwing out of proportion) – of realities, to show more clearly the features that matter in those realities, which, if merely copied or reported inventorily, might possibly be observed, but would more probably be overlooked. Hence 'realism' is not Art.   (Aug 1890, in *Life*, pp. 228-9)

For Hardy, the 'actual proportions and order of things', what in the poem 'Heiress and Architect' he called 'the law of stable things', was change-as-decay. The feature in change-as-decay that most appealed to his idiosyncratic way of seeing things – that is, to his nostalgic yearning for a lost past – was the impossibility of regeneration (of restoration, redemption, or return). His idiosyncratic way of seeing and feeling (his nostalgic idealism) led him to disproportion realities in order to bring out the inevitably hopeless human struggle against the deteriorative tendency, against the death-wardness, he saw in nature, in his traditional culture, and in individual lives.

Hardy's most complete theoretical account of his deterioristic view of things and of the difficulty plaguing the artist who would counter deterioration with illusion was made not in a literary but an architectural context, in 'Memories of Church Restoration', a talk he prepared for delivery before the Society for the Protection of Ancient Buildings in 1906.[45] Hardy joined the Society in the early 1880s because, as he said in 'Memories', he had come to despise 'active destruction under saving names', whether through pulling down, regularizing varied styles, or shifting irregular details for practical or other reasons. Such practices violated men's memories, he said, and cited by way of example the case of two brothers who, upon returning to their native place after many years' absence to attend the funeral of their father, quarrelled violently about the exact location of the family pew, long since removed by a restorer of churches. Such alterations violated the 'human interest in an edifice', Hardy argued, as well the aesthetic interest, which he then discussed at some length.

Though Hardy found abhorrent the alteration of any feature of an old building, he approved what he called 'the honest reproduction of old shapes in substituted materials'. He approved substitution because he thought this process accorded with 'the actual process of organic nature herself, which is one continuous substitution. She is always discarding the matter, while retaining the form', always, in biological terms, discarding the individual while retaining the species. Having granted this much, however, he would grant no more, for to prefer form to matter, the species to the individual, would be to ignore and thus to obliterate the individual, the particular, and the unique. Because Hardy ranked the 'human interest' of a building above its architectural or aesthetic interest, he opposed any attempt to submerge concrete, individual realities in a universal reality. A law of nature was of interest to him mainly for its effect on individual lives. And so, a society for the protection of ancient buildings was needed, he believed, to preserve two attributes of Gothic artistry:

> The first is uniqueness; such a duplicate as we have been considering can never be executed. No man can make two pieces of matter exactly alike. . . . It is found in practice that even such an easily copied shape as, say, a traceried window, does not get truly reproduced. The old form inherits, or has acquired, an indefinable quality – possibly some deviations from exact geometry (curves were often struck by hand in medieval work) – which never reappears in the copy, especially in the vast majority of cases where no nice approximation is attempted. (*PW*, p. 214)

The would-be restorer of Gothic is caught here in the same dilemma as the artist who 'recognizes the impossibility of really reproducing on canvas all that is in a landscape' (*Life*, p. 216). But where the artist can illude and distort on behalf of an underlying truth and thereby avoid the problem of actual reproduction, the restorer can only imitate imperfectly and therefore only falsify. Restoration, Ruskin had said, is a lie. A 'material' lie, Hardy here adds, that precipitates a 'spiritual' one:

> The second, or spiritual, attribute which stultifies the would-be reproducer, is perhaps more important still, and is not artistic at all. It lies in human associations. The influence that a building like Lincoln or Winchester exercises on a person of average impressionableness and culture is a compound influence, and though it would be a fanciful attempt to define how many fractions of that compound are aesthetic, and how many associative, there can be no doubt that the latter is more valuable than the former. . . . I think the damage done to this sentiment of association by replacement, by the rupture of continuity, is mainly what makes the enormous loss this country has sustained from its seventy years of church restoration so tragic and deplorable. The protection of an ancient edifice against renewal in fresh materials is, in fact, even more of a social – I may say a human – duty than an aesthetic one. It is the preservation of memories, history, fellowship, fraternities. Life, after all, is more than art, and that which appeals to us in the (maybe) clumsy outlines of some structure which had been looked at and entered by a dozen generations of ancestors outweighs the more subtle recognition, if any, of architectural qualities. The renewed stones of Hereford, Peterborough, Salisbury, St. Albans, Wells, and so many other places, are not the stones that witnessed the scenes in English chronicle associated with those piles. They are not the stones over whose face the organ notes of centuries 'lingered and wandered on as loth to die,'[46] and the fact that they are not, too often results in spreading abroad the feeling I instanced in the anecdote of the two brothers. (*PW*, pp. 214–15).

Hardy finally argued for the preservation rather than the restoration of ancient buildings because he believed that, once shaped and used, a building was both artistically and humanly unique and therefore unreproducible. Its chief value was that it preserved, in its smudges and smears, the continuity of human associations, a 'spiritual attribute' that the author of such a poem as 'Old Furniture' (*CP*, p. 485) understood from the heart.

Like the two brothers of the anecdote, and like so many of Hardy's protagonists, the speaker in 'Old Furniture' has returned to his old home after an absence. But he is more fortunate than most of Hardy's homecomers, because the traces of his past have not been tampered with. He can sit amid 'relics of householdry' that date from the days of his mother's mother and lovingly meditate upon them:

> I see the hands of the generations
>   That owned each shiny familiar thing
> In play on its knobs and indentations,
>   And with its ancient fashioning
>   Still dallying . . . .

After recreating from traces on clock, violin and hearth the hands, the fingers and even the faces of his dead ancestors, he gently chides himself for this attempt at an imaginative restoration:

> Well, well. It is best to be up and doing,
>   The world has no use for one to-day
> Who eyes things thus – no aim pursuing!
>   He should not continue in this stay
>   But sink away.

Like the hopelessly devoted lover of 'She, to Him, III' (*CP*, pp. 12–13), the poet in 'Old Furniture' – in spite of his self-rebuke – is torn between a compelling personal desire to be true to the past and an obligation to 'souls of Now, who would disjoint / The mind from memory, making Life all aim'. 'The world' cherishes 'aim' because it for the most part sees a law of progress at work where the poet sees a law of decay. It regards as mere sentimentality what is for him the only sensible response to tragic reality, which is to distort the actual, that is, the decaying, order of things by creating an illusion of restoration to show the 'features that matter' – the preservation of the dead in the memory of the living in defiance of inevitable decay.

At one point in 'Memories' Hardy with wry humour suggested that, since churches must be used and 'ruinous' churches are virtually useless, the 'ideal' solution to the problem would be to enclose the old church in 'a crystal palace' so that it would be available for viewing and then to build alongside it a new, utilitarian structure 'for services'. This fanciful plan (reminiscent of George Somerset's scheme for the ruined Stancy Castle at the end of *A Laodicean*) is the architectural equivalent of the strategy in 'Old Furniture', in which for a brief, sweet moment the dead are indeed raised:

> On the clock's dull dial a foggy finger,
>> Moving to set the minutes right
> With tentative touches that lift and linger
>> In the wont of a moth on a summer night,
>>> Creeps to my sight.
>
> On this old viol, too, fingers are dancing –
>> As whilom – just over the strings by the nut,
> The tip of a bow receding, advancing
>> In airy quivers, as if it would cut
>>> The plaintive gut.
>
> And I see a face by that box for tinder,
>> Glowing forth in fits from the dark,
> And fading again, as the linten cinder
>> Kindles to red at the flinty spark,
>>> Or goes out stark.

Hardy was divided between a dreamy wish to have things as they had been and a hard-headed conviction that – except imaginatively – they could never be so. As an architect and church-restorer he sought to preserve old buildings because they could not be reproduced, especially in their human associations. As a poet and a novelist he distorted and disproportioned reality to at once avoid the impossible work of reproducing it and yet still fulfil the necessary task of carrying that reality to the reader. Such a disproportioning of reality was in Hardy's view neither a merely eccentric nor a narrowly subjective rendering of things; for he believed that the seer-poet who watched 'that pattern among general things which his idiosyncrasy move[d] him to observe, and describe[d] that alone' was 'going to nature', with the result 'no mere photograph, but purely the product of the writer's own mind' (*Life*, p. 153; June 1882). Hardy's expressive–mimetic view of his art may seem a self-contradictory one, but his purpose, to show by distorting the reality of decay the 'features that matter', in particular the human struggle against decay, and thereby to preserve the unreproducible, is consistent throughout his writing.[47] It is the basis of the vision 'ghast and grim' in the early poems. It is near the centre of the vision of the novels, which may be divided into narratives of successful or thwarted return and narratives of successful or thwarted restoration. It is one of the overriding concerns of the later poems, of whose view of things Hardy resolved to say no more in the last poem of *Winter Words*:

> Let Time roll backward if it will
> (Magians who drive the midnight quill
>   With brain aglow
>   Can see it so),
> What I have learnt no man shall know.

> (*CP*, p. 390)

The Dynasts with its evolutionary meliorism is his magnificent but qualified attempt at a counterstatement. His mythic 'Wessex', 'a partly real, partly dream-country', was for a time the perfect expression of his desire to show 'what mattered' in a world of decay; for in Wessex he could set side by side as it were an enduring image of the old and a record of its inevitable and irreversible decline.

The restoration of ancient churches, like the uprooting of persons from the homes of their childhood, ruptures continuity, deprives aim of memory, and calls upon the artist to do two things: to show the working of the natural law of decay; to show what matters in the face of it, the pathos, the beauty, and the wonder of the human struggle (almost always futile) to thwart it. The artist who shows this is awake to what Hardy called 'the tragical mysteries of life' (*Life*, p. 185).

2 'Thinking o' Perfection': the Novels and Poems to 1875

> I sometimes am afraid that he'll never get on, . . . all through his seeing too far into things – being discontented with make-shifts – thinking o' perfection in things, and then sickened that there's no such thing as perfection.   (*DR*, ch. 8, pt 3)

For Thomas Hardy the years between 1862 and 1875 were, as has been seen, years of unsettling movement and decisive personal change. On Maundy Thursday (17 April) 1862, he had left his Dorset home of nearly twenty-two years for London; after five years in the great metropolis he had returned, in poor health, to live once again in the family cottage at Higher Bockhampton. Though the old homestead was to be his headquarters for the next seven years, he frequently left it for visits to London, to Weymouth (where he lived for a time in 1869–70), and after 1870, to Cornwall. The seven years (1867–74) at home were undoubtedly years of social and intellectual readjustment, for after five years as 'an isolated student cast upon the billows of London with no protection but his brains' he had returned to rural Dorset an angry critic of politics, society and religion, as can be seen in what remains of 'The Poor Man and the Lady' (1867), his first and never-published novel (*Life*, pp. 56ff). The seven years from 1867 to 1874 were also years of romance. A shadowy love affair with Tryphena Sparks, a first cousin of sixteen, began a short time after his homecoming in July 1867. It ended, possibly on a note of bitterness, in 1872 or 1873,[1] probably because by 1872 Hardy was in love with Emma Gifford, whom he had met two years before while on a visit to Cornwall to undertake the restoration of the church of St Juliot, near Boscastle. Finally, these were years of tremendous anxiety, even of despair, about his vocation. Was he to be an architect or a writer, and if a writer, a poet (his deepest wish) or a serial novelist? He flirted with the idea of becoming a clergyman, of writing art-criticism, and even of going on the stage. His earliest attempts at poetry had been rejected by London editors and his first attempts at fiction were faring little better.

'The Poor Man and the Lady' was turned down by Macmillan, then by Chapman and Hall, and then by Tinsley (in 1869). *Desperate Remedies*, written in 1869–70, was rejected by Macmillan, then accepted by Tinsley (in 1871) with an agreement that Hardy pay £75 against the cost of publication. The *Spectator* came down hard on it, and Hardy never forgot his bitterness when he read the review: 'at the time he wished that he were dead' (*Life*, p. 84). *Under the Greenwood Tree* (1872) he sent first to Macmillan; it was returned with an offer to reconsider, a proposition that Hardy apparently viewed as a rejection, for he set it aside until Tinsley asked for it in the spring of 1872. It sold poorly. No wonder he wrote the date 'July 1871' beside the following passage in his copy of *Macbeth*: 'Things at their worse will cease, or else climb upward / To what they were before' (*Life*, p. 85). 'Climb upward' things indeed did, for with the publication of *A Pair of Blue Eyes* (1873) and *Far From the Madding Crowd*, and with his marriage to a 'girl of grace', Hardy would seem to have been well on his way to success and personal happiness by the autumn of 1874. But if we look more closely – not only at the first five novels and the early chapters of the *Life*, but also at some of the poems of the 1860s and at some later poems about the 1870s – we find that 'things at their worse' had, in one crucial sense, not ceased at all.

What do the poems of the 1860s, the late poems about the 1870s, and the novels of 1867–74 have in common? The first six chapters of the *Life*, as has been seen, suggest an answer. They have in common deteriorism, the view that time, history and consciousness are caught up in an irreversible process of decline or decay. All is a falling away from a primal felicity and perfection. The *Life*'s at times triumphal account of the rise of Thomas Hardy from rural obscurity to the apex of the world of letters is challenged repeatedly by melancholy reflections on the decline of the Hardys. Especially in his later years, Hardy had a strong sense of himself as one of the last survivors of a dying line.[2] Neither his brother, Henry, nor his sisters, Mary and Kate, ever married; and he himself was childless, a circumstance that disturbed him to the end of his days.[3]

The *Life* is more, of course, than the melancholy rumination of a lonely, childless octogenarian. It is a careful self-portrait shaped, like much of the prose Hardy wrote after 1890, by a strong desire to justify himself as a thinker of positive thoughts on God, nature and human life. That he should have concealed some unflattering details about his birth and his first marriage was at least consistent with this desire. But in its portrait of a human life the *Life* resembles the novels and many of the poems; for the career of its central figure is viewed not only as a movement toward ripeness and fulfilment (which Hardy's career in its external aspects surely was), but as a decline, a fading away, from an early grace and felicity. Within this somewhat paradoxical view, growth becomes a metaphor of decay and spiritual death; for removal from the first – that is to say, the best – time is irremediable.

HOPE UNBLOOMS: THE POEMS OF THE 1860s

The personae of the poems of the 1860s are, almost all of them, saddened or embittered observers of irremediable loss. In 'Discouragement' (1863–7; *CP*, p. 829), an indignant poet describes the ruin of Mother Nature by a 'lord' who thwarts her hopes and plans for perfection. 'His defiling hand' mars her plans for bloom and beauty. He causes the loves and dreams of her human creatures to depend on chance or on error; and this is disheartening, the death of hope, the cause of 'visions ghast and grim'. The faint suggestion in this poem that Mother Nature has been sexually defiled makes it a weird variant on one of Hardy's favourite stories, the story of the ruined maid. In place of a pure maiden we have the all-creating, perfection-seeking Mother; in place of sexual assault we have ruin stemming from the defective order of things. Not a single life but the source of all life is attacked and besmirched. Not the perfect innocent but the matrix of perfect innocence is violated, and not just once, but again and again; for her ruin is continual. She fails as predictably as she hopes, as regularly as she plans for 'bloom and beauty', as frequently as she attempts to make a 'perfect mould'. Though it is not clear whether nature's brutal master is man, or chance, or God, it is clear that there is defect – irremediable defect – at the heart of things.[4] Here Hardy exhibits nature in much the way he would come to exhibit himself, as a 'simple self that was' brought to ruin by time and by experience ('Wessex Heights', *CP*, pp. 319–20).

Cynical rejection of a simpler self is the strategy of 'Melia in the 'Ruined Maid' (1866). 'Melia is a former country girl whose life as a prostitute in the town has brought her not ruin but fine clothes, polished manners and leisure, all in striking contrast to an old friend from the country, whose virtue and hard work have brought her misery and want:

> '– I wish I had feathers, a fine sweeping gown,
> And a delicate face, and could strut about Town!' –
> 'My dear – a raw country girl, such as you be,
> Cannot quite expect that. You ain't ruined', said she

> (*CP*, pp. 158–9)

Vice has its reward, virtue its punishment. The poem exhibits respect for 'Melia's refusal to look back in regret or to make the worst of things. But such disdain for lost innocence is rare in Hardy. Sad disillusionment is the usual response.

This is certainly the view in 'The Temporary the All', the undated poem that Hardy placed at the head of the dozen or so poems of the sixties that open *Wessex Poems* (1898). In it a man reflects with bitterness on his belief, in his 'flowering youthtime', that temporary friendships and loves, interim dwelling places and deeds, were but previsions of ideal ones to come. He has learned from experience that the true friend or the 'Wonder of women' never appears, that the 'visioned hermitage' is never built, the 'high handiwork' never completed. In sum, the idealistic hopes and dreams of youth are delusions; and there is no compensation in experience or in growth, for growth is a steady falling away from an early glory and gleam. Perfection, he discovers is behind, not before, him (*CP*, p. 7). In 'Amabel' (1865) a similar man notes with increasing resentment the signs of decay in the woman he once loved: 'her ruined hues' and 'custom-straitened views', her gown 'once rose, now earthen brown', her once lively step now 'mechanic' and slow, her laugh no longer sweet (*CP*, pp. 8–9). Amabel has withered, and her poet lover can do nothing but muse on this and on the ironic fact that though lovers fade 'Love's race' endures. He resolves to say no more and bids his fading love farewell 'Till the last Trump'. There is a cutting irony in this goodbye, for it echoes a phrase from St Paul's great chapter on mankind's redemption through Christ: 'Behold, I shew you a mystery; We shall not all sleep, but we shall all be changed, in a moment, in the twinkling of an eye, at the last trump: for the trumpet shall sound, and the dead shall be raised incorruptible. . . . O death, where *is* thy sting? O grave, where is thy victory?' (1 Corinthians 15: 52–5). No such 'mystery' comforts Amabel or her lover. Both are victims of 'time the tyrant'; for both, joy lies slain and hope 'unblooms'.

The verb is used, of course, in 'Hap' to signify absolute negation, the failure of a seed of hope to germinate, sprout, grow and blossom ('Why unblooms the best hope ever sown?'). But it also suggests deterioration, the reversal of the action denoted by the verb 'blooms', thus signifying that hope unwinds, moves backward in a process of devolution and disintegration toward the nothingness that preceded life. Lurking behind 'Hap' as well as the other poems of the sixties is the cry of outraged innocence heard in 'Tess's Lament':

> I cannot bear my fate as writ,
>   I'd have my life unbe;
> Would turn my memory to a blot
> Make every relic of me rot,
> My doings be as they were not,
>   And gone *all trace of* me.

> (*CP*, pp. 175–7)

'Heiress and Architect' (1867) is Hardy's most complete early statement of his view that, in a phrase from the poem 'Genetrix Laesa', 'all is sinking / To dissolubility' (*CP*, p. 770). An heiress, brimming with the desire to build a 'visioned hermitage', is shown the ghast, grim reality with regard for which she must build by an architect, a man of 'cold, clear view' who speaks on behalf of something he calls 'the law of stable things' (*CP*, p. 75). She asks first for a design that will admit the sounds and scents of sweet nature. He warns, by way of response, that 'winters freeze'. She then asks for a house of many windows that will show her beauty to passers-by. He warns that she will fade, grow sick of soul, and seek solitude. She relents and asks only for 'a little chamber' richly ornamented, 'a Paradise / Wherein my Love may greet me!' He reminds her that love also wanes and that the 'sweet work' of the chamber will serve only to remind her of the inevitable, that she will lose her love. Overwhelmed by the contrast between the glow of her dream and the gloom of her architect, she asks in desperation that he build for her a loft atop a winding stair, a place where she might grieve in solitude. He completes her lesson in the deterioristic nature of things by telling her that the stair must be made wide enough to allow her final descent, in her coffin. In this closing image of winding descent, punctuated with the brutal 'For you will die', we have another instance of unblooming or 'unbecoming', of an inevitable deterioration, identified here as a law of nature. The architect designs and builds 'as the rule declares'. The heiress's life must follow the same pattern. 'Dream of the City Shopwoman', a poem of the 1860s not published until 1922, is a companion poem and a variation on the theme of decay-in-growth.

In 'Dream', the folly of seeking joy in a defective world is the discovery of another kind of woman altogether, a lowly shopwoman who yearns for a safe-haven in marriage and life in a rural nook:

> Within a cot of thatch and clay
> We'd list the flitting pipers play
> Our lives a twine of good and gay
> Enreathed discreetly;
>
> Our blithest deeds so neighbouring wise
> That doves should coo in soft surprise,
> 'These must belong to Paradise
> Who love so sweetly.'
>
> Our clock should be the closing flowers,
> Our sprinkle-bath the passing showers,
> Our church the alleyed willow bowers,
> The truth our theme.
>
> And infant shapes might soon abound
> Their shining heads would dot us round
> Like mushroom balls on grassy ground . . .
> – But all is dream!

> (*CP*, p. 609–10)

This working-class vision of the earthly paradise, vulgar but sincere, is much like the vision of the heiress at the other end of the social scale. Like the heiress, the shopwoman seeks a paradise in love and an ideal home. Her snug country cottage and its cooing doves remind us of the heiress's 'little chamber . . . with swan and dove/

Ringed thickly, and engrailed with rare device / Of reds and purples'. And shopwoman like heiress must fail because nature decrees that all things decay; that is, that youth must disintegrate into age, hope into disappointment, love into indifference, life into nothingness. The movement of consciousness, like the movement of the stars and the universe of which they are a part, is toward death and disorder:

> O God, that creatures framed to feel
> A yearning Nature's strong appeal
> Should writhe on this eternal wheel
> In rayless grime;
>
> And vainly note, with wan regret,
> Each star of early promise set;
> Till death relieves, and they forget
> Their one life's time!

There is unusual injustice in the failure of the shopwoman, because, unlike the heiress, she is knowing and prudent. She and her mate have made their lives 'a twine of good and gay / Enwreathed *discreetly*' (emphasis added). Their dreamt-of retreat to a rural haven is, she knows, a delusion; the true movement of a human life is not back to a happier time but forward and down to death. Yet neither her knowledge nor her discretion helps her. The failure of the two women is echoed in another poem of the 1860s, 'The Two Men' (*CP*, pp. 77–9), in which two youths of equal preparation and promise set off on entirely different paths only to meet the same ignominious end. The first rejects 'the Market's sordid war' and is true to his beloved as he labours long and hard to further 'Truth and Purity'. He seeks 'to mend the mortal lot / And sweeten sorrow'. The second 'liked the winnings of the mart', but, too idle to pursue them, deceived his first love in order to make a profitable marriage. One is a base, the other a noble man; but both fail. The idealist and the opportunist, like the heiress and the shopwoman; suffer a common fate: 'He perished in the pauper sty / While his old mate lay dying nigh'. The three poems share an Ecclesiastean note of futility: 'Though the wise be better than the fool, yet both have one event'.

In sum, the poems of the 1860s urge that 'a radiance has waned' ('Her Initials'), that 'excellencies' of a primal moment have faded

('She, to Him: i'), and that – most crucial – all is beyond remedy or recall. But within this 'ghast' vision of the unregenerateness of things, Hardy shaped poetic images of great beauty of feeling, images so pure that one wonders if the lost ideal were not somehow elusively present between and behind his lines, luring the poet on as it were. In these poems, for all the sense of loss, the yearning for the thing lost recalls though it does not recover the thing lost; so that both the dream and the futility of the dream, both what might be called the Heiress-impulse and the Architect-impulse in Hardy, are shown and honoured. What is it that holds, pleases, and moves us in the following?

> Snow-bound in woodland, a mournful word,
> Dropt now and then from the bill of a bird,
> Reached me on wind-wafts; and thus I heard,
>   Wearily waiting – . . . .
>
>   ('Postponement', *CP*, p. 11)

> Perhaps, long hence, when I have passed away,
> Some other's feature, accent, thought like mine,
> Will bring you back to what I used to say,
> And bring some memory of your love's decline.
>
>   ('She, to Him: ii', *CP*, p. 15)

> Amid the happy people of my time
> Who work their love's fulfilment, I appear
>
> Numb as a vane that cankers on its point,
> True to the wind that kissed ere canker came:
> Despised by souls of Now, who would disjoint
> The mind from memory, making Life all aim.
>
>   ('She, to Him: iii', *CP*, p. 16)

> He stood by a pond that winter day,
> And the sun was white, as though chidden of God,
> And a few leaves lay on the starving sod;
>   – They had fallen from an ash, and were gray.
>
>   ('Neutral Tones', *CP*, p. 12)

What holds and pleases us, I think, is a beauty of language and rhythm deriving from Hardy's devotion to the austere beauty of the irrefutable truth 'Once lost, always lost'. Also, and of this one must be less certain, there is here a beauty deriving from memories of early intimations of a lost good. What moves one is the sadness of each spokesman, a sadness pure enough and intense enough to purge our own capacities for grief. We come away from these poems renewed even though *and* because they proclaim there is no renewal. This is almost, though not precisely, the point of 'A Young Man's Exhortation' (1867). Here Hardy opposes poetry to 'care', to 'Life's louring', and to girdling time as the instrument with which to 'tender back / All that . . . [the] soul contains'. He thereby defies death and preserves the 'preciousness of dreams':

> For what do we know best?
> That a fresh love-leaf crumpled soon will dry,
> And that men moment after moment die,
> Of all scope dispossest.
>
> If I have seen one thing
> It is the passing preciousness of dreams;
> That aspects are within us; and who seems
> Most kingly is the King.

> (*CP*, pp. 601–2)

In an important sense, the deteriorism of the early poems is less serious in itself than it is as an occasion for expression of a profoundly sad truth and its attendant beauty. Hardy sought, to borrow one-half of a phrase from 'The Two Men', to 'sweeten sorrow'. But, as his first attempt in fiction would show, he sought also, to quote the other half of the same phrase, to 'mend the mortal lot'.

'THE POOR MAN AND THE LADY'

That a poet of loss and 'unbloom' should write a satiric, reforming first novel was in several ways appropriate. 'The Poor Man and the Lady' (1867) was 'a sweeping dramatic satire, . . . the author's views . . . being obviously those of a young man with a passion for reforming the world' (*Life*, p. 61). Satiric prose must have seemed to Hardy in 1866–7 a constructive, and a salable, alternative to pessimistic poetry. But for Hardy to turn to social satire from 'Hap', 'Neutral Tones', 'At a Bridal', 'Her Dilemma' and other poems of the 1860s was for him merely to seem to change his subject, which was always the defect not just in men and in society, but in nature itself. Hardy would exhibit his true scope as a satirist in *Jude*, where his scathing attack on social ills is at bottom a bitter lament that not just a law of decay should prevail in nature, but a law of cruelty as well. Hardy's target is the universe, the entire order of things. In any case, in the late 1860s Hardy could find no publisher for his spirited indictment of 'the squirearchy and nobility, London society, the vulgarity of the middle class, modern Christianity, church-restoration, and political and domestic morals in general' (*Life*, p. 61). And so, this story of Will Strong, son of a rural tranter who succeeds as a London architect, seeks without success to win the hand of a squire's daughter, and, in bitter disappointment, takes up radical reform politics, became, in 1878, *An Indiscretion in the Life of an Heiress*,[5] the story of Egbert Mayne and Geraldine Allenville's futile attempt to recover time past. So far as can be told from its remnants, 'The Poor Man' fused social satire with the story of the return of a native. A young man seeks to 'mend the mortal lot' at the same time that he seeks the irrecoverable best time in his own life. The urge to reform society is thus the by-product of thwarted nostalgia.

The orphaned son of an artist who married a farmer's daughter, Egbert is a social anomaly, an educated young man living with his grandfather, Farmer Broadford, a tenant on the estate of Squire Allenville, and at the same time teaching the children of Tollamore. He is attracted to Allenville's daughter, Geraldine, and she to him, when he saves her from injury after her clothing has become entangled in a threshing machine. Though much in love, both are disturbed by the 'sin' of crossing class lines and they therefore decide to part. Annoyed at Mayne's readiness to comply in this (he has his pride), Geraldine urges her father to remove old Broadford from the spot he has occupied for many years. When Broadford dies, in part from distress at having to leave his old place, Geraldine blames herself for the old man's death and turns to Mayne for forgiveness and relief from guilt. He convinces her that she is innocent, restores her thereby to a semblance of her former self, and wins back her love. At this moment of forgiveness social differences count for nothing: 'They spoke and acted simply as a young man and woman who were beset by common troubles, and who had like hopes and fears' (*ILH*, I, ch. 6). Geraldine loves Egbert because, though he is her social inferior, he and he alone can free her from guilt; loving him is a guarantee of, perhaps a repayment for, innocence. But not a simple innocence, for Geraldine knows she can never be as she was. And she is slightly perverse in preferring the redeemed state to the innocent one: 'Do you forgive me entirely? . . . Say "Yes". It is sweeter to fancy I am forgiven than to think I have not sinned' (ibid.). In this love scene, possibly the first Hardy ever constructed, the bond is sealed not with passion but with forgiveness. Variations on this situation will recur at crucial moments throughout the novels: Elfride will seek forgiveness of Knight, Bathsheba of Boldwood and of Oak, Fancy Day of Dick Dewey and Parson Maybold, Clym Yeobright of his mother and his wife, Henchard of Elizabeth-Jane, and, of course, Tess of Angel Clare. It is comedy when granted, tragedy when forgiveness is refused.

The next crisis in this slight narrative re-enacts the first. The lovers have again separated, and after five years Egbert, now a successful author, seeks to revive the earlier relationship. But things are not as they were, for Geraldine has become a woman who knows well the strength of the 'world's customs':

> It is well for you to remember that I am not the sophisticated girl I was when you first knew me. For better or for worse I have become complicated, exclusive, and practised. A woman who can speak, or laugh, or dance, or sing before any number of men with perfect composure may be no sinner, but she is not what I was once. She is what I am now. She is not the girl you loved. That woman is not here.   (II, ch. 3)

Faced with this truth, Mayne takes to aimless wandering. When he learns that Geraldine is to marry a nobleman, he returns in despair to his native Tollamore. A short time later, Geraldine, as nostalgic as she is capricious, rejects Lord Breton and returns to Tollamore herself. She is reunited with Egbert at an isolated woodland retreat, Monk's Hut, where she confesses her love and her wish to be to him what she once was. They marry secretly, return to the hut, and 'by rigorously excluding all thoughts of the future . . . felt happy with the same old unreasoning happiness as of six years before, now resumed for the first time since that date' (II, ch. 6).

As their first crisis was settled through forgiveness, their second is settled through return to a place of earlier happiness. This suggests a connection between forgiving and returning. And indeed there is a connection, for a particular kind of temporal illusion is in play in both. To forgive is to say, in effect, it is as it was between us before the offence. To forgive perfectly is therefore to undo the ravages of time and to thwart guilt and remorse by wholly human means. It is to repeat, or at least to nearly repeat, time past. Perfect forgiveness is for Hardy that rarest, most precious illusion – the restoration of things past without denial that change is decay. To return to an earlier place after a long absence is analogous to forgiveness. There is change and yet there is continuity. Geraldine cherished Mayne's forgiveness because forgiven error is sweeter than innocence; by analogy, returning to rustic Tollamore after five years in London is sweeter than never having departed. Hardy must have known well from his own experience of homecoming the particular pleasure involved.

The three blissful days at Monk's Hut are a consciously constructed illusion that time has been turned back.[6] In the words of 'A Young Man's Exhortation', they 'exalt and crown the hour / That girdles [them], and fill it full with glee / Blind glee, excelling aught could ever be / Were heedfulness in power' (*CP*, p. 601). But their idyll, their illusion of time-regained, must be brief; for Geraldine, drawn by guilt and duty to make amends to her stern, unforgiving father, is stricken fatally as she waits, perplexed, to see him: 'I hardly know . . . how I can explain to my father, or what could be done to reconcile him to us' (*ILH*, II, ch. 7). Redemption through forgiveness or return ends here, for Squire Allenville will not forgive. At Geraldine's deathbed he tolerates the presence of Egbert only when he despairs of his daughter's life. She dies unrelieved by his forgiveness, and her failure is given cosmic overtones: 'Her weak act of trying to live seemed a silent wrestling with all the powers of the universe' (ibid.). She fails because though she had known better she had attempted the impossible, the reinstatement of time past. Her folly is foreshadowed in Mayne's bewilderment upon his return to 'his old country nook' after five years in London.

When he reaches the 'old home of his mother's family', Mayne looks nostalgically for familiar things, for he is determined to renew old ties. But he finds that change has marked the face of things. 'Middle-aged men were a little more round-shouldered, their wives had taken to spectacles, young people had grown up out of recognition, and old men had passed their second childhood' (II, ch. 4). He visits the school where five years before he had taught the village children and met often with Geraldine. He visits the site of his grandfather's cottage, now pulled down. He hastens from this familiar spot because he finds the effect of memory to be 'otherwise than cheerful' (ibid.). He is so deeply moved by sight of the old places or their remnants that he wishes he had never been so 'reckless' as to return (ibid.). His mood is associated (via the chapter's epigraph) with the mood of the Preacher of Ecclesiastes: 'Then I said in my heart, "As it happeneth to the fool, so it happeneth to me; and why was I the more wise?"' (Ecclesiastes 2:15). The Ecclesiastean sense of a short-lived humanity upon an ageless earth, of life as an endless series of cycles in which the individual, whether wise or foolish, counts for nothing, is strong throughout Hardy. Yet, if he shares the Preacher's sense of the vanity of all things, as an agnostic humanist he must reject the Preacher's justification: 'Fear God, keep the commandments: for this is the whole duty of man. For God shall bring every work into judgment, with every secret thing, whether it be good, or whether it be evil.' And though he embraces the Preacher's pessimism – 'There is no remembrance of former things' – he is by his love of former things compelled to seek their renewal or at least their preservation.[7]

In so far as it preserves aspects of 'The Poor Man and the Lady', *An Indiscretion in the Life of an Heiress* is a faithful reflection of the 1860s, when Hardy pondered the question of regeneration in some of his earliest poems and when, in July 1867, he returned to live at his native Bockhampton after five years in London. Yet it transcends the immediate circumstances of its composition, for it assimilates Hardy's personal experiences of change to a myth of lost felicity as old as Plato's *Phaedrus* and the Book of Genesis and as recent for Hardy as Wordsworth's *Prelude* and Charlotte Brontë's *Jane Eyre*. It is the first embodiment of a myth underlying almost all of Hardy's fiction – the soul's yearning for a lost joy associated with ideal love and beauty.[8] There was a stage of existence, Hardy's novels suggest, that was blissful, tranquil, and good. Call it Eden,[9] childhood, first love, or pre-industrial rural England. The ideal state is disturbed by change, by growth, by aliens, or, more typically in Hardy, by natives who have departed, returned with new ideas, and cannot help but disrupt the primal order. The typical protagonist of this story is torn by a sense of irretrievable loss because he is attempting to recover a lost happiness while struggling against defects of self or of society and while moving through a natural or an architectural landscape that thwarts or mocks his attempt; for what he is attempting is against the nature of things. His division resembles Hardy's own: he is as attracted emotionally to regeneration or repetition as he is convinced intellectually that it is impossible.

DESPERATE REMEDIES (1871)

Geraldine's futile attempt to gain redemption through return anticipates the plight of Cytherea Aldclyffe in *Desperate Remedies*, a novel whose very title suggests Hardy's early interest in questions of restoration and regeneration. Cytherea Aldclyffe is a woman with a past. Some thirty years before we meet her in the novel, she had loved a young architect, Ambrose Graye, but left him because she found herself with child by another man, a cousin. In middle age, wholly by chance, Cytherea meets the angelic Cytherea Graye, the daughter of the man she had loved and lost in her youth. She is moved deeply when she discovers that Graye, out of loyalty to her, had given her name to his daughter. His nostalgic gesture makes the younger Cytherea, in Miss Aldclyffe's remorseful eye, a reincarnation of her lost innocent self. Not only does the middle-aged Cytherea seek the youthful Cytherea's companionship by retaining her as her personal maid; she seeks sexual intimacy with her. And this is not all. She also tries to use the innocence of the girl to redeem the guilt of her son, Aeneas Manston, a man of dark deeds and darker thoughts. Thus, though *Desperate Remedies* can be described as a sensation novel in the manner of Wilkie Collins, it is also an unusual kind of morality play, as D. H. Lawrence was the first to suggest:

> The people . . . as far as the plot is concerned, are not people: They are the heroine, faultless and white; the hero, with a small spot on his whiteness; the villainness, red and black, but with more red than black; the villain, black and red; the murderer, aided by the adulteress, obtains power over the virgin, who, rescued at the last moment by the virgin knight, evades the evil clutch. Then the murderer, overtaken by vengeance, is put to death, whilst Divine Justice descends upon the adulteress. Then the virgin unites with the virgin knight, and receives a Divine Blessing. That is a morality play, and if the morality were

vigorous and original, all well and good. But between-whiles we see that the virgin is being played by a nice, rather ordinary girl.[10]

Lawrence's remarks, though in some ways severely reductive, identify Hardy's wish to show, in non-theological terms, the working of sin, of chance and of a limited human power for redemption or remedy.

Hardy's 'virgin' is the childlike Cytherea Graye, a naïve able to draw 'new sensations from old experience' because she looks 'with children's eyes at . . . ordinary scenery' (*DR*, ch. 2, pt i). Her 'brightness of nature' and readiness to 'take advantage of any adventitious restoratives' (ibid.) sustain her through the four affronts to her innocence that shape the story: her father's death; Edward Springrove's fickleness in love; Miss Aldclyffe's lovemaking and her insistence that Cytherea marry Manston; and Manston's all-out attempt on her virginity. Her entry into the world and into adulthood begins when she sees her father plunge to his death from a church tower: 'She unknowingly stood . . . upon the extreme posterior edge of a tract of her life, in which the real meaning of Taking Thought had never been known. It was the last hour of experience she ever enjoyed with a mind entirely free from a knowledge of that labyrinth into which she stepped immediately afterwards' (ibid.).

Scarcely recovered from this shock, she falls in love with Edward Springrove. In his love, she thinks, she has found a substitute for that happy time of pure feeling, that time free from thought, before her father's death. Their first embrace creates a perfect bliss like that achieved by Geraldine and Egbert during their three days at Monk's Hut:

> It was the supremely happy moment of their experience. The 'bloom' and the 'purple light' were strong on the lineaments of both. Their hearts could hardly believe the evidence of their lips.
> 'I love you, and you love me, Cytherea,' he whispered.
> She did not deny it; and all seemed well. The gentle sounds around them from the hills, the plains, the distant town, the adjacent shore, the water heaving at their side, the kiss, and the long kiss, were all 'many a voice of one delight', and in unison with each other.   (ch. 3, pt ii)

This is indeed felicity, but in just a few moments it is 'dead and gone', for Edward confesses to a treachery he will not name (his betrothal to another); and this ruins all for Cytherea. From this second moment of joy and loss, Cytherea's career declines toward two conclusions: one in marriage to Springrove after a narrow escape from Manston; the other (our chief concern here) in playing the redeemer of the guilt-ridden Miss Aldclyffe. The title-phrase 'Desperate Remedies' may be taken to refer in an interestingly ambiguous way to both Edward's breathtaking rescue of Cytherea from Manston, and to Cytherea's redemption of Miss Aldclyffe by her forgiveness. To parallel a melodramatic rescue and a sincere act of redeeming forgiveness in this way is perhaps to suggest by the implausibility of the first the implausibility of the second: Cytherea's redemption of Miss Aldclyffe is made to seem as unlikely as Springrove's preservation of Cytherea's honour.

This is, of course, to force an analogy, but it suggests the value of Lawrence's remarks, which deserve to be extended. The virgin begins her movement toward the adulteress, the murderer, and the virgin knight after being expelled by Death from the Garden of Thoughtlessness. She even compares herself and her brother, Owen, to the crestfallen Adam and Eve of Genesis 3:17: 'We desire as a blessing what was given us as a curse [toil], and even that is denied' (*DR*, ch. 3, pt iii). Springrove finds Cytherea a creature of 'Arcadian innocence' (ibid.). Their first meeting is to him 'Eden-like', and at its end he experiences 'a hopeless sense of loss akin to that which Adam is said by logicians to have felt when he first saw the sun set and thought in his inexperience that it would return no more' (ch. 2, pt iv). But Cytherea's strength is not her innocence; her strength is her unsentimental resolve to get on with life in spite of misfortune and loss. Speaking to Owen of the intense joy of loving Springrove, she can yet dismiss it 'with dignity': 'What is he to me? Nothing. I must dismiss such weakness as this – believe me, I will. Something far more pressing must drive it away. I have been looking my position steadily in the face, and I must get a living somehow' (ch. 3, pt ii). Though Hardy cannot resist taking a swipe at such courage and resolve in a woman,[11] his point is clear. Far from being a mere damsel in distress, Cytherea Graye is the heroine of a drama of redemption; and the fate of Miss Aldclyffe is in her hands.

Miss Aldclyffe, in this view of the novel, is less the adulteress than the temptress, one who seeks to subvert innocence because she is forever cut off from her own innocence. Like Milton's Satan, she hates what is irretrievably lost to her and seeks, for the most part unwittingly, to bring to ruin those who might enjoy it. And so she at one point confronts Cytherea 'like a tall black figure standing in the midst of fire' only moments after the maiden, 'with an imagination fresh from nature', had been gazing at a sunbeam and 'picturing a wonderful paradise on the other side as the source of such a beam' (ch. 4, pts i and ii). Racked with guilt and remorse, Miss Aldclyffe wants more than merely 'the sympathy of a pure girl like [Cytherea]' (ch. 6, pt i). The meaning of the oft-discussed lesbian scene is not only that Miss Aldclyffe desires Cytherea's person, but also that she desires to take on Cytherea's innocence: 'I long to be what I shall never be again – artless and innocent, like you' (ibid.). She is angry, not jealous, when she learns that Cytherea has kissed a man – 'You are not, after all, the innocent I took you for' – because that former self, *that* Cytherea Bradleigh, who for her Cytherea re-embodies, must be pure and undefiled. She has her own undoing in mind when she rebukes Cytherea Graye in these remarkably frank words:

> Yes, women are all alike. I thought I had at last found an artless woman who had not practised or been practised upon by the arts which ruin all the truth and sweetness and goodness in us. Find a girl, if you can, whose mouth and ears have not been made a regular highway of by some man or another! Leave the admittedly notorious spots – the drawing-rooms of society – and look in the villages – leave the villages and search in the schools – and you can hardly find a girl whose heart has not been *had* – is not an old thing half worn out by some He or another! If only men knew the staleness of the freshest of us! . . . You are as bad as I – we are all alike; and I – an old fool – have been sipping at your mouth as if it were honey because I fancied no wasting lover knew the spot. But a minute ago, and you seemed to me like a fresh spring meadow – now you seem a dusty highway!
> (ch. 4, pt i).

If this is the passion of lesbian love, it is also the passion of nostalgic yearning for lost innocence. Miss Aldclyffe, remarks the sceptical narrator, '*seemed to be completely won out of herself* by contact with a young woman whose modesty was absolutely unimpaired, and whose artlessness was as perfect as was compatible with the

complexity necessary to produce the due charm of womanhood'
(ch. 8, pt i; emphasis added).

Aeneas Manston, the unhappy product of Miss Aldclyffe's
youthful indiscretions, also seeks redemption through Cytherea;
and in this regard it should be noted that the most sensational
episodes of the story – a missed meeting between Manston and his
wife, her supposed death by fire, his killing, concealment and burial
of her – are the unavoidable results of his attempt to break with his
dark past in order to begin life anew with the radiant Cytherea. For
Cytherea is Manston's Jane Eyre, the only saviour imaginable for
a sinner of unnamed sins who believes, much like Charlotte Brontë's
Rochester, that he is 'dammed past redemption' (ch. 19, pt ii). But,
unlike Rochester's, Manston's remedy must fail, an inevitability
Hardy conveys through his description of the church in which the
doomed man proposes marriage to his would-be redeemer:

> Cytherea and Manston walked into the porch, and up the
> nave. . . . Everything in the place was the embodiment of decay:
> the fading red glare from the setting sun, which came in at the
> west window, emphasizing the end of the day and all its cheerful
> doings, the mildewed walls, the uneven paving stones, the wormy
> pews, the sense of recent occupation, and the dank air of death
> which had gathered with the evening. . . .   (ch. 12, pt vi)

The oppressive atmosphere of decay causes Manston to avoid
flattery and Cytherea to feel 'almost ashamed to be seen walking in
such a world'. In this gloom they agree to marry.[12] The decision
prompts Manston to ask for a kiss, a favour Cytherea feels obliged to
refuse because they are, as she puts it, 'too near God'. At this phrase,
Manston 'gave a sudden start, and his face flushed. She had spoken
so emphatically that the words "Near God" echoed back through
the hollow building from the far end of the chancel.' The irony here
stems from the contrast between setting and statement: how can
they be near God in a church and a world marked by decline and
decay? This clash between the reality of decay and the possibility of
regeneration occasions the words, somewhat familiar, that follow:

> 'What a thing to say!' he exclaimed; 'surely a pure kiss is not
> inappropriate to the place!'
> 'No,' she replied. . . . 'I don't know why I burst out so – I can't
> tell what has come over me! Will you forgive me?'

'How shall I say "Yes" without judging you? How shall I say "No" without losing the pleasure of saying "Yes"?' He was himself again.

'I don't know,' she absently murmured.

'I'll say "Yes",' he answered daintily. 'It is sweeter to fancy we are forgiven, than to think we have not sinned; and you shall have the sweetness without the need'.   (ch. 12, pt viii)

Manston repeats almost exactly the words of Geraldine to Egbert upon being forgiven by Egbert for the death of Farmer Broadford, but there is an important difference. In *An Indiscretion*, forgiveness is a prelude to love; here it is a charade at which the unregenerate Manston plays in his attempt to forget the ghast, grim truth that the law of decay prevails over the hope of grace, the inevitability of death over the possibility of an everlasting life. Manston knows from the beginning what Geraldine and Egbert only come to know.

In the end, it seems impossible fully to explain the cause of Manston's anger, guilt and melancholy. Though he covets Cytherea as a last hope of happiness in a 'wretchedly conceived' universe, Manston has no hope of deliverance, divine or human. He not only rejects Providence; he is convinced that Providence actively mocks and torments him. When he learns that he is denied Cytherea because his first wife still lives, his language is that of Job: 'O my lost one! O my Cytherea! That it should come to this is hard for me!' Tis now all darkness – "a land of darkness as darkness itself; and of the shadow of death without any order, and where the light is darkness"' (ch. 14, pt iii; cf. Job 10: 20–2). If in some ways inexplicable, Manston is important as a rehearsal for the similar but greater Michael Henchard of *The Mayor of Casterbridge* (1886). Like Henchard, Manston writes his will before withdrawing to die after losing in the struggle against an irremediable flaw in his make. A clue to Hardy's intention in him may lie in his Virgilian–Byronic name, Aeneas Manston. Like Byron's Manfred, Manston is burdened with a mysterious, inexpiable sin. And he possesses Aeneas's overwhelming sense of loss without his sense of destiny or his gift of divine favour. Manston is an image of unregenerate man.

Cytherea's choice of Manston over Springrove out of duty to her brother is a kind of fall from which she is rescued by the efforts of Raunham and especially Springrove. But, in spite of what Hardy in 1889 called the novel's 'mystery, entanglement, and moral obliquity', *Desperate Remedies* does not conclude with a facile formula for happiness. Its tight chronological structure – it covers a precisely mapped period of 31 years, 5 months, 3 days and 9 hours from December 1835 to 24 June 1867 – is an implicit refutation of Miss Aldclyffe's desperate attempt to turn back the clock. And the idea that forgiveness can remedy the evil of the past, embodied most movingly in Cytherea's forgiveness of Miss Aldclyffe as the older woman lies near death, is simply set alongside another idea, embodied in Manston's suicide in the Casterbridge jail, the idea that evil is irremediable. The 'denouement in forgiveness'[13] is simply set beside the denouement in death, a juxtaposition forced upon Hardy by the struggle within him between his residual belief in a redemptive theology and an emerging view of things as irremediably deteriorative.

Like a medieval morality play, *Desperate Remedies* is concerned with the forgiveness of sin; unlike a morality, it points to a human source of forgiveness and redemption. Manston is damned, seeks amendment through Cytherea, and fails. Miss Aldclyffe errs, is contrite, confesses, and seeks and wins forgiveness. But her redeemer is Cytherea, not a merciful God in heaven:

> 'Can you forgive me?'
> 'I do forgive you. Not in a hasty impulse that is revoked when coolness comes, but deliberately, and sincerely: as I myself hope to be forgiven, I accord my forgiveness now'.　(ch. 21, pt iii)

There is no denying the sincerity and force of this language, nor the fact that in Cytherea, if not in Manston or Miss Aldclyffe, hope of a divine grace is alive. But that supernatural force is passive, withdrawn, and it is Cytherea's love and self-sacrifice – like Viviette Constantine's and Tess Durbeyfield's later – that brings good out of evil. But even this achievement is checked, for Cytherea's is not the last word. Even in this strand of the narrative, which ends with Cytherea's marriage to Springrove (Lawrence's 'virgin knight'), happiness is qualified. The sacred ceremony is overshadowed by the appearance of a black-garbed stranger who aids the Carriford bell-ringers on the wedding day. 'I come to see the wickedness of the land', he explains, after rejecting one ringer's suggestion that he may be of 'the devil's brood'. The reviewer for the *Spectator* who accused the anonymous author of *Desperate Remedies* of 'prying into the ways of wickedness' was right.[14] He would have been more correct, however, had he said that his unknown author was 'prying' into the limited remedies for evil in a radically defective world; for in making a redeemer of Cytherea, the author of *Desperate Remedies* was secularizing 'inherited theological ideas and ways of thinking'.[15] In such a world forgiveness loses, in the words of another commentator, 'not only its religious sanctions but its deep moral relevance; at best it is a sensible strategy for meliorating pain'.[16]

'MAN'S GOODNESSE': *UNDER THE GREENWOOD TREE* AS COMEDY OF FORGIVENESS

Rightly regarded as the most nearly perfect of the early novels, *Under the Greenwood Tree* (1872) is also Hardy's most complete exhibition of the human powers of redemption that reside in the community and the family. It is frequently argued that *Greenwood Tree* was salvaged from the wreckage of 'The Poor Man and the Lady', and it indeed seems probable that some of the rustic scenes originated there. But *Greenwood Tree* is too well constructed, too subtle in its irony and use of allusion, to be derivative in any important sense.[17] Hardy not only changed from a first-person to a third-person narrative; he also turned from social satire to pastoral comedy. More important, he made Fancy Day's return to her native Mellstock after a lengthy absence the central, unifying event in his narrative. In 'The Poor Man' at least in those elements of it said to be preserved in *An Indiscretion in the Life of an Heiress*, Egbert's return to Tollamore is placed late in the story (like Springrove's return to Carriford in *Desperate Remedies*), and is subordinated to the love story and the social criticism. But Fancy's return occurs early and the effects of her return shape the entire narrative. The painfulness of homecoming is at the heart of *Greenwood Tree*, making it the prototype of *The Return of the Native* and *The Woodlanders*.

If *Greenwood Tree* derives in an important sense from 'The Poor Man', it is because it fuses two elements from it – the motif of return and the search for regeneration – into a story of regeneration through return. Because she finds love and forgiveness among those she has left and returned to, Fancy Day accomplishes what Geraldine Allenville could not.

Fancy's homecoming kindles a series of conflicts, and all of them are settled harmoniously. She encourages the attentions of Dick Dewey, is opposed by her father, feigns illness at the advice of a witch, and is indulged by her doting parent. But Fancy is not easily satisfied. She next flirts with Farmer Shiner and is forgiven by Dick; she accepts Maybold's offer of marriage while betrothed to Dick, then turns back to Dick, and Maybold, though shattered, forgives her. Finally, the venerable members of the Mellstock Quire, not without bitter complaint, withdraw in a peaceful, dignified way to make room for the barrel organ that Maybold, Shiner, and especially Fancy introduce. As one critic has said, the novel raises communal values above personal and individual ones. Its strength is its profound 'sense of the linkage of people into families, and of families into communities, and of communities into the wider fellowship still of the succeeding generations of men'.[18] There are other examples of a unique capacity for reconciliation in Mellstock. The foolish Thomas Leaf is not mocked, confined, or banished; he is made a welcome part of the community and its activities, and in the end seems not so foolish. The marriages of the Deweys and the Days are stable because the tranter and the keeper, with patient affection, tolerate their wives' eccentricities.

Because tolerance, good humour, and love are alive in Mellstock, Fancy can be both an agent of disruption and a source of orderly change. As teacher, as musician and as wife, she presides, in a distinctly amusing way, over the 'fall' of a traditional order. And this, it seems, is why she is ushered into the novel on Christmas Eve by an 'ancient body of minstrels' singing an 'ancient and time-worn hymn, embodying a quaint Christianity':

I

Remember Adam's fall,
    O thou Man
Remember Adam's fall
    From Heaven to Hell
Remember Adam's fall;
How he hath condemned all
In Hell Perpetual
There to dwell.

II

Remember God's goodnesse,
    O thou Man
Remember God's goodnesse,
    His promise made.

Remember God's goodnesse
He sent his Son sinlesse
Our ails for to redress;
    Be not afraid!

III

In Bethlehem He has born
    O thou Man
In Bethlehem He was born
    For mankind's sake.
In Bethlehem He was born,
    Christmas-day in the morn;
Our Saviour thought no scorn
    Our faults to take.

IV

Give thanks to God alway
    O thou Man:
Give thanks to God alway,
    With heart-most joy.
Give thanks to God alway
On this our joyful day:
Let all men sing and say
    Holy, holy!

(*UGT*, 1, ch. 4)

Sung by the Quire to bring Fancy to her window, the hymn recounts the cardinal events of the Christian story – the fall, the condemnation, God's mercy, and man's redemption through Christ.[19] In the manuscript version of the novel (in the Dorset County Museum), Hardy used only the first two lines of the hymn; he added the remainder, with its account of the Atonement, later, possibly in 1912. In so doing he inserted an explicit account of the traditional scheme of redemption that it is one of his purposes in the novel to set gently aside as a remnant of 'a quaint Christianity'. In this traditional view, sinful men are wholly in the land of a wise and merciful God whose son carries out His loving design for them. In the 'modern' view set forth in the novel, an analogous and wholly human scheme of redemption is presented. In this view, men are in the hands of men, and (even worse) of women. *Greenwood Tree* is the story of a pastoral Eden's invasion by new ways in the person of the fascinating homecomer who charms all the men she meets. In the Christmas Eve scene mentioned above, for example, the Adamic Dick Dewey is stunned by Fancy's beauty and is a lost soul forever after. It might even be said that the 'fall' of Dick and the traditional order of Mellstock is a 'fortunate' one, the forgiveness and forbearance inspired by Fancy's actions being the secular equivalent of the Divine mercy inspired by Eve's. Though the comic elements of the novel invite this optimistic view of evil and disruption, it is impossible to go very far with it. For the thematic structure of *Greenwood Tree* is essentially that of *Desperate Remedies* and 'The Poor Man', and of such a poem as 'The Ruined Maid'. Innocence is lost (Cytherea's, Geraldine's, Dick's and Mellstock's, 'Melia's); reconciliation and atonement come about through wholly human means: Egbert forgives, Dick forgives, Cytherea forgives, Mellstock is tolerant and patient, 'Melia laughs ironically. But at this point of reconciliation, in every case, we are brought up short. The movement toward redemption is blocked by an evil beyond the reach of intelligence, of love, or of laughter. Thus Squire Allenville's refusal to forgive Geraldine, Manston's inexpiable guilt, and Fancy's incurable capriciousness are discords that, finally, cannot be harmonized. In sum, the 'fortune fall' of Mellstock is qualified by Hardy's use of irony to show that things in Mellstock are neither so placid nor so happy as they seem.

This bucolic world is no paradise; in it pain always accompanies forgiveness. There is, for example, something besides paternal love in Reuben Dewey's 'smile of miserable satire' at learning that Dick loves Fancy (*UGT*, ii, ch. 3). Dewey knows well the price of harmony in a marriage in which the man is the woman's social inferior. When the girls' chorus, led by Fancy, drowns out the playing of the Quire, Mr Spinks's laughing acknowledgement ('We useless ones had better march out of church, fiddles and all') contains a 'horrible bitterness of irony', a 'ghastliness' understood only by other members of Quire (ii, ch. 6). When Dick asks the money-minded Keeper Day for Fancy's hand in marriage, he is leaning on the top rail of Day's pig-pen, contemplating a 'whitish shadowy shape . . . moving about and grunting'. Dick's anguish at Day's blunt refusal is anticipated by the shriek of 'some small bird that was being killed by an owl in an adjoining wood' (iv, ch. 2). Then there is Enoch, Mr Day's trapper, who entertains political views 'very damaging to the theory of master and man' in the view of Day (ii, ch. 6). Enoch scoffs at the trust in Providence among the ''twas to be' school of thinkers on the subject of marriage (II, ch. 6). He cynically reminds Day that the keeper's sole motive in killing thousands of honey bees is purely and simply monetary: "Tis the money. . . . For without money man is a shadder!' (IV, ch. 4). But cynics are punished in Mellstock, and so Enoch is placed in the stocks, then banished, allegedly for drunkenness. The closing episode of the story is not simply the communal ritual of marriage – symbol of harmony and regeneration – under the spreading greenwood tree. It is that *and* Enoch, bearer of the name of the son of Cain, working alone in a distant turnip field, excluded from the festivity because he sees, like the wise fool Leaf, that chance, money, and greed play a part – perhaps as great a part as intelligence and love – in human affairs. His cynicism, it should be noted, is matched by a cynicism about the nature of women exhibited throughout the novel, which ends ominously, with a secret that Fancy will not tell Dick.[20] It is incautious to acknowledge the insistent realism of *Greenwood Tree* and yet to urge that it is a pastoral novel that 'perceives rural life in lyrical tones', maintains a 'nostalgic quality', and depicts 'stylized and charming' rustics in a 'peaceful and idyllic' love story.[21] In *Greenwood Tree* the elements of disorder, implacable and immune to human means of remedy, are simply kept beneath the surface, though they threaten to break through at every turn.

If we ask several questions – What if Fancy's reforms had been openly opposed?, What if Keeper Day had persisted in his opposition to Dick?, What if Dick and Maybold had refused to forgive Fancy her whimsies? – we find ourselves in the world of Hardy's next novel and on the brink of tragedy, which for Hardy unfolds when men and women find the defects in nature and in themselves that lie beyond their limited powers of remedy. Hardy knew 'the tragedy that underlies Comedy if you only scratch it deeply enough' (*Life*, p. 439). In *A Pair of Blue Eyes* (1873) he penetrated to the tragic substrata of comedy: Stephen Smith (unlike Fancy Day) cannot go home again, and Henry Knight (unlike Parson Maybold) cannot forgive a capricious and erring sweetheart.

A PAIR OF BLUE EYES (1873)

In *Under the Greenwood Tree* Hardy used verbal and dramatic irony to temper nostalgia stemming from his use of materials from private experience; for Mellstock is based on Stinsford, the tranter's cottage on Hardy's birthplace at Higher Bockhampton, and Fancy, at least in part, on his sister Mary and perhaps his cousin Tryphena, both of whom were schoolmistresses.[22] In *A Pair of Blue Eyes* cosmic irony, an irony of fate deriving from a sense of the unregenerateness of things, counters not just nostalgia but hope, hope raised by the beginning in 1870 of the second great emotional experience of Hardy's life, his love for, courtship of, and marriage to Emma Lavinia Gifford. What I wish to suggest is that between 1870 and 1874 Hardy thought he had recaptured in his love for Emma the ideal bliss that he thought he had lost forever when he left Higher Bockhampton and the sphere of his mother, in 1862. That he connected the security of childhood with his affection for Emma is clearly suggested in the poem 'I Was the Midmost':

> I was the midmost of my world
>   When first I frisked me free,
> For though within its circuit gleamed
>   But a small company,
> And I was immature, they seemed
>   To bend their looks on me.
>
> She was the midmost of my world
>   When I went further forth,
> And hence it was that, whether I turned
>   To south, east, west, or north,
> Beams of an all-day Polestar burned
>   From that new axe of earth

(CP, p. 666)

The shift from 'I' to 'She' between the first line of the first stanza and the first of the second suggests that Hardy somehow recaptured an aura of his childhood in his courtship of Emma. 'She' assumes the role for him of the 'immature' child, and as a reincarnation of his earlier self becomes a new centre for his life. A similar displacement enters into Henry Knight's love for Elfride Swancourt in *A Pair of Blue Eyes*, as it had in Cytherea Aldclyffe's love for Cytherea Graye.

In order to shape materials of such intensely private significance, Hardy had to use again the autobiographical techniques of 'The Poor Man', *Desperate Remedies* and *Under the Greenwood Tree*. So it is not surprising to find in Stephen Smith, Elfride Swancourt's second lover, a homecomer of modest origins (like Mayne and Springrove) whose work is architecture (like Springrove's), and who seeks the hand of a lady (as do Mayne and Dewey). However, if Smith is something of an author-figure, it was Henry Knight the reviewer, Elfride's third lover, whom Hardy would later describe as a man like himself (*Life*, p. 74). The connection between Hardy and Knight is important, because Knight resembles those characters in earlier novels (Geraldine, Miss Aldclyffe, Manston) who are hopelessly estranged from an earlier happiness and innocence. Hardy's associating himself with the repressed, nostalgic Henry Knight suggests a personal basis for these earlier figures, as well as for their important successors in the novels: Farmer Boldwood, Clym Yeobright, Angel Clare, Sue Bridehead, Edred Fitzpiers and Jocelyn Pierston. But, if there is self-portraiture in *A Pair of Blue Eyes*, it is divided, as at least one critic has recognized, between Smith, the native who cannot return, and Knight, the fastidious, ascetic intellectual who cannot recover his lost innocence by loving an innocent woman.[23] In this division, however, there is a unity: both Smith and Knight learn that the past is irretrievable. And this is Elfride's lesson as well. She discovers that she cannot make amends to Knight for her indiscretions with Jethway and Smith. 'Can one be pardoned', she wonders with Hamlet, 'and retain the offence?' (*PBE*, ch. 27).

To this twofold assertion – no return to or recovery of things past, no redemption for the sinner – Hardy, by use of architectural setting, added a third: no restoration of the old. In *Blue Eyes* he attempted to build an ambitious analogy between the difficulties of spiritual renewal and the difficulties of architectural restoration. I am referring not just to the all-too-sudden collapse of the tower of Endelstow Church at the precise moment that Knight discovers Elfride's past loves and bemoans his ruin in the words of Milton's Adam: 'Fool'd and beguiled: by him thou, I by thee!' (ch. 31). This heavy-handed attempt to parallel the careers of men and of buildings merely hints at a deeper analogy at work in the novel that Hardy himself would describe in his 1895 Preface to the novel. There he spoke of *Blue Eyes* as 'an imaginary history of three human hearts, whose emotions were not without correspondence' with the 'wild and tragic features' of the rugged Cornish coast and 'the crude Gothic art of the ecclesiastical buildings scattered along it'. He went a step further: 'To restore the gray carcasses of a medievalism whose spirit has fled seemed a not less incongruous act than to set about renovating the adjoining crags themselves'. Though he does not take it, a third step seems possible: the restoration or renovation of human hearts must be equally incongruous. There can be no return for Smith, no recovery for Knight, no redemption for Elfride, because their lives correspond to the disintegrating rocks of the water-worn coast and the crumbling stones of the churches along it.

Before looking further into Hardy's account of the unregenerateness of things in *A Pair of Blue Eyes*, however, it would be well to pause to describe the dream-like experience that he preserved in both its romantic setting and its lyrical, highly allusive use of language. And for this we must turn to some of his late poems about Emma and her marvellous Cornish world. Emma appealed to Hardy because, as he would suggest in the poem 'She Opened the Door', she freed him from a stifling world-weariness:

> She opened the door of the West to me,
>   With its loud sea-lashings,
>   And cliff-side clashings
> Of waters rife with revelry.
>
> She opened the door of Romance to me,
>   The door from a cell
>   I had known too well,
> Too long, till then, and was fain to flee.
>
> She opened the door of a love to me,
>   That passed the wry
>   World-welters by
> As far as the arching blue the lea.

> (*CP*, p. 773)

In the poem 'Ditty (E. L. G.)' (1870), Hardy contemplates his wife-to-be living in a Cornish home 'that no spot on earth excels'. Though he admits that chance alone brought them together, he believes he has grown better through contact with a 'Sweet' who lives 'by the bough the firstling browses'. Emma's love has restored him to a state untainted by getting and spending, a state of purity from which he fears he will again fall if he breaks with her. For she brings to him, as he urges in 'Without, Not Within Her', a strange revivifying power:

It was what you bore with you, Woman,
    Not inly were,
That throned you from all else human,
    However fair!

It was that strange freshness you carried
    Into a soul
Whereon no thought of yours tarried
    Two minutes at all.

And out from his spirit flew death,
    And bale, and ban,
Like the corn-chaff under the breath
    Of the winnowing-fan.

              (*CP*, p. 647)

In 'The Seven Times', a poem recounting seven visits to Cornwall over the years, Hardy recalled that on the first visit 'Life was clogged in me with care' (*CP*, pp. 687–8). And in 'As 'Twere To-night', he remembered this same first moment of meeting with his 'girl of grace' as the beginning, in Dantean phrase, of 'a new life' (*CP*, p. 582). By restoring his spirit and relieving his worries about getting on in the world, Emma won him out of doubt in life itself. 'For Life I Had Never Cared Greatly' speaks of a despair in the 1860s caused by 'conditions of doubt' overcome, at least for a time, by 'symphonies soft and sweet colour':

    It [Life] courted me then,
      Till evasions seemed wrong,
  Till evasions gave in to its song,
And I warmed, until living aloofly loomed duller
    Than life among men.

              (*CP*, p. 537)

In the second decade of the twentieth century Hardy would look back to the 1870s as years of intense joy deriving from 'certain starry thoughts' and from a sustaining 'vision' that Emma, of all his associates, most encouraged. He had met her at a time when literary failures had made him doubt his prospects as a writer. In her he found a sensitive, genteel woman with literary interests, and one who was pleased to copy a good deal of manuscript and to talk with him of 'plots, possible scenes, tales and poetry, and of his own work' (*Life*, p. 72). At a time when his parents and friends (especially Horace Moule) were advising him to take the practical course, Emma urged upon him the course he most dearly wished to follow: 'to adhere to authorship, which she felt sure would be his true vocation' (*Life*, p. 87). 'With that rapid instinct which serves women in such good stead, and may almost be called preternatural vision', Emma recognized and encouraged the artistic impulse in the 'constitutional tendency to care for life only as an emotion and not as a scientific game' (*Life*, pp. 82, 87).

Emma's open, trusting ways suggest that what was probably most attractive about her for Hardy was her childlikeness. The shift from 'I' to 'She' between the first and the seventh lines of 'I Was the Midmost' (noted above) was possible only because the 'She' was, even at age thirty, still fresh and innocent enough to re-embody the childhood 'I' of the poet. And, as any reader of Emma's *Recollections* (1911) will discover, she preserved some of the traits of a dreamy, credulous child throughout her life:

> The front-door bell rang, and the architect was ushered in. I had to receive him alone, and felt a curious uneasy embarrassment at receiving him alone, especially so necessary a person as the architect. I was immediately arrested by his familiar appearance, as if I had seen him in a dream. . . . The day we were married was a perfect September day – the 17th of the month – 1874 – not of brilliant sunshine, but wearing a soft sunny luminousness; just as it should be.
>
> I have had various experiences, interesting some, sad others, since that lovely day; but all showing that an Unseen Power of great benevolence directs my ways; I have some philosophy, and mysticism, and an ardent belief in Christianity and the life beyond this present one, all which makes any existence curiously interesting. As one watches *happenings* (and even if should occur unhappy happenings), outward circumstances are of less import-ance if Christ is our highest ideal. A strange unearthly brilliance shines round our path, penetrating and dispersing difficulties with its warmth and glow. (*Life*, pp. 69–73)

That Emma's dreamy way of seeing things appealed to Hardy is confirmed by the fact that he based some of his finest lyrics on passages from her memoirs.[24] Her ardent redemptive faith was, from his point of view, part and parcel of her winning ingenuousness; it can only have deepened his sense of her as a re-embodiment of his own earlier consciousness, a consciousness from which he, like his own Henry Knight, had fallen away. This active, graceful, trusting woman encouraged her architect to be true to his poetic genius, and he, out of love and gratitude, immortalized her in Elfride, the heroine of *A Pair of Blue Eyes*. But here commences a mystery, for *A Pair of Blue Eyes* is no more a celebration of feminine grace and goodness than it is an account of the growth of genius. It is the sometimes grim history of Elfride's emotions 'as modified by the creeping hours of time' (*PBE*, ch. 1).

What is remarkable about *A Pair of Blue Eyes* is that it is so severely self-critical a brand of autobiographical fiction. If Knight and Elfride resemble Hardy and Emma, and there is evidence they do, then how is one to explain that by 1873, a year before his marriage, Hardy was contemplating the destructive whimsicality of a heroine much like his wife-to-be and the emotional inadequacy of a hero much like himself? One reply is that Elfride and Knight do not in these respects resemble their originals. It seems more likely, however, and the other novels tend to confirm this, that Hardy used figures like himself and Emma in his tragic story because he believed that his own life was following a tragic pattern; that is, he believed that his life was, like Henry Knight's, a decline from an irretrievable simplicity and purity. Knight, like Hardy in 1870, is a thoughtful man of about thirty, and one for whom the glory and the gleam of childhood was fading under the influence of work and life in London. He is characterized repeatedly with allusions to Wordsworth's Intimations Ode, the very poem on which Hardy would draw to describe the beginning of his own marital troubles in the late 'seventies (*Life*, p. 124). In Elfride, Knight finds 'a fair vestal' living in 'a little paradise of flowers and trees' (*PBE*, chs 1, 2). Endowed with a 'Miranda-like curiosity and interest', the vestal knows 'no more about the stings of evil report than the native wild-fowl knew of the effects of Crusoe's first shot' (chs 2, 11). For Knight, to love such a creature is to be 'lulled by a peaceful sense of being able to enjoy the most trivial thing with a childlike enjoyment' (ch. 20). It is to enjoy a vicarious innocence (ch. 32). But Elfride is also his idol, and he comes to love her with a religious devotion: 'A religion was building itself upon you in my heart. I looked into your eyes, and thought I saw there truth and innocence as pure and perfect as ever embodied by God in the flesh of woman. Perfect truth is too much to expect, but ordinary truth I *will have* or nothing at all' (ch. 34). Knight turns to Elfride, it seems, only because he cannot have perfect truth or innocence. And his imperious need for 'ordinary truth', by which he means absolute sexual innocence, is Elfride's undoing. For, when he refuses to forgive her indiscretions with Jethway and Smith, he drives her to self-hatred, to the desperate remedy of marriage to Lord Luxellian, and to eventual death in childbirth.

Elfride's errors are minor and unpremeditated – she had flirted with Felix Jethway, a boy of the village, years before, and later, wholly on impulse, had nearly eloped with Stephen Smith. But for Knight, as for the novel's narrator, a degree of misogyny enters in. Elfride's 'actual innocence' is less important than her essential fickleness, and she is made to pay heavily for all her 'sins'. Her childish flirtation with Jethway led indirectly to his death; this is revenged by his mother, the Widow Jethway, who pursues Elfride and punishes her by enabling the precise Knight to learn of Elfride's past. Knight can no more forgive Elfride than can the half-crazed mother, and Elfride's failure to find forgiveness is made to seem just because there is something indefinably treacherous in her. It is difficult 'to see the form and substance of her features when conversing with her' (ch. 1). The Wordsworthian yearning for 'thoughts that lie too deep for tears' which lights her face proves to be a less-than-ideal yearning, for she is consistent in only one thing, her drive to charm and possess a man. She is made to move with something like an unconscious propensity – though ever upward on the social scale – from Jethway, to Smith, to Knight, to Luxellian. During her first meeting with Smith she sings for him Shelley's 'When the Lamp is Shattered', a lyric in which woman is depicted as the frail cradle, home, and bier of love. She unwittingly brings Knight to her trysting places with Smith – one of them also the tomb of Jethway. Though she has a 'superlative capacity for being wounded' (ch. 4), she is hardly to be admired for this, since her powers of recovery are suspiciously rapid. Hardy seems fond of the idea that deep natures do not mend or forgive easily. Elfride's is not a deep nature:

> Elfride possessed special facilities for getting rid of trouble after a decent interval. Whilst a slow nature was imbibing a misfortune little by little, she had swallowed the whole agony of it at a draught and was brightening again. She could slough off a

sadness and replace it by a hope as easily as a lizard renews a diseased limb.   (ch. 14)

Elfride is a strange mixture of the naive and La Belle Dame Sans Merci: 'She will say things worthy of a French epigrammatist, and act like a robin in a greenhouse' (chs 7, 18). Mindless vacillation marks her way of making the momentous decision to elope with Smith. She tosses the reins of her horse, Pansy, over its head, thinking the animal will turn toward home and away from Plymouth, where Smith waits. But because Pansy prefers corn to grass, she ambles toward the stable at Plymouth; and her 'decision' profoundly affects the future of Elfride, of Knight, and of Smith. The association of Elfride's behaviour with that of a lizard, a robin and a horse, taken with her seemingly automatic movement from Jethway, to Smith, to Knight and to Luxellian, suggests that Hardy viewed her as a creature of emotion and instinct, a creature whose heart juggles with her brain (ch. 11). On the decisive journey to St Launce's and Plymouth, all Elfride 'cared to recognize was a dreamy fancy that today's rash action was not her own. She was disabled by her moods' (ibid.). Once in London with Stephen, she suddenly changes her mind and insists that they return immediately to Endelstow. This might seem the admirable working of conscience, but when Stephen gives way she is disappointed, for she has 'her sex's love of sheer force in a man, however ill-directed' (ch. 12). It is precisely Knight's superior manner and force of mind that make him attractive to her. But Knight's ideas, especially his obsession with purity, will destroy her. For Knight loves 'philosphically rather than romantically' (ch. 20).

Knight is too refined and fastidious, too attached to perfection, to live happily in an imperfect world. Like the personae of some of the poems of the 1860s, Knight yearns for a joy that he has lost; unlike them, he believes he can recover it in the person of his beloved. In him, as in Cytherea Aldclyffe, Hardy explored the sexuality of nostalgia and revealed it to be an asexuality, a ruthless, relentless desire for purity, 'an invincible objection to be any but the first comer in a woman's heart' (ibid.). Knight's lost innocence can be recovered only by capturing the love of an innocent girl. And if the substitute fails, as Elfride does fail for Knight, then something like immortal opportunities have been lost:

There had passed away a glory, and the dream was not as it had been of yore. Perhaps Knight was not shaped by Nature for a marrying man. Perhaps his lifelong constraint toward women, which he had attributed to accident, was not chance after all, but the natural result of instinctive acts so minute as to be undiscernible even by himself. Or whether the rough dispelling of any bright illusion, however imaginative, depreciates the real and unexaggerated brightness which appertains to its basis, one cannot say   (ch. 30).

Hardy, even for him, is unusally circumspect here. What he is saying is that Knight's aversion to women may stem from chance, from nature, or from his experience with Elfride. But, whatever the cause, the effect is the death of immortal possibilities, as the allusion to Wordsworth's great Ode makes clear. That allusion may recall for us that shortly after meeting Elfride Knight had discovered that 'the glory and the dream he formerly found' in the Lakes of Killarney had mysteriously departed them (ch. 20).[25] The Ideal had moved from 'that romantic spot' into Elfride. But he can love Elfride, or the Ideal he believes resides in Elfride, only in her, the imperfect vessel's, absence. For Henry Knight, love dies on contact.

> Stephen fell in love with Elfride by looking at her: Knight by ceasing to do so. When or how the spirit entered into him he knew not. . . .
>
> Knight's experience was a complete disproof of the assumption that love always comes by glances of the eye and sympathetic touches of the fingers: that, like flame, it makes itself palpable at the moment of generation. Not till they were parted, and she had become sublimated in his memory, could he be said to have even attentively regarded her.
>
> Thus, having passively gathered up images of her which his mind did not act upon till the cause was no longer before him, he appeared to himself to have fallen in love with her soul, which had temporarily assumed its disembodiment to accompany him on his way.   (ibid.)

For Henry Knight, time, history, and consciousness are not, finally, aspects of a process of irreversible decline from a primal moment of perfection. He reveals this in his hope that Elfride can be that lost time's re-embodiment. Falling in love with Elfride is for him 'gentle innocent time – a time, which, though there may not be much of it, seldom repeats itself in a man's life, and has a peculiar dearness when glanced at retrospectively' (ch. 20). When she proves to be an imperfect reincarnation, he thinks himself an Adam betrayed, an exile from paradise. He is ruthless in his frenzy over loss because he cannot accept its finality: 'The man of many ideas, now that his first dream of impossible things was over, vibrated too far in the contrary direction; and her every movement of feature – every tremor – was taken as so much proof of her unworthiness' (ch. 34).

The cure for Knight's nympholeptic yearning – a cure he cannot stomach – is knowledge, knowledge that his nostalgia, his remembrance of things past, is contradicted by nature's law of decay. As Knight dangles, in a much-celebrated episode, over the Cliff Without a Name, 'hand in hand with the world in its infancy', eye to eye with a fossilized trilobite, he might come to see the folly of nostalgic idealism and its impulse to regard as unchanging a morality produced by one, and that the merely human, phase of the life-process engraved by time on the rock to which he clings. He might see the absurdity of attempting to recover the glory and the dream of yore. Though face to face with a petrified image of time as a series of unique, unrepeatable events, he treats Elfride as though she had violated an enduring, unchanging moral law. When he refuses to forgive her he forgets that the impulsiveness that led to a flirtation and a near-elopement also moved her to make from her undergarments a rope with which to save his life. A more discreet woman might have hesitated. But Knight values the Idea over its imperfect embodiment, and Hardy suggests – in perhaps the most trenchant bit of self-criticism in the novel – that he does so because he is by nature averse to women.[26]

GABRIEL OAK AND THE 'ART WHICH DOES MEND NATURE'

In *A Pair of Blue Eyes* Hardy exhibited in Henry Knight the folly of an idealizing nostalgia unchecked by knowledge that decay is a law of nature. Hardy's people always end worse than they began, and Smith, Elfride and Knight fully illustrate this. But *Far from the Madding Crowd* (1874) repudiates this view of the course of things. In this, his first major novel, Hardy diagnosed various ills of men and women, their pride, impulsiveness, and sentimentality, and various defects of nature, its 'rule' of chance and its indifference, and in Gabriel Oak offered two remedies – self-renunciation and un-sentimental acceptance of the pastness of the past. In *Far from the Madding Crowd* the law of decay seems temporarily suspended, even reversed. The illusion at its end, at least from one point of view, is of things as being better than they were in the begining. The wicked Troy and the volatile Boldwood have been removed from the scene; the erratic Bathsheba has wed the steady, stable Gabriel Oak, and harmony has been restored to Weatherbury. Both hero and heroine have known and have overcome misfortune; nature is ailing, but Oak is a skilful physician, and Bathsheba, finally, a willing patient. Of course, this ending is happy only if we ignore the suffering that precedes it, and only if we set aside what the novel suggests about the nature of Bathsheba and of womankind. The pressing question behind *Madding Crowd* – How well can men and women remedy the defects of human and non-human nature? – was implicit in *A Pair of Blue Eyes*, particularly in the episode on the Cliff Without a Name, to which we may now return for a moment.

Elfride's rescue of Knight as he dangles from the cliff suggests that human intelligence can triumph over nature, here personified as a grim female presence making a 'treacherous attempt to put an end' to the lovers (*PBE*, chs 21, 22). This malicious Mother, as Knight learns, has 'moods in other than a poetical sense: predilections for certain deeds at certain times, without any apparent law to govern or reason to account for them'.

> She is read as a person with a curious temper; as one who does not scatter kindnesses and cruelties alternately, impartially, and in order, but heartless severities or overwhelming generosities in lawless caprice. Man's case is always that of the prodigal's favourite or the miser's pensioner. In her unfriendly moments there seems a feline fun in her tricks, begotten by a foretaste of her pleasure in swallowing the victim. (ch. 22)

Though 'active, lashing, eager for conquest', and 'pitiless' in her determination, nature can be thwarted, at least intermittently, by unselfish love. Knight offers his body that Elfride might use it as a ladder upon which to climb to safety; Elfride then fashions a rope from her undergarments to save Knight from falling to certain death. But the struggle against defective nature does not end here, as might seem to be the case. The lovers' struggle against external or non-human nature is counterpointed by a struggle within, their struggle against their worst selves. At the same time Elfride is saving Knight, she is betraying Stephen Smith, whom she had promised to marry upon his return from abroad and who is actually visible to her on board a steamer bringing him home to Endelstow. She carries with her, and loses in her efforts to save Knight, a receipt for Stephen's gift of £200, earnest against his ability to marry her. Nature, Hardy would have us see in this scene, is just as surely, though perhaps even more elusively, at work in the inconstant Elfride as 'she' (nature) is in the rain, the wind, and the Cliff Without a Name. 'Lawless caprice' governs both Elfride and feminized nature. Elfride's 'rush of exultation' at having saved Knight merges with 'a defiance of duty to Stephen, and a total recklessness as to plighted faith' (ch. 22).

Elfride's trembling impressionability is matched by Knight's sexual diffidence. A 'peculiarity of nature' prevents him from kissing Elfride during 'those moments of impulsive embrace in the pelting rain'. When he looks upon her clad only in 'her diaphanous exterior robe', he sees not the throbbing form of a woman passionately in love with him, but the figure of one 'as small as an infant' (ch. 22). He is, it seems, as emotionally inadequate as she is emotionally overcharged. Though he now blesses her for such complete devotion, he will later reject her for the, to him, unforgivable sin of having kissed another man. In the episode on the cliff, then, external nature is shown to be defective; and Knight and Elfride – though capable of limited remedies – are shown to be the defective offspring of a marred Mother. Knight can make a ladder of his body to save Elfride, Elfride a rope of her petticoats to save Knight, but they cannot correct the flaws of their natures. Nor can they alter 'the chance of things' that brought them together: a throbbing woman hungry for love, and a man 'whose emotions had been drawn out long and delicate by . . . seclusion like plants in a cellar' (ch. 30). In *Far from the Madding Crowd*, which Hardy began to write while still at work on *Blue Eyes*, this encounter between an imperfect but amending humanity and a defective non-human nature continues, with Bathsheba the impassioned, unstable woman, Boldwood the repressed lover, and Oak a wholly new factor in the struggle. Gabriel Oak is a new kind of character in Hardy's fiction – a man whose intelligence and self-mastery enable him both to control his own impulses and to study and repair the misworking of external nature. But the extent of his power over the serious defects he finds in human nature – in Bathsheba, in Troy, in Boldwood – is left tantalizingly uncertain.

Hardy's view of nature in *Madding Crowd* has usually been defined by association with certain prominent pastoral elements in the novel.[27] Nature, in this view, is a moral norm and Oak, as protagonist, is its imitator and champion. Though helpful in accounting for some of the elements of traditional pastoral in the novel, this argument fails to explain the complexity in Hardy's conception of Oak and Oak's rural world, which is, I believe, expressive of a 'new' idea of nature and of man's place in nature that is diametrically opposed to the idea of nature inherent in traditional pastoral. This 'new' idea, we may note in passing, strongly resembles John Stuart Mill's concept of nature and of man's duty in nature in his essay 'Nature' (written in the 1850s and published in 1874). Put briefly, Mill's view is that art is that activity in nature whose purpose is to amend or improve nature. The duty of man is to be an artist in the broadest sense: he is to study and to improve nature rather than merely to imitate or follow her.[28]

It is possible to discern three senses of nature at work in *Madding Crowd*: nature-as-law, nature-as-impulse, and nature-as-art. The first is nature as 'the Creative and regulative power [feminine in gender] which is conceived of as operating in the material world . . . as the immediate cause of all its phenomena' (*OED*). The second, nature-as-impulse, is 'the inherent dominating impulse (in men and animals) by which action or character is determined, directed, or controlled' (*OED*). The third, nature-as-art – Shakespeare's 'art which adds to nature' – is the skill to adapt the things of nature to the purposes of man, purposes that are, however, nature's own. Hardy used the first two aspects of nature to convey his encompassing sense of nature as, on the one hand, a compelling force working mischievously through humans (especially women), and, on the other, a creative, regulative force working outside human consciousness. These two aspects were for him complementary, as one might say that the realms of psychology and physics are complementary. At the same time, he was exploring the powers and the boundaries of each, of nature-as-impulse and nature-as-law. He arranged the people of his novel according to their relationships to nature in this dual sense. It is one point of the novel that Bathsheba, even more than Elfride in *A Pair of Blue Eyes*, is an agent of nature-as-impulse. Farmer Boldwood, like Henry Knight a victim of sexual repression, and Fanny Robin, a mere vessel of emotion, are similarly moved. This is also the plight of the rustics and the animals in the novel, which is the first, it should be noted, in which human and animal lives are suggestively intermingled. Thus Bathsheba, even more than Elfride, is described with allusions to plants and animals; and the cycle of her emotional life is made to correspond to the cycle of the seasons.

It is a second point of the novel that nature-as-law and as-impulse can be understood and even controlled to a significant degree by a man of Oak's self-mastery and intelligence. Oak can control nature-as-impulse at work in himself and at the same time guide, with some success, the working of nature-as-impulse and nature-as-law in the persons and events around him. He somehow transcends the working of nature-as-law, perhaps because in him, as his many healing, mending, and saving acts suggest, the third (and somewhat paradoxical) aspect of nature in the novel, nature-as-art, is in ascendance. *Far from the Madding Crowd* is 'about' Oak's heroic and usually successful efforts to counter the misworkings of nature – both as-impulse and as-law – with love and intelligence, which is to say, with art. And Bathsheba, portrayed as an inherently flawed agent of nature-as-impulse, of unconscious nature, is the chief object of Oak's attention. This makes for an odd sort of love story and invites a new view of Bathsheba.

It is a commonplace in criticism of the novel to describe Bathsheba as one who develops through misfortune from a vain, egotistical girl into a wise, sympathetic woman.[29] There is something to this view, for, at least superficially, Bathsheba changes for the better between her arrival at Norcombe, penniless and alone atop a wagon loaded with her few possessions, and her marriage to Oak amidst order and prosperity at Weatherbury some three years later. She learns to sympathize with Fanny Robin, seeks to make amends to Farmer Boldwood, acts courageously in the face of Troy's violent death, and marries the exemplary Gabriel Oak. However, there is much in Bathsheba for which a developmental view like this cannot account. Take for instance the following passage, typical of others:

> Bathsheba was no schemer for marriage, nor was she deliberately a trifler with the affections of men, and a censor's experience on seeing an actual flirt after observing her would have been a feeling of surprise that Bathsheba could be so different from such a one, and yet so like what a flirt is supposed to be. She resolved

never again, by look or by sign, to interrupt the steady flow of this man's [Boldwood's] life. But a resolution to avoid an evil is seldom framed till the evil is so far advanced as to make avoidance impossible.   (*FMC*, ch. 18)

One thing here is in radical conflict with a 'transformist' view of Bathsheba: she is an unconscious agent of evil. Her actions are not within her control. This implies what indeed proves to be the case, that for Bathsheba moral growth, even when it occurs, must be slight and fitful. Hardy's attitude to her, veiled somewhat by the conventions of pastoral comedy, is that of the compassionate sceptic; he sympathizes with her irrationality (she is not, after all, wholly responsible for her condition) at the same time as he deplores its consequences.

Bathsheba's root affliction is vanity, 'woman's prescriptive infirmity', as Hardy terms it in his description of her self-admiring entry into Norcombe atop a wagon loaded with her belongings:

The picture was a delicate one. Woman's prescriptive infirmity had stalked into the sunlight, which had clothed it with the freshness of an originality. A cynical inference was irresistible by Gabriel Oak as he regarded the scene, generous though he fain would have been. There was no necessity whatsoever for her looking in the glass. She did not adjust her hat, or pat her hair, or press a dimple into shape, or do one thing to signify that any other intention had been her motive in taking up the glass. She simply observed herself as a fair product of Nature in the feminine kind, her thoughts seeming to glide into far off likely dramas in which men would play a part . . . .   (ch. 1)

What the self-smitten Bathsheba and the fascinated Oak both see as a lovely image is in truth the root and stem of much of the mischief of the novel. Bathsheba will encourage Oak's attentions, then forget him when her fortunes rise and his plunge; she will entice Boldwood, then ruin him by turning to Troy. Deserted by Troy, she will re-engage Boldwood as 'a kind of repentance'. But in this, her effort to make amends, she will be thwarted by Troy's carefully contrived return and his sudden death – at the hand of Boldwood, who will then try to kill himself. Bathsheba will be driven to despair by the knowledge that her childish, whimsical act of sending a Valentine to Boldwood had brought madness, murder, near-suicide and a

possible execution in its wake. Fortunately, Boldwood's death
sentence is reduced to a term in prison, Bathsheba recovers, and the
novel ends with her marriage to her first lover, Oak, who has
remained loyal throughout.

Up to a point, Bathsheba's moral history parallels Troy's. Just as
she entices Boldwood, he seduces Fanny Robin. Just as his attempt
to make amends is mockingly overthrown by the rain and the
gargoyle on Weatherbury Church, her attempt to atone is thwarted
by his malice and deceit. Both, in a phrase from the poem 'To Meet,
or Otherwise', fail to 'undo the done' (*CP*, p. 310). But here
similarities end. Troy is portrayed to a degree as one capable of
better things who has been pushed into error by the circumstances of
his birth, by his profession as a soldier, and by the susceptibility of
women to his gallantry. His vanity and heartlessness are not seen as
inherent or incurable. Bathsheba, in striking contrast, is presented
as one who errs because she is a woman and therefore innately and
irremediably flawed.

The view that women are inherently infirm pervades *Madding
Crowd*. Bathsheba's weakness when she inexplicably refuses to pay
the toll at Norcombe is 'what it always is' in women – vanity. She
refuses to thank Oak when he pays it for her, because 'in gaining her
a passage he had lost her her point, and we know how women take a
favour of that kind' (ch. 1). When she saves Oak from death by
suffocation in his hut, she is described as 'that novelty among
women – one who finished a thought before beginning the sentence
with which to convey it' (ch. 3). But in fact she is no thinker, for hers
is an 'impulsive nature under a deliberative aspect. . . . Many of
her thoughts were perfect syllogisms; unluckily they always remained thoughts. Only a few were irrational assumptions; but,
unfortunately, they were the ones that most frequently grew into
deeds' (ch. 20). In her presence, Oak is a Samson in danger of being
unmanned, Boldwood an Adam in peril of fatal temptation (chs. 3,
17). Having charmed Boldwood, she is blind to the extent of her
power over him: 'When women are in a freakish mood their usual
intuition, either from carelessness or inherent defect, seemingly fails
to teach them this, and hence it was that Bathsheba was fated to be
astonished today' (ch. 17). Faced with Boldwood's ardent proposal
of marriage, she begins to feel 'that she was inherently the weaker
vessel. She strove miserably against this femininity which would
insist upon supplying unbidden emotions in stronger and stronger
current' (ch. 31). Bathsheba herself believes that she is the 'weaker

vessel', as when she warns her workfolk against taking advantage of her womanliness: 'Don't any unfair ones among you . . . suppose that because I'm a woman I don't understand the difference between bad goings-on and good' (ch. 10). Humiliated by Troy's continuing love for Fanny, she admits inferiority: 'Tell me the truth, Frank. I am not a fool, you know, although I am a woman, and have my woman's moments' (ch. 41). Rendered nearly speechless by Boldwood's renewed devotion after Troy's disappearance, she describes what may be an ultimate handicap: 'It is difficult for a woman to define her feelings in language which is chiefly made by men to express theirs' (ch. 51).

Henery Fray inveighs against the villainy of womankind; Laban Tall is afflicted with a shrewish wife; the workwomen Temperance and Soberness, despite their names, are 'yielding women', as in fact are Fanny and Bathsheba herself. At one point the temperate Oak, mortified by Bathsheba's rebuke when he injures a sheep he is shearing for her, murmurs half-seriously the bitter words of Ecclesiastes 7:26: 'I find more bitter than death the woman whose heart is snares and nets' (ch. 22). An 'element of folly . . . *almost* foreign to her [Bathsheba's] intrinsic nature' [emphasis added] colours and permeates her whole constitution:

> Bathsheba, though she had too much understanding to be entirely governed by her womanliness, had too much womanliness to use her understanding to the best advantage. Perhaps in no minor point does woman astonish her helpmate more than in the strange power she possesses of believing cajoleries that she knows to be false – except, indeed, in that of being utterly sceptical on strictures that she knows to be true. (ch. 29)

And so, when Bathsheba comes under the influence of Troy, his deceit – quite consistently within the novel's misogynistic point of view – is seen less as an expression of his damnable depravity than as a response, almost excusable, to Bathsheba's 'strange power . . . of believing cajoleries':

> The wondrous power of flattery in *passados* at woman is a perception so universal as to be remarked upon by many people almost automatically as they repeat a proverb, or say they are Christians and the like, without thinking much of the enormous corollaries that spring from the proposition. Still less is it acted

upon for the good of the complemental being alluded to. With the majority such an opinion is shelved with all those trite aphorisms which require some catastrophe to bring their tremendous meanings thoroughly home. When expressed with some amount of reflectiveness it seems coordinate with a belief that this flattery must be reasonable to be effective. It is to the credit of men that few attempt to settle this question by experiment, and it is for their happiness, perhaps, that accident has never settled it for them. Nevertheless, that a male dissembler who by deluging her with untenable fictions charms the female wisely, may acquire powers reaching to the extremity of perdition, is a truth taught to many by unsought and wringing circumstances. And some profess to have attained to the same knowledge by experiment as aforesaid, and jauntily continue their indulgence in such experiments with terrible effect. Sergeant Troy was one.   (ch. 25)

One what? We are scarcely certain just what Troy was or is as we thread our way through this labyrinthine account of the evil that can come of women's supposed love of flattery. Troy, we know, is an oily-tongued cajoler who relishes the rewards of his deceit. What is so odd is that Troy's heartless philandering draws less of Hardy's censure than Bathsheba's susceptibility to deceit. Perhaps the peculiarly male sophistry in this produces the involuted style. A certain contempt for woman disarms censure of her deceiver. It is not, however, my chief purpose here to examine Hardy's attitude to women, except in so far as it affects his view of Bathsheba's capacity for moral growth.[30]

Hardy's problem with Bathsheba seems to have been this: how to show moral growth in a member of the sex decreed infirm by long-standing custom. A degree of external improvement might be hoped for, but the logic of the underlying premise – 'prescriptive infirmity', 'carelessness of inherent defect', 'weaker vessel' – is against essential improvement. Bathsheba is vain, capricious, domineering, impulsive, coquettish and helpless before flattery: 'I want someone to tame me; I am too independent', she confesses to Oak during the courtship at Norcombe (ch. 4). She is tamed – that is, reduced from wildness to tractability and usefulness. Like a spirited mare, she is broken to harness. She submits to Troy's wiles, to Boldwood's claim on her balky conscience, and to Oak's steady example. Except in a limited sense, however, it is difficult to see this as moral growth, for rational self-awareness is almost wholly absent.

Her essentially irrational character is curbed, not transformed, by the sensational events of three years; for at the end of the novel we find her re-enacting her earlier attempt to shape an environment in which she is the focus of male attention. Her manner changes, but her instinct to charm and control a man remains what it was.

When, after Troy's death and Boldwood's imprisonment, Oak re-enters Bathsheba's life, reserve and sadness give way to a comic bit of male fantasy, the taming of a shrew; for Oak's plan to leave Wessex and Weatherbury for California moves Bathsheba to pursuit of him. But Hardy does not allow this playful turnabout to conceal the truth that Bathsheba's new humility cloaks her old vanity, her inherent need to charm and dominate a man. Stung by the thought that Oak, 'her last old disciple', has abandoned her, she is once more on the hunt for an admirer (ch. 56). On Christmas Day, exactly one year after the shock of Troy's death, she examines her heart only to find it 'beyond measure strange that the subject of which the season might have been supposed suggestive – the event in the hall at Boldwood's – was not agitating her at all; but instead, an agonizing conviction that everybody abjured her – for what she could not tell – and that Oak was the ringleader of the recusants'. She has mistaken Oak's delicate concern for her position as an attractive widow for betrayal of a presumed obligation to serve and worship her. The language of the episode suggests even more. 'Disciple', 'abjured' and 'recusants' are the words of a religionist, in this case the words for the thoughts of a once-idolized woman longing for re-enshrinement. The words recall with grim fidelity that only three years before she had sent Boldwood the fatal Valentine because she was annoyed at his 'nonconformity' (ch. 13). He was, in her view, 'a species of Daniel in her kingdom who persisted in kneeling eastward when reason and common sense said that he might just as well follow suit with the rest, and afford her the official glance of admiration which cost nothing at all'. When she learns from Oak of his imminent departure for America, she weeps bitterly, but not at the thought of losing him: 'She was aggrieved and wounded that the possession of hopeless love from Gabriel, which she had grown to regard as her inalienable right for life, should have been withdrawn just at his own pleasure in this way' (ch. 56). Still governed by irrational urgings, she has not changed in essence since the days at Norcombe, three years before. She is perhaps worse, for her acts are now those of a woman of station and of experience.

On the eve of the wedding there is 'a certain rejuvenated appearance about her: – "As though a rose should shut and be a bud again!"':[31]

> Repose had again incarnadined her cheeks; and having, at Gabriel's request, arranged her hair this morning as she had worn it years ago at Norcombe Hill, she seemed in his eyes remarkably like the girl of that fascinating dream, which considering that she was just only three or four-and-twenty, was not very wonderful.
>
> (ch. 56)

There is irony in Bathsheba's seeming to Oak 'remarkably like' the girl at Norcombe, and folly in his indulging a nostalgic attempt to recreate the girl of that time, the girl, we recall, whom he had watched admire herself in a mirror 'as a fair product of nature in the feminine kind' while thinking of 'dramas in which men would play a part – vistas of possible triumphs – smiles . . . suggesting that hearts were imagined as lost and won' (ch. 1). Is Hardy suggesting that the redoubtable Oak is but another victim of this fair product of nature? The answer, at least in part, must be yes. Vanity still governs Bathsheba, and Bathsheba still entrances Oak. But it must be said also that Oak, aware of her vanity from the start, is a willing victim who enjoys his own kind of victory. Though Bathsheba is essentially the same, her circumstances have changed drastically. Her circle of male admirers has been reduced by two-thirds, and her 'absolute hunger' for affection, a stable law of her flawed nature, can be satisfied only by Oak, the sole survivor of the trio. Oak has Bathsheba, so to speak, where he wants her – in a position from which she can turn only to him for the support and love that are her infirm nature's deepest needs. The 'happiness' in this ending, and there can be no doubt that we have here happiness of a kind, grows up, as Hardy says, 'in the interstices of a mass of hard prosaic reality'.[32] The nature of that reality is best seen by studying Oak's special kind of heroism within the defective world of the novel.

OAK AS AGENT OF RATIONAL NATURE

If Bathsheba is the infirm agent of irrational impulse, the other characters of the novel are scarcely exemplary. Boldwood is completely unhinged by Bathsheba's harmless Valentine because, even before coming under her influence, he had lived in a delicate state of emotional equilibrium. Rejected by her, he neglects his farm and succumbs to fantasy; to keep Troy from her, he first attempts to bribe, then murders, the deceitful and mocking sergeant. Troy is Boldwood's antithesis, as openly self-indulgent as Boldwood is self-repressive. He gets Fanny with child, turns whimsically from marrying her, then takes up with Bathsheba and proceeds to destroy the order of Weatherbury Farm. Rebuffed in his belated attempts to make amends to the dead Fanny, he returns, out of spite it seems, to bedevil Bathsheba and Boldwood. Fanny, Troy's victim, is a sympathetic figure – hardly, it would seem, a target of the novel's censure of infirm womankind. And yet, in the misogynist context of this novel, it is difficult not to view her as but another daughter of Eve – weak, impressionable and dependent, though more sinned against than sinning. As the case of Fanny would suggest, the novel's rustics, if at times quaint and picturesque in manner and speech, are not simple swains. The hen-pecked Laban Tall, those 'yielding' workwomen Temperance and Soberness, the sanctimonious Joseph Poorgrass, whose thirst delays Fanny's burial and brings about the disastrous meeting between Bathsheba and Troy beside Fanny's coffin, are not the worst of them. Henery Fray is a back-biting gossip, and Bailiff Pennyways is a thief. And the whole lot of them accede readily to Troy's forceful invitation to drink brandy and water at the Harvest Supper, with stupefaction and the near ruin of the grain stores by the rain the result.

Though superior to the flawed and foolish persons around him, Gabriel Oak is hardly perfect: his 'defects were patent to the blindest, and [his] virtues were as metals in a mine' (ch. 29). His great strength is that he is not nostalgic; because he can forget and forgive he lives in expectation. Though not indifferent to the claims of the past, he knows its irretrievable pastness. Hardy reveals this early, by invoking what at first seems an inappropriate and forced analogy between Oak and Milton's Satan. Oak peeps into the hut in which Bathsheba and her aunt are feeding two cows and sees Bathsheba 'in a bird's eye view, as Milton's Satan first saw Paradise' (ch. 2). Satan's attitude upon first seeing Paradise combined envy with regret for his own loss of paradise. Though Oak's wish is not, like Satan's, to destroy Paradise so as to in some way to defy the Almighty, his situation is like Satan's in that he too has lost his original place. Gabriel Oak the third (we think of Thomas Hardy the third) has abandoned his original calling as a shepherd, the calling of his father and grandfather before him. Unlike them he seeks to own the flock he tends; he seeks the status of an independent farmer, a status that will enable him to seek the hand of a girl like Bathsheba. And by the end of the novel he will have achieved his goal. But, for Hardy, to rise is to fall, to develop is to decay; Oak's point of view is that of a fallen angel because he is a rising shepherd. Better to reign at Weatherbury than to serve at Norcombe! An ambitious shepherd named, ironically, Gabriel and a rebellious archangel named Satan are momentarily associable because, for Hardy, to abandon one's original place is to fall from a primal felicity.[33] Oak, we slowly realize as we contemplate the association, is one of Hardy's displaced persons – a native abroad, like Mayne, Smith and Springrove, even a spiritual exile like Henry Knight, looking for a paradise in love to replace the lost paradise of childhood. But Oak differs drastically from his predecessors because he does not wish to go home again; nor does he wish to be a shepherd once more, though he is capable of taking up the shepherd's crook when misfortune strikes. He differs profoundly from Knight in that he has no need for his well-beloved to be spotless and pure.

Oak harbours no illusions of returning to or reinstating an earlier, happier time. Because he is free of nostalgia, he habitually does two things: he observes the working of things as they are, and he acts to correct the misworking in what he observes. In the opening chapter, when he watches Bathsheba preening herself atop the wagon, sees her refuse to pay a toll, then pays it for her, he observes the misworking of female nature and moves to avert the consequences. He also falls in love – hopelessly in love – with the infirm creature whom he observes and aids. He can love her in spite of her vanity and impulsiveness because he is not distracted – like a Knight or a Boldwood – by a notion of the ideal woman. He loves the imperfect individual before him, not the lost ideal, associated with childhood, that she imperfectly or only temporarily embodies. When ruined by the loss of his flock (ch. 5) Oak does not, like Troy at the spitting of the gargoyle (chs 45, 46), conjure up then curse a jeering Providence. Because he does not observe the world through a preconceived idea of what it should be, he is free to observe it as it is, in all its imperfection, then to act to improve it. And he has great success with it; much more than he has with his imperfect human brethren.

Oak's way of controlling the fire that threatens Bathsheba's corn illustrates his ability to perceive the laws of physical nature and then exploit them to good ends. His firm instructions to the confused labourers reflect a clear understanding of the laws by which things burn: 'Stop the draught under the wheatrick! . . . Get a tarpaulin, quick! . . . Stand here with a bucket of water and keep the cloth wet' (ch. 6). By moving the tarpaulin between the rick and its source of air, by keeping the tarp wet to prevent its flapping or burning, by beating off the sparks until the dry corn can be dampened, Oak obeys and by obeying controls the natural process called burning. His method here – to bring separate things into contact and to engage other natural forces – is also his method when he saves the bloated sheep:

> He had . . . taken from his pocket the instrument of salvation. It was a small tube or trochar, with a lance passing down the inside; and Gabriel began to use it with the dexterity that would have graced a hospital-surgeon. Passing his hand over the sheep's left flank, and selecting the proper point, he punctured the skin and rumen with the lance, retaining the tube in its place. A current of air rushed up the tube, forcible enough to have extinguished a candle held at the orifice. (ch. 21)

Oak saves the sheep by freeing the vapours swelling their intestines to move, like waters seeking their own level, into the surrounding atmosphere. Before going on to the great storm episode – the scene of Oak's most difficult encounter with nature – it might be well to note some of the similarities (noted above) between Oak's skilful acts and John Stuart Mill's view of the duty of man in his essay 'Nature'.

Mill's view of nature in this essay published in the same year as *Madding Crowd* is, like Hardy's, a repudiation of the idea of nature as a moral guide or teacher. As one commentator has put it, the vigour of Mill's essay derives from his attack on 'the appeal to "nature" which underlay theories of natural law, [for which] Mill shared to the full the utilitarian hatred'.[34] Mill summarized his argument, with remarkable terseness, as follows:

> The word Nature has two principal meanings: it either denotes the entire system of things, with the aggregate of all their properties, or it denotes things as they would be, apart from human intervention. In the first of these senses, the doctrine that man ought to follow nature is unmeaning, since man has no

power to do anything else than follow nature; all his actions are done through and in obedience to some one or many of nature's physical or mental laws.

In the other sense of the term, the doctrine that man ought to follow nature, or, in other words, ought to make the spontaneous course of things the model of his voluntary actions is equally irrational and immoral: Irrational, because all human action whatever, consists in altering, and all useful action in improving, the spontaneous course of nature. Immoral, because the course of natural phenomena being replete with everything which when committed by human beings is most worthy of abhorrence, anyone who endeavoured in his actions to imitate the natural course of things would be universally seen and acknowledged to be the wickedest of men. . . . Whatever in nature gives indication of beneficent design proves this beneficence to be armed only with limited power; and the duty of man is to co-operate with the beneficent powers, not by imitating but by perpetually striving to amend the course of nature – and bringing that part of it over which we can exercise control more nearly into conformity with a high standard of justice and goodness.

Mill dismisses the view by which 'nature is opposed to art, and natural to artificial' because 'art is as much nature as anything else; and everything which is artificial is natural – art has not independent powers of its own: art is but the employment of the powers of nature for an end'.

Hardy and Mill agree on two points: both reject the romantic dictum to follow nature because both reject the idea of nature as an ideal state free from the taint of things human; both think of nature as 'the entire system of things', including humanity, and therefore think of all human actions as occurring 'through and in obedience to some one or many of nature's physical or mental laws'. Hardy's conception of Gabriel Oak is compatible with Mill's view that 'all useful action [consists] in improving the spontaneous course of nature' by co-operating with the 'beneficent powers' of nature. Oak's way of extinguishing the fire and saving the sheep is most suggestive of Mill's description of the 'office of man' that follows his statement that 'art is as much nature as anything else':

[The duty of man] is . . . a very limited one; it consists in moving things into certain places. We move objects, and by doing this bring some things into contact that were separate, or separate others which were in contact; and, by simple change of place, natural forces previously dormant are called into action and produce the desired effect. Even the volition which designs, the intelligence which contrives, and the muscular power which executes these movements, are themselves powers of nature.

By applying trochar and lance to the swollen flanks of the sheep, by moving the tarpaulin between the burning and the as yet unburnt ricks, Oak calls dormant natural forces into action to produce the desired effects. We are reminded of this by his flute-playing atop windy Norcombe Hill at the beginning of the novel: 'Suddenly an unexpected series of sounds began to be heard in this place up against the sky. They had a clearness which was to be found nowhere in the wind, and a sequence which was to be found nowhere in nature' (ch. 2). As flute-player, as extinguisher of fire, and as healer of the ailing sheep, Oak calls into play natural forces to produce a desired effect. This is his artistry, to act according to nature in order to improve nature, to be nature in its rational, self-amending form.

In the sensational storm scene (chs 36, 37) the three aspects of nature exhibited in the novel (nature-as-law, as-impulse, and as-art) are brought into an interesting interplay. Nature-as-law, as 'creative, regulative power' for the moment benignly maternal, warns Oak of imminent foul weather by sending a 'direct message' in the forms of slug and toad. Nature in this mood seems benevolent enough, though in the form of the violent electrical storm she will display 'sinister', 'lurid', and destructive faces as well. The fields are 'sallow with the impure light' and the lightning leaps 'with the spring of a serpent and the shout of a fiend'. At the first peal of thunder it is hardly credible to Oak and Bathsheba 'that such a heavenly light could be the parent of such a diabolical sound' (ch. 37). Confronted with natural forces that are at once beautiful and lethal, at once helpful and destructive, Oak observes then acts to parry the threat in what he observes. First, he translates the message sent him by the Great Mother in garden-slug and toad. Next he seeks the aid of the revellers in the barn, of fellow humans capable like him of rational acts but now, under the influence of Troy, reduced to a state of unconciousness. Oak is as far removed from his drunken fellow beings as he is from the storm about to break and the dumb creatures whose instinctive movements he translates into thought and saving actions. The correspondence here is between nature-as-law and nature-as-impulse, between the 'dance of death' in the heavens ('leaping, striding, racing around, and mingling together in unparalleled confusion') and the revel in the barn ('convulsions, spasms, St. Vitus's dances, and fearful frenzies'). As we might expect, Bathsheba – though at this point sensible and helpful – is placed in the ranks of the irrational. The ricks are exposed because of the 'instability of a woman', help unavailable because of the reckless arrogance of Troy.

Oak, nature-as-art, stands apart from creative, regulative nature in one of 'her' violent moods and from inherent, dominating nature in one of its typical spasms. He works, first alone, then with the aid of Bathsheba, to protect the grain from the storm. Mill's 'moving things into certain places' – in this case tarpaulins and thatch – again comes to mind. When lightning threatens, Oak makes an effective lightning-conductor from an iron ricking-rod and a length of chain.[35] Nature-as-law storms, nature-as-impulse snores drunkenly, nature-as-art labours to correct and repair. The scene captures with some precision Hardy's complex sense of man's relation to nature in the novel, a complexity revealed in the various similes he uses to describe the drunken labourers: their hair, lying 'in every conceivable attitude except the perpendicular', resembles 'mops and brooms'; their breathing forms 'a subdued roar like London from a distance'; Poorgrass is 'curled round in the fashion of a hedgehog'; and water drips 'into the neck of the unconscious Mark Clark, in a steady, monotonous drip, like the dripping of a stalactite in a cave' (ch. 36). As Hardy himself noted at this point, 'man, even to himself, is a palimpsest, having an ostensible writing, and another beneath the lines'.

But if Oak can save the grain from the storm, he is powerless to save the next victim of nature's misworking. On the road back to his cottage after the storm, he meets Boldwood and learns that the morose farmer, distracted by Bathsheba's turn to Troy, has allowed his corn stores to go to ruin. Saddened by this waste, Oak tries to preserve what he can by assuming some of Boldwood's duties. But it soon becomes clear that the working of defective nature in Boldwood is beyond Oak's ministrations. And this is so because 'material causes and emotional effects are not to be arranged in regular equation. The result from capital employed in the production of any movement of a mental nature is sometimes as tremendous as the cause itself is absurdly minute' (ch. 17). Such 'great issues from little beginnings' are beyond even Oak's patience, strength and ingenuity. He can control flames fed by wind and straw, and he can master the heat of his own devotion to Bathsheba; but how can he block the draught that feeds the 'great flame' of Boldwood's idealized passion and 'the little wildfire' that ignited it? (ch. 18). The roots of inherent, dominating nature, of nature-as-impulse, are deep and elusive. And in Troy Oak encounters an even greater enigma, a rational man who deliberately indulges and encourages the irrational in himself and in those around him. Troy is as clever as Oak in perceiving nature's laws, but he chooses to turn them to evil rather than to good ends. He understands Bathsheba's vanity and courts it with flattery. He understands the rustics' appetite for brandy and for the company of a social superior and exploits these things. He understands both Boldwood's hopeless devotion to Bathsheba and Bathsheba's desperate wish to make amends to Boldwood, and he mocks and thwarts both in their efforts. His sword demonstration proves him a master of a destructive art which may be seen, like the science of war itself, as a rationalization of the lethal forces of nature. He is as skilful with his rapier as Oak is with the surgical lance. Both Oak and Troy are rational and intelligent men, but one serves good and the other evil. Hardy does not reveal why, though he is tempted occasionally, as has been seen, to blame Troy's villainy on the women he deceives. He can suggest a monstrousness in Troy's acts by making him analogous to the gargoyle on Weatherbury Church – it thwarts him in his attempt to make amends to Fanny as he thwarts Bathsheba in her attempt to make amends to Boldwood. Troy's propensity for evil, when not attributed to the influence of the women around him, is left in mystery.

It is here, in the view that imperfect men and women are unalterably what they are, that Hardy differs markedly from the perfectibilitarian Mill. Hardy might accept Mill's proposition that 'nature denotes the entire system of things' including humanity; he might accept Mill's injunction that men 'strive to amend the course of nature'. But he parts with Mill when he depicts the all-amending, all-mitigating Oak confounded by the plight of a Boldwood irreparably injured by a prescriptively infirm Bathsheba and later denied union with her by a cruel, contriving Troy. Oak can extinguish fire, guard against the ravages of rain and wind, cure ailing sheep, and even master his own desires and disappointments; but amendment of the evil contrived by rational

beings is beyond him – unless, Hardy suggests, he can develop a
taste for the imperfect and the infirm, a sense of the beauty in defect.
Oak achieves his end with Bathsheba by seeing and accepting her
infirmity, then suffering patiently the effects of it until her infirmity
and his need can be joined. His role is summed up succinctly in a
remark he makes while munching a piece of bacon that had fallen to
the ground: 'I never fuss about dirt in its pure state, and when I
know what sort it is' (ch. 8). Roy Morrell has rightly described this
statement as 'a precise metaphor of what Oak has been doing in the
wider sphere of life'.[36]

Oak's hearty appetite suggests his unhesitating acceptance of the
imperfect in man and nature, and this is one antidote for the
fastidiousness of a Henry Knight and the blind idealism of Farmer
Boldwood. Knight must have purity in Elfride because union with a
purity supposedly in her is for him the equivalent of reunion with a
lost glory of childhood. When he does not find it in her, he rejects her
with the peculiar moral heartlessness of a thwarted idealist. Oak,
something of an unsentimental fallen angel, knows the irremediable
defect of nature and takes it as his duty to make the most of the
chancefulness and changefulness of things. He accepts the loss of his
flock, then the loss of his beloved Bathsheba, and works patiently
toward recovery. He confronts fire, storm, and disease, and uses
tarp, rod, and lance to keep loss to a minimum. He labours
throughout to reduce the effects of the folly of Bathsheba, Troy, and
Boldwood. In none of these does he succeed completely, but in all he
manages to accept loss and to make what gains he can. He is neither
a rebel against nor an imitator of nature's laws. He is instead a
student of them who uses them to good ends.

Hardy's ambitious attempt in *Far from the Madding Crowd* to
define man's role in nature brought to an end the first phase of his
exploration of a personal and mythic drama in which a radiant
dream-world, simple and good, has deteriorated into a complex
and faulty one. In the world of this drama, history is decline,
maturing is decaying, and disillusionment is the unavoidable
condition of living. As has been suggested, Hardy found a
touchstone for this view, at least up to a point, in Wordsworth's
Intimations Ode, a poem he quoted throughout his fiction as well as
on a crucial occasion in the *Life*, the January night in 1879 when the
troubles of his marriage make him and Emma feel, like Elfride and
Knight, that 'there had past away a glory from the earth' (p. 124).
Hardy was at one with the poet who recalled a time when every

common sight seemed 'apparelled in celestial light', the poet for
whom things once seen were seen no more. For Hardy, as for
Wordsworth in the Ode, 'there [had] past away a glory from the
earth'. Though the idealism of Wordsworth's famous fifth stanza
must have appealed to Hardy, the realism of the last ten lines of that
stanza must have appealed even more:

> Heaven lies about us in our infancy!
> Shades of the prison-house begin to close
>   Upon the growing Boy
> But he beholds the light, and whence it flows,
>   He sees it in his joy;
> The Youth, who daily further from the east
>   Must travel, still is Nature's Priest
>   And by the vision splendid
> Is on his way attended;
> At length the Man perceives it die away,
> And fade into the light of common day.

If Hardy found in Wordsworth another poet who lamented the loss
inherent in growth, he parted with him in seeing no compensation
for that unavoidable loss. There is for Hardy only grief for loss, no
'strength in what remains behind'. Wordsworth's enduring 'primal
sympathy' is vitiated for Hardy by time, chance, experience and
knowledge. Contemplation of human suffering produced in him not
'soothing thoughts' but profound sadness mingled with pity,
indignation, and despair. Hardy's people are deprived of a 'faith
that looks through death', and their years bring isolation and regret
rather than wisdom or calm. The child in Hardy's fiction (e.g.
Johnny Nunsuch in *The Return of the Native*, Father Time and young
Jude Fawley in *Jude the Obscure*) is not 'father to the Man' because
privy to an everlasting source of truth and beauty. Hardy's children
are prematurely adult and like his adults are victims of 'the
hypocrisy of things'. He himself had been a child who did not want
to grow up. Nature he learned to regard not a benevolent mother
but an 'arch-dissembler': 'A child is deceived completely; the older
members of society more or less according to their penetration;
though even they seldom get to realize that *nothing* is as it appears'
(*Life*, p. 176).

3 'Nothing Backward Climbs': the Futility of Return in *The Return of the Native*, *The Woodlanders* and *The Well-Beloved*

The creation of Gabriel Oak brought to a hopeful end a first phase of Hardy's exploration of the drama of regeneration. After *Far from the Madding Crowd* Hardy would find it possible to exhibit human powers of amelioration or remedy comparable to Oak's only in the minor narratives he called 'romances', 'fantasies' or 'novels of ingenuity'. There would be, of course, the meliorism of *The Dynasts*; but that is evolutionary, its source non-human rather than human nature. A sense of tragic irremediability in things can be said to govern in the major novels, which Hardy called narratives of 'character and environment'. Even more distinctly than before 1874, the pattern of Hardy's fiction after that year is vacillatory, an alternation between comedic displays of regenerative possibilities and tragic depictions of the impossibility of renewal. And so, after the pastoral comedy of *Far from the Madding Crowd*, he moved to social comedy in *The Hand of Ethelberta* (1876), then to tragedy in *The Return of the Native* (1878); then to 'romance' and 'ingenuity' in *The Trumpet-Major* (1880), *A Laodicean* (1881) and *Two on a Tower* (1882); then to tragedy and tragi-comedy in *The Mayor of Casterbridge* (1886), *The Woodlanders* (1887), *Tess* (1891) and *Jude* (1895); and, finally, to 'fantasy' in *The Well-Beloved* (1892, 1897). After the creation of Oak, Hardy found it possible to exhibit regenerative heroics only in admittedly fanciful or severely attenuated forms.

This state of affairs may explain why in 1875 and 1876 Hardy turned from the story of restoration to the story of return or homecoming, which to this point in his fiction had been a secondary one. It had been a subordinate element in 'The Poor Man', in *Desperate Remedies*, and in *A Pair of Blue Eyes*, and had emerged full-blown for the first time in *Under the Greenwood Tree*. In *The Return of the Native* and *The Woodlanders* – the latter sketched in the mid seventies[1] – Hardy again would use the story of homecoming that he first perfected in *Under the Greenwood Tree*. But why should he have turned from stories about the difficulty of restoration to stories about the difficulty of homecoming? There are probably two answers. First, the story of return and the story of restoration are in fact stories about the difficulty or impossibility of return or restoration and derived for Hardy from the same truth, that time or consciousness is a process of decay inherently opposed to regenerative beliefs or schemes. And so, his taking up the story of return did not require a change in essential outlook. Second, he could turn to the story of (no) return after 1874 because by then he had found it to be his own story, a particular aspect of private experience that he could turn into an allegory of universal human experience, a dramatic image of the homelessness, the unavoidable estrangement from the good and the pure, that time and growth visits on us all. To turn to the story of return from the story of restoration was to continue to trace 'that pattern among general things which his idiosyncracy move[d] him to observe' (*Life* [1882], p. 153).

The basic elements of the story of return or homecoming are relatively simple. A former rustic (Fancy Day, Clym Yeobright, Grace Melbury) returns to his or her native place (Mellstock and Yalbury Wood, Egdon Heath, the Hintocks) after a long sojourn in the city. The homecoming kindles discord, suffering, even causes death within the rustic community; for the homecomers' acquired tastes and opinions clash with the rural ways of their families and neighbours, as well as with those homely ways within themselves that, long repressed, are stirred by the return. This internal – external clash of values crystallizes in every case around the choice of a mate. Each of the homecomers is attracted to prospective partners of contrasting styles and values. Each must choose between an 'alien' lover (Vicar Maybold, Eustacia Vye, Edred Fitzpiers), who may represent a substitute for the lost childhood dream and a 'native' lover (Dick Dewey, Thomasin Yeobright, Giles Winterborne) associated with childhood. At the same time, the homecomer seeks to please an ambitious, intrusive parent (Keeper Day, Mrs Yeobright, George Melbury) torn between a desire to see his child rise in the world and a wish to preserve the old ties. The struggle to choose a mate is suggestive then of the struggle to choose between the childhood ideal of innocence and simplicity and the adult ideal of love. In every case the marriage decision signals the 'meaning' of the return.

Under the Greenwood ·Tree, which through acts of forgiveness ends with the 'happy' marriage of Fancy and Dick, renders the comedy of return, in which Dick is both love object and symbol of innocence. However, in this novel's undercurrent of irony and cynicism we catch a glimpse of the tragic world of *The Return of the Native*, in which we are shown the working of revenge (not forgiveness) through two shattered marriages and three untimely deaths. Clym's yearning is divided irreconcilably between mother and lover. *The Woodlanders*, which ends with Grace and Giles's marriage-masquerade at One-Chimney Hut, the death of Giles, and the precarious reunion of Grace and Fitzpiers, is a mixed spectacle best described as the tragi-comedy or, more precisely, the irony of the return of a native.[2] Grace's changeability (or is it her good sense?) is set off against Marty's grim fidelity to the lost beloved, and we are left somewhere between amusement and pity.

Though *The Well-Beloved* (1897) – first published as *The Pursuit of the Well-Beloved* in 1892 – departs in some ways from the pattern of the earlier returns, it is intimately related to them. In fact, it may be said to be a portrait of the helplessly nostalgic temperament that found expression in the almost-compulsive writing and rewriting of the story of homecoming. Jocelyn Pierston seeks not a lost joy connected with an early environment, but an elusive ideal of beauty and truth that for him resides in several women of his native Isle of Slingers. Pierston's returns to the Isle at twenty-year intervals are the expression of a nympholeptic yearning that transforms the women he loves there into carriers of the elusive ideal. Furthermore, it seems most significant that the marble of the isle, the artist hero's home, is literally the raw material of his art. As sculptor, Pierston shapes images of the ideal from the marble taken from his father's quarry on the Isle. In a somewhat similar way, Hardy, as novelist, transformed the lives and places of Dorset and neighbouring counties into the stuff of Wessex. Perhaps Hardy had this in mind when he wrote to Sir George Douglas (in March 1897) that *The Well-Beloved* was a 'fanciful, tragi-comic, half-allegorical tale of a poor Visionary pursuing a Vision'.[3] Hardy's phrase describes not only Pierston's (and his own) spiritual yearning, but also his shifting, recurring use of the return motif throughout the four novels of homecoming: comedy in *Greenwood Tree*, tragedy in *The Return*, irony in *The Woodlanders*, fantasy in *The Well-Beloved*. Throughout the stories of return, Hardy seems a 'poor Visionary', a seer assuming various disguises, modes and voices in his quest for a lost moment, meaning and harmony whose imperfect re-embodiments torment his conscience because he at once worships and abhors them. The seeker's contempt for the things he loves has two sources. First, the object of his love is always imperfect, and never, as Henry Knight discovers, the pure reincarnation. Second, the object is frequently homely or in other ways remindful of the humbler station he had abandoned to undertake his quest. But to hate what he once loved is to incur guilt and regret. And so, if the telling and retelling of the story of return is the pursuit of a vision, it is also an attempt to make amends to the home, to the family, and to the class abandoned for the pursuit. Hardy was too humane and too loyal to his past to be a pure visionary; thus his suggestive phrase, ' "a poor Visionary pursuing a Vision" '. This mixture of guilt and longing is first revealed in *The Hand of Ethelberta*, the heavily autobiographical novel that followed *Far from the Madding Crowd*.

THE HAND OF ETHELBERTA (1876)

Hardy's situation between 1874 and 1876 was much like that of Ethelberta Petherwin, the heroine of his next novel.[4] His remark that *Ethelberta*, his sixth novel, had 'nothing whatever in common with anything he had written before' has gone unchallenged since he made it (*Life*, pp. 102–3). And it is possible to see why, for at first glance this satiric novel of manners (just the sort of novel he said he did not wish to write) seems to depart entirely from the romantic narratives that preceded it. But this is not the case if we recall that social satire was prominent in 'The Poor Man', and that class conflict, a strong element in *Ethelberta*, has a place both in *A Pair of Blue Eyes* and *Under the Greenwood Tree*. Furthermore, the situation of Ethelberta Petherwin – a gifted native of Wessex who writes poetry, 'tells' novels for profit, and marries above her station as the daughter of servants – is in essence the predicament not just of Hardy himself but also of *déracinés* such as Egbert Mayne, Edward Springrove, Stephen Smith and Fancy Day. Like them, like Clym Yeobright of *The Return* and Grace Melbury of *The Woodlanders*,

Ethelberta is an uprooted native of Wessex. The structure of her story differs from that of Clym or Grace because she is depicted not upon her return to her native Wessex but during her sojourns in various cities and towns. The shift from a romantic to a realistic mode in *Ethelberta* is in part a response to a shift of setting and perspective. But the subject – the troubled consciousness of an uprooted native – is the same.

Ethelberta's movements between London, Angelbury, Knollsea, Sandbourne, Melchester and Paris – distinctly remindful of Hardy's own moves between 1874 and 1876 – are disturbed both by her longing for her earlier, simpler life in Wessex and by guilt for having abandoned her family and station. She has learned that 'the only feeling which has any dignity or permanence or worth is family affection between close blood-relations'.[5] Both by marriage outside her class and by education that has raised her above her class, she has estranged herself from her modest origins. A quarrel about the propriety of some of her poems with Lady Petherwin, her mother-in-law, leaves her penniless and forces her to 'keep base life afoot' (cf. *Life*, p. 102) by reciting prose narratives of her own invention. When the support of her parents (who are servants) and many siblings falls wholly on her shoulders, she decides that she must find a wealthy husband, even though she loves a poor musician named Christopher Julian. Courted by Eustace Ladywell, Alfred Neigh and Viscount Mountclere, she finally chooses the last, an enormously wealthy old nobleman. With this choice her self-betrayal is complete. As at the expense of home and family she had turned to letters and society, and at the expense of poetry had turned to prose, so now, at the cost of sincere feeling, she has turned to wealth and high station – and in a particularly repulsive form, for Mountclere is a practised womanizer. This might constitute Ethelberta's moral failure, as something similar will constitute Tess Durbeyfield's; and her story might thus be seen as another version of the story of ruined innocence. But Ethelberta's moral compromise is depicted as a function of economic necessity. Like a Gabriel Oak observing and obeying the laws of nature, Ethelberta observes and obeys the economic and social 'laws' that drive her up and away from the simple good of her beginnings. Like Oak, she masters nostalgic yearning. And, even more emphatically than he, she is portrayed as a Satanic creature because she is rootless and unsentimental. Ethelberta is no innocent abroad, but that more complex thing, a person of scruple and principle forced to compromise her convic-

tions by her need for money. Like Oak, like Clym and Grace, like
Hardy himself seeking in the 1870s to live life as an emotion rather
than a science of climbing,[6] she rises in station only to fall (in her
own eyes) in moral worth. For all these *déracinés*, estrangement from
origins is the equivalent of moral ruin; and, because their estrangement is necessary and unavoidable, their ruin is tragic. As Raymond
Williams has said so well,

> It is common to reduce Hardy's fiction to the impact of an urban
> alien on the 'timeless pattern' of English rural life. Yet, though
> this is sometimes there, the more common pattern is the relation
> between the changing nature of country living, determined as
> much by its own pressures as by pressures from 'outside', and one
> or more characters who have become in some degree separated
> from it yet who remain, by some ties of family, inescapably
> involved. It is here that the social values are dramatized, in a very
> complex way, and it is here that most of the problems of Hardy's
> writing seem to arise.[7]

Thus the chief moral reality of *Ethelberta* is not the foibles of the
upper classes or the corruption of rural innocents by wicked
urbanites. The central moral concern of the novel is Ethelberta's
unavoidable betrayal of family loyalty, of artistic integrity, and of
true love for money and getting on in the world.

Hardy knew the bitter terms of this dilemma, for he, like
Ethelberta a poet by instinct and preference, wrote *Ethelberta* and
his earlier novels for much the same reason that Ethelberta tells first-
person narratives in the manner of Defoe to leering or stupid
fashionables – 'to keep base life afoot'. Hardy's only first-person
narrative, 'The Poor Man and the Lady', was also modelled on
Defoe (*Life*, p. 61). Though usually thought of as purely stylistic,
Hardy's debt to Defoe, considered in the context of *Ethelberta*, can be
seen to be thematic as well. *Robinson Crusoe* is the story of a boy who
leaves home against his parents' wishes in search of adventure and
fortune – that is, in search of money – which Ian Watt in his classic
study of the novel has called 'fortune in its modern sense'. As Watt
says, 'the hypostasis of the economic motive logically entails a
devaluation of other modes of thought, feeling, and action; the
various forms of traditional group relationship, the family, the
guild, the village, the sense of nationality – are all weakened, and so,
too, are the competing claims of non-economic recreations'.[8]

Among such profitless recreations we might include literary art, unless it be the profitable art of writing (or telling) prose fictions.

Ethelberta can neither accept her father's advice to keep to her old class (*HE*, ch. 7) nor her brother's to stay in her adopted one (ch. 17). Though she keeps her family near her by employing them as her servants, she cannot open her heart to them, for they have grown uneasy with her refinement. She wishes herself dead when she sees that her ambition has, in her mother's cruel word, 'tempted' the family from the simplicities of rural life in Wessex (ch. 23). She pines for 'an hour of childhood over again in a romp with the others', for when she sets 'the years from her infancy to her first look into town against those linking that epoch with the present, the former period covered not only the greater time, but contained the mass of her most vivid impressions of life and its ways' (ch. 26).[9] At this recollective moment, Hardy – as we might expect – invokes Wordsworth (and through Wordsworth Milton) to lend epic grandeur and gloom to the plight of his native in exile.

The occasion is a pilgrimage to Milton's grave at Cripplegate Church, London, inspired by Mrs Belmaine's flippant quoting from Wordsworth's 'London. 1802': 'Milton! Thou shouldst be living at this hour / England hath need of thee' (ch. 27).[10] Ethelberta, fresh from reading a life of Milton, takes up *Paradise Lost* and reads from Book I (lines 671ff.) while standing before the poet's tomb: 'Mammon led them on / Mammon, the least erected spirit that fell / From Heaven.' The quotation is more than ornamental, for it is read 'not many yards from the central money-mill of the world', and the implication of the juxtaposition is clear. By betraying class and kin, by pursuing material wealth at the cost of poetry and sincere love, Ethelberta, like one of Milton's fallen angels, has lost her paradise – that is, her simpler, purer life of the imagination. Now she dearly wishes that she could 'get a living by some simple, humble occupation, and drop the name Petherwin, and be Berta Chickerel again, and live in a green cottage as we used to when I was small' (ch. 28). As Ian Watt has noted, migrants from one social station to another often see their 'dissatisfaction with "the state wherein God and Nature has placed [them] as [their] original sin"', which is really the 'dynamic tendency of capitalism itself, leaving home, improving on the lot one was born to'. Mr·Chickerel's tart comment on Ethelberta's nostalgic wish to be as she once had been – 'No use your going into high doctrine like that. . . . You chose your course. You have begun to fly high and you had better keep there' – recalls the striking encounter between a duck and a hawk with which the novel opens.[11]

The opening scene of *Ethelberta* is set on the eastern edge of Egdon Heath, near Anglebury. There Ethelberta watches a duck dive from the sky into the protective depths of a pond to elude a hungry hawk, a predator in the motion of whose wings is seen a 'satanic moodiness'. Usually regarded as an expression of Hardy's Darwinism,[12] the probable Dantean source of this episode has been ignored. The dramatic chase almost surely derives from Canto XXII (lines 130ff.) of the *Inferno*, where Ciampolo escapes the talons of a demon by diving into the boiling lake: 'E'en thus the water-fowl, when she perceives / The falcon near, dives instant down, while he / Enraged and spent retires'.[13] This is a Dantean as well as a Darwinian opening whose meaning is not simply that Ethelberta is like a poor bird caught up in a struggle for survival. The duck, we infer, endangers its life when it moves too far beyond its native element; by returning it is saved. The episode may seem to foreshadow Ethelberta's perilous flights out of Wessex into high society and 'high doctrine' and to suggest that return to her native element is the best cure for such folly. But Ethelberta does not return to her green cottage in Chickerel; she ends as Lady Mountclere. More important, the 'satanic moodiness' in the hawk's motion is present also in her view of herself as a 'Mammon' of sorts, and in the 'satanic mood' of her poems (*HE*, ch. 36). She knows that she is one who, deprived of 'the select and sequent gifts of heaven, blood, and acres', must exploit her 'subversive Mephistophlean endowment, brains', if she is to rise in the world (chs 24, 31). In short, Ethelberta is to be associated with *both* duck and hawk, for she is not only the pursued (by no fewer than four admirers) but also the pursuer (of knowledge, of fame, of a rich husband). And in that pursuit, like Milton's Mammon and Dante's Ciampolo, she has sinned by wandering far from truth and love. Because she has chosen expediency over inner truth, the rejected good becomes a paradise from which she is banished and a rack on which she is tortured. 'My God, what a thing am I', she cries, when, at Corvsgate Castle with a group of fashionables, she falsely denies knowledge of the donkey with 'clumsy trappings of rustic make, and [a] needy woeful look of hard servitude' that carried her from Knollsea. She sees, to her horror, that she is ashamed of her 'history and extraction' and that in despising her origins she is destroying her first, best self and thus the source of her poetry.

But for all her nostalgia and regret, Ethelberta does not go home again. Like Gabriel Oak, she rejects nostalgia. She indeed considers retreating to some rural place where she can 'give the rudiments of education to remote hamleteers'.[14] But, when opposed by her parents for this wish to 'go down in the scale', she consults Mill's 'Utilitarianism' and decides that 'personal interests . . . are not to be considered as paramount' (ch. 36). For the sake of her family she decides to sacrifice herself, her poetry, and her dream of a simpler life:

> She had begun as a poet of the Satanic school in a sweetened form; she was ending as a *pseudo*-utilitarian. Was there ever such a sad transmutation effected before by the action of a hard environment? It was not without a qualm of regret that she discovered how the last infirmity of a noble mind[15] had at length nearly departed her. She wondered if her early notes had had the genuine ring in them, or whether a poet who could be thrust by realities to a distance beyond recognition as such was a true poet at all. Yet Ethelberta's gradient had been regular: . . . from soft and playful Romanticism to distorted Benthamism. Was the moral incline upward or downward?   (ibid.)

The question is never answered. 'Realities' rule Ethelberta, as they rule Oak; and like him she makes the most of them. She not only guarantees her family's security by marrying the wealthy Mountclere, but soon has the frolicsome old nobleman under her control. She has played her hand well. She can even accept the sadly ironic fact that her marriage, though undertaken wholly in the interest of her family, has widened – given the family's class jealousy – the break with them she had sought to heal. Ethelberta sees what a Clym Yeobright does not see, that material enrichment must precede poetry and 'a serene comprehensiveness' (*RN*, III, ch. 2). She would understand well the following words of Henry Knight: 'It is without doubt a misfortune for a man who has a living to get, to be born of a truly noble nature. A high soul will bring a man to the workhouse . . .' (*PBE*, ch. 19).

Ethelberta has been described, too emphatically I think, as Hardy's attempt 'somehow [to] conceal his own humble origins', both from the general public and from Leslie Stephen and Emma.[16] In some ways this must be true, for Hardy's turn from pastoral fiction to social comedy in 1874–5 was in part caused by a reviewer

who thought *Madding Crowd* the work of a 'house-decorator' (*Life*, p.
102). However, as has been noted, in Ethelberta Petherwin Hardy
continued to explore the divided feelings of such earlier figures as
Mayne, Springrove and Smith. And, for any student of Hardy's life
in its relation to his fiction, Ethelberta's situation must seem often a
thinly veiled version of Hardy's between 1870 and 1876. In fact, on
at least one occasion in the novel Ethelberta's situation suggests a
strong urge on Hardy's part to reveal rather than to conceal his
humble origins. I am thinking of how, in her last public perform-
ance as a story-teller, Ethelberta suddenly decides to replace her
'naive' first-person method of narration (the method of Defoe and
'The Poor Man') with the sincere autobiographical 'I'. She does this
because she has decided, in a moment of guilt, 'to show herself as she
really was . . . and so get rid of that self-reproach which had by this
time reached a morbid pitch, through her sensitiveness to a situation
in which a large majority of women would have seen no falseness'
(ch. 38). What Ethelberta feels forced to divulge here is that by birth
she is not a lady, but the daughter of servants. If Hardy chose to tell
Ethelberta's story in order to baffle claims that the author of
Madding Crowd was of humble beginnings, or to conceal his origins
in some other way, he wrote a story perilously close to his own. His
mother, Jemima, a cook and servant before marrying the second
Thomas Hardy in 1839, was the daughter of a servant, George
Hand, who died in 1822 and left Jemima, her mother, and her six
siblings with so little money that they required support from the
Poor Law Overseers of the parish of Melbury Osmund (Dorset) for
fourteen years. One cannot help but wonder if Hardy did not write
this frequently personal narrative containing sensitive details from
his family's history with the tacit consent of the readers – in
particular Jemima and Mary – within his own family. Far from
writing 'out of his system the Hardy who was one of the people who
toiled and suffered' in *The Hand of Ethelberta*,[17] Hardy seems bent on
confessing, at least to the few who would understand, an undying
but troubled allegiance to them, an allegiance he had already
explored in *A Pair of Blue Eyes* and *Under the Greenwood Tree* and
would explore again in *The Return of the Native* and *The Woodlanders*.

I suggest this because it seems doubtful, first of all, that anyone
can write away the self deriving from the circumstances of his
earliest days. It is no less a social than a biological impossibility, and
Hardy believed strongly in heredity. It is also doubtful that Hardy
wanted to escape entirely the world of the Dorset Hardys and

Sparkses. Whatever his mother's hardships, he himself had never been one of those who had toiled and suffered. On the contrary, his mother seems to have taken great pains that none of her children, and especially not her talented eldest, should go down in the scale. And none of them did. Mary and Kate became schoolmistresses, Henry inherited the family business, and Thomas became one of the great writers of the age. It was no mean achievement for any mother, much less the daughter of a servant, to rear such a family, and the Hardy children must have known from their earliest days the powerful love, pride and ambition that made their achievements possible. As much as anything, this atmosphere of family pride and achievement must have made Hardy's memories of his early days, like Ethelberta's, Clym's and Grace's, sweet and powerfully appealing, an emblem of ideal happiness. Far from looking on as ones who had escaped, Ethelberta, Clym and Grace long to return, but they find return devilishly difficult and find themselves deeply divided in their feelings toward the people and places left behind. Hardy's actual movements between 1867 and 1883 suggest that he was at one with his protagonists in this. Would he have returned to Dorset in 1867 and remained until 1874 if the appeal of home were not a powerful one? Would he have returned again in 1883 (over Emma's objections) to build his permanent home if he wished to cut himself off? And, if *Ethelberta* is an attempt to conceal his origins, why is its heroine moved to reveal hers in public? Because, quite probably, Ethelberta, like her author, was both attracted and repelled by her origins. Her impulse to be loyal and to confess vies with her impulse to conceal. This complication of feeling and motive reflects the experience of an author who from age sixteen had lived between two worlds, the world of architecture, society, and letters, and the world of his rural beginnings. His crisis was, as Raymond Williams has said, the 'crisis of the relation between education and class, relations which in practice are between intelligence and fellow-feeling'. Out of this relation came the creative tension, which for Hardy was in 'his own lived history, within a general process of change which could only come clear and alive in him because it was not only general but, in every detail of his feeling, observation, and writing, immediate and particular'.[18] Through the cautious self-scrutiny and self-portraiture of this faulty comedy of manners, Hardy touched the tragic subsurface of his own history that would find more powerful expression in *The Woodlanders* and *The Return*.

SON AND LOVER: THE DILEMMA OF CLYM YEOBRIGHT

The tragedy of *The Return of the Native* (1878) grows out of the nostalgia that drives Clym Yeobright to do precisely what Ethelberta chooses not to do: to leave the great world (in Clym's case, Paris) to return to the Wessex world of his infancy and childhood. Clym does this, we are at first told, for an altruistic reason: he wishes (as Ethelberta for a short time wished) to educate the rustics of Egdon. We learn his deeper motive, however – reunion with his mother and with the powerful maternal presence called Egdon Heath – when he falls in love with Eustacia Vye. In several ways, *The Return* is thinly veiled autobiography, an extension of the confessional impulse discernible in *The Hand of Ethelberta*. Critics have long recognized similarities between Egdon and the environs of Higher Bockhampton, between the forceful Mrs Yeobright and the ambitious Jemima Hardy, and, of course, between Clym and Hardy. Hardy must have found it difficult when the time came to introduce his genteel wife to the plain folks at Bockhampton. If, as Robert Gittings has suggested, Emma was half-ignorant of her talented husband's modest background when she married him, the difficulties for Hardy must have been enormous.[19] One can only wonder if it did not slowly dawn on Emma, who in the 1870s was frequently involved in the production of the novels, that from the beginning her husband had been writing about his own social and psychological dilemma, that the plight of Mayne, of Springrove, of Smith, of Fancy Day and of Ethelberta was in essence his plight. If she did, perhaps she began to see as well that the *Heimweh* of these uprooted figures was combined in their author with a fastidious idealism, a powerful nostalgia like that of Henry Knight, rooted in a mother-devotion that made falling in love and marrying as gross a betrayal of first things as leaving home had been. What is more likely is that she, as well as some of the members of Hardy's immediate family, read the novels, detected some resemblances between art and life, but did not perceive the turmoil contained in them. How much more one would like to know – in order to understand better the emotional content of *The Return* – about Thomas and Emma's Christmas visit to Higher Bockhampton in 1876 and about the circumstances surrounding the sad note in the *Life* for 13 August 1877: 'We hear that Jane, our late servant, is soon to have a baby. Yet never a sign of one is there for us' (p. 116). Was there a connection between this personal disappointment and the note, exactly one month earlier, that the 'sudden disappointment of a hope leaves a scar which the ultimate fulfilment of that hope never entirely removes' (*Life*, p. 116). Or between this and the vow made two months earlier (June 1877), and echoed in the opening chapter of *The Return*, to look nature's defects in the face and make them 'the basis of a hitherto unperceived beauty'? (*Life*, p. 114). Though we can never know precisely how closely *The Return* reflects Hardy's private anxieties, it is worth noting that in the novel the maimed (blinded), quiescent Clym and the passionate Eustacia soon learn that they are incompatible. Wildeve (Eustacia's paramour and the father of Thomasin's child), and not Clym, is the sexually potent one.

With this we enter uncertain ground. A novelist's responsibilities in his private relationships cannot be equated with his responsibilities as a writer without confusing the truth of life and the truth of fiction. The 'truth' that Hardy attempts to convey to us in such a novel as *The Return* has to be judged not by its historical accuracy but by its concreteness, its internal logic, and its inclusiveness as a criticism of life. The 'truth' that Hardy attempted to exhibit in *The Return* is the law of nature that he had contended with from the beginning – that all is change and all change decay – that, in social terms, 'You can't go home again.' Thus homecoming and its attendant hope of personal and social renewal must be seen as futile and destructive, even unnatural. But what is most striking here is the way Hardy chose to shape this second version of return. Not with the elements of pastoral romance, as in *Under the Greenwood Tree*, not with the conventions of social realism as in *The Hand of Ethelberta*, but in the pattern of classical tragedy, with a natural setting both pervasive and articulate, he traced – with probably Hamlet and Oedipus his chief analogues – the struggle of a man much like himself to resolve conflicting loyalties to his mother and his native place on the one hand, and to his wife and the world beyond Egdon on the other. The wonder of *The Return* when we see it emerging from such lesser predecessors as *Ethelberta* and *Greenwood Tree* is the finish of its structure and the daring of its vision. Hardy suddenly found it possible to cast private experience in tragic form, and in doing so unleashed a devastatingly critical self-portrait. He coolly diagnosed the cause of Clym's nostalgia, showed the folly and destructiveness of it, then declared it incurable. In so far as *The Return* is self-portraiture, it is unflinching self-analysis and self-censure; at the same time, it implies acceptance of the incurable defective self and of that defective order of things which both made it so and prevents its remedy.

On one level, Clym's return from Paris to Egdon is cultural drama – his attempt, like Fancy's in *Greenwood Tree* and Grace Melbury's in *The Woodlanders*, to regain his position among the people and places of his childhood. He mingles with the heath folk, welcomes the silences and shadows of Egdon, and even embraces the opportunity to work as a furze-cutter when partial blindness blocks his plan to open a school for the rustics. Against his mother's, then his wife's, strong protests he comes home to stay. He ends as the faithful keeper of his mother's house and grave, and as a preacher of moral homilies to uninterested rustic congregations. Though Clym returns to stay, he cannot reinstate himself in the rural society that nurtured him. The rustics of *The Return*, unlike the townsfolk of *Greenwood Tree*, are narrow, rigid and unforgiving toward deserters. Fancy Day is reassimilated (not without mutterings and bad omens); Clym is kept apart and therefore fails in this aspect of his return. He fails as well on a second, more potent, level of return – the psychodrama in which he at once resubmits to and contests the power and influence of his mother. This attempt to recover a prenatal quiescence and security – suggested perhaps in his 'death' and resurrection from the waters of the weir, and in his affection for the heath – fails disastrously; and Clym is left with what one critic has called 'a tender after-view of the oedipal conflict'.[20]

Here it is helpful to pause to contrast Clym's homecoming with that of Grace Melbury of *The Woodlanders*, for, though the two novels have much in common, their differences are even more important. Grace's return confronts her with the paradox of culture-in-nature, a paradox produced by the novel's monism, its view, reminiscent of the encompassing view of nature in *Madding Crowd*, that human and non-human nature are one. Grace returns to the Hintocks, to her father and to Giles Winterborne expecting serenity, simplicity, and renewal of things past; she discovers instead Fitzpiers, Mrs Charmond and the fact that she cannot choose but go on. Clym's return – to the rustics and to Egdon, to his mother and to the preconscious roots of self – confronts him with an internal wilderness, a dark tangle of emotions that he can neither explain nor elude. Throughout *The Return*, from its wonderfully evocative opening, through its heavily allusive and lyrical middle, to its divided conclusion, Hardy – like Clym trying hopelessly at one point to explain to his mother why he has returned to Egdon –

suffered in the writing of his novel a 'hopelessness of being understood' because 'logic . . . [was] almost too coarse a vehicle for the subtlety of the argument' (*RN*, III, ch. 2). Clym's unconscious longing for the condition of boyhood and infancy clashes with his conscious desire to study, to marry, and to work to improve his part of the world. Grace breaks the circle by admitting that sentiment (her girlish attachment to Giles) and morality (her father's wish to make amends to John Winterborne by marrying her to Giles) are less important than getting on with her life. Having looped back, she moves forward again in obedience to the law of change and decay that rules all things. But Clym, overwhelmed by remorse and unable to turn from his mother to his wife, burrows deeper and deeper into the dark roots of consciousness.

Soon after his arrival at Bloom's End on Christmas Eve, Clym begins the hopeless task of reintegration. With his mother he sponsors a Christmas party for the heath folk. A Christmas party is a feature of *Greenwood Tree* (I, chs 7, 8) and *The Woodlanders* (chs 9, 10) as well. In the former it is an occasion for comedy, as Dick and Farmer Shiner, both smitten with love for Fancy, vie for her favour. In the latter it is a tragi-comic moment, for Giles's awkward and homely preparations provoke laughter at the same time as they mark his utter alienation from Grace's refined ways. In *The Return*, the Christmas party (II, chs 4–6) is the occasion of the St George play, in which the tragic folly of Clym's return is indirectly conveyed. The St George ceremony originated in pagan ceremonies whose purpose was 'to secure the regeneration of earth, animals, and humans through sympathetic magic'; in keeping with this purpose, death and resurrection, the latter usually effected by a physician, were important themes in the play.[21] In *The Return*, however, this traditional purpose is all but obliterated. Eustacia holds both mummers and mumming in contempt; she joins the ancient ceremony only so that she might come secretly into the presence of Clym. The mummers themselves are unenthusiastic; they play their parts with so little excitement that the reader wonders, with the narrator, 'why a thing that is done so perfunctorily should be kept up at all' (II, ch. 4). This 'fossilized survival' is watched uncritically by Clym because it gratifies his romanticism, his love of the old for its own sake, and his nostalgia, his wish to recover an earlier, happier time in both his own life and the life of the race. Hardy's point seems to be that Clym's attempt to secure redemption through return is as foolishly atavistic as the attempt through the play to secure regeneration through sympathetic magic. Associated with Christ on the one hand and with modern reformist thought on the other,[22] Clym may be seen in fact as analogous to the quack doctor (with 'his little bottle of alicampane') who appeared in all versions of the play. That is, Clym is the physician who cannot heal his own wounds, the reformer who neither reforms himself nor his people. The law of decay overwhelms him, just as it overwhelms all myths of regeneration.

In at least one instance, Clym's actions resemble those of the worshipper in primitive myth who tried to renew things through sympathetic magic and sacrifice. The primitive worshipper, writes Karl Young, 'fancied that by dressing himself in leaves and flowers, and by hanging such objects on trees, he could encourage the earth to re-clothe itself with verdure; or that by putting to death some representative of the principle of life and subsequently reviving him, he could bring about a repetition of this act on a comprehensive scale by the mighty forces that govern the physical world'.[23] Clym, at the urging of nostalgia rather than religion, attempts a comparable renewal. He chooses Egdon and 'some rational occupation among the people I know best' over the idleness and vanity of the diamond trade in Paris. Later, in preparation for marriage and school-teaching he takes up residence in a lonely hut at Alderworth. When hard study partially blinds him, he puts on the rough clothes of a furze-cutter and appears, even to the discerning eye of his mother, as a denizen of the heath:

> He appeared of a russet hue, not more distinguishable from the scene around than the green caterpillar from the leaf it feeds on. . . . The silent being who thus occupied himself seemed to be of no more account in life than an insect. He appeared as a mere parasite of the heath, fretting its surface in his daily labour as a moth frets a garment, entirely engrossed with its products, having no knowledge of anything in the world but fern, furze, lichens, and moss. (IV, ch. 6)

The man who as a boy had been 'so inwoven with the heath that . . . hardly anybody could look upon it without thinking of him' (III, ch. 1) returns to the heath to recover the springtime of his life by awakening some of his earliest sensations:

He was permeated with its scenes, with its substance, and with its odours. He might be said to be its product. His eyes had first opened thereon; with its appearance all the first images of his memory were mingled; his estimate of life had been coloured by it; his toys had been the flint knives and arrowheads which he found there, wondering why stones should 'grow' to such odd shapes; his flowers, the purple bells and yellow furze; his animal kingdom the snakes and croppers, his society, its human haunters. . . . He gazed upon the wide prospect as he walked, and was glad. (III, ch. 2)

The death of Mrs Yeobright as a result of the wholly unintentional collaboration of Clym, Wildeve, Christian and Diggory may suggest the primitive ritual of killing the king in order to guarantee the renewal of the community's vitality and welfare, for the resurrection of the dead king had been the most significant element of the myth and ritual pattern.[24] But Mrs Yeobright's death no more brings renewal than Clym's return to Egdon brings reinstatement; in this hint at the dying king motif, as in the use of the St George play, the regenerative element must be discounted. Hardy cannot accommodate it to his sense of time, history and human consciousness as aspects of the deteriorative course of things. This same deteriorism governs the drama of guilt and sorrow, of thwarted restoration, that is always for Hardy an integral part of the story of return.

Books v and vi of *The Return* (excluding the reunion of Diggory and Thomasin that Hardy provided in his 1912 amendment) is a study in the irreparable at whose centre is a bewildered Clym trying to make amends to both his dead mother and his estranged wife. Clym has learned from Johnny Nunsuch that his mother died broken-hearted because she thought she had been turned away from Alderworth by Clym. He is staggered by the thought that the injury done her 'could never be rectified' (v, ch. 1). He now finds himself morally in the same blind alley in which he finds himself socially because he cannot return. He craves his mother's forgiveness; that is, he wants to be to her what he was before the incident at Alderworth and the quarrel at Bloom's End. This denied him, he cries out for an ultimate peace in death or at least for torture at the hand of God: 'If there is any justice in God let Him kill me now. He has nearly blinded me, but that is not enough. If he would only strike me with more pain I would believe in Him forever!' (v, ch. 1). When he learns that it was Eustacia who ignored Mrs Yeobright's knock at Alderworth, he turns on her in fury; but even his desire for revenge is cooled by devotion to his mother: 'Phew – I shall not kill you. . . . I did think of it; but – I shall not. That would be making a martyr of you, and sending you to where she is; and I would keep you away from her till the universe comes to an end' (v, ch. 3). He even echoes his mother's scandalous reason for rejecting Eustacia: his 'How could there be any good in a woman that everybody spoke evil of?' (v, ch. 3) echoes Mrs Yeobright's 'Good girls don't get treated as witches, even on Egdon' (iii, ch. 2).

Clym simply cannot free himself from the oppressive influence of his mother and her values. Johnny Nunsuch's statement to him that his face at the moment he learns of Eustacia's 'guilt' is like Mrs Yeobright's in her last anguish reunites Clym with his mother in a horribly ironic way: the two are fused, in the words of one critic, 'in a common expression; it is the mask of tragedy which Oedipus wore after his incestuous love of Jocasta was terminated'.[25] In all of this Clym sacrifices his former luminousness of mind, derived from study of advanced ethical thought of his time, to his mother's jealous moralizing. He moves into her house at Bloom's End (a name itself suggestive of sterility and deterioration) to put it in order, for 'it had become a religion with him to preserve in good condition all that had lapsed from his mother's hands to his own' (v, ch. 6). His hope that Eustacia will return to him is less a loving gesture toward her than a fear that he had been too harsh with 'his mother's supplanter' (ibid.). He admits to Thomasin that a man can be 'too cruel to his mother's enemy', and he writes to Eustacia pleading unusual provocation and begging her to return to him. But chance, or honest error on the part of Captain Vye, conspires with his reluctance, and a reconciliation is thwarted. In any case, Clym's attempt to gain Eustacia's forgiveness is feeble in comparison with his desire for reinstatement with his mother. And neither Eustacia's death nor his own near-death and return to life in the weir alters this. For him there is no renewal, just the same mother-worship, conventional moralizing, and moral masochism ('My great regret is that for what I have done no man or law can punish me' – v, ch. 9). Clym's lapse into timid conventionality draws Hardy's special scorn: Clym is one of those, lacking in sternness, who hesitate 'to construct a hypothesis that shall . . . degrade a First Cause . . . and, even while they sit and weep by the waters of Babylon, invent excuses for the oppression which prompts their tears' (vi, ch. 2). He frequents his beloved heath because it is familiar, maternal, and thus the temporary solution for his frustrated yearning. He is moved toward marriage with Thomasin not by her mature and gentle loveliness but by the sight of flowers 'revived and restored by Thomasin to the state in which his mother had left them':

> He recalled her [Thomasin's] conduct toward him throughout the last few weeks, when they had often been working together in the garden, just as they had formerly done when they were boy and girl under his mother's eye.   (vi, ch. 1)

> Years ago there had been in his mother's mind a great fancy about Thomasin and himself. It had not positively amounted to a desire, but it had always been a favourite dream. That they should be man and wife in good time, if the happiness of neither was endangered thereby, was the fancy in question. So that what course save one was there now left for any son who reverenced his mother's memory as Yeobright did?   (vi, ch. 3)

Full of devotion to an idealized mother, Clym, both as a man and as a preacher, ends as a mother-obsessed son:

> Yeobright sat down in one of the vacant chairs, and remained in thought a long time. His mother's old chair was opposite; it had been sat in that evening by those who had scarcely remembered it was there. But to Clym she was almost a presence there now as always. Whatever she was in other people's memories, in his she was the sublime saint whose radiance even his tenderness for Eustacia could not obscure. But his heart was heavy; that mother had *not* crowned him in the day of his espousals and in the day of the gladness of his heart.[26] And the events had borne out the accuracy of her judgment, and proved the devotedness of her care. He should have heeded her for Eustacia's sake even more than for his own. 'It was all my fault,' he whispered. 'O, my mother, my mother! would to God that I could live my life again, and endure for you what you endured for me!'   (vi, ch. 4)

His discourses to people were to be sometimes secular, and sometimes religious, but never dogmatic. . . . This afternoon the words were as follows: – 'And the king rose up to meet her, and bowed himself unto her, and sat down on his throne, and caused a

seat to be set for the king's mother; and she sat on his right hand.
Then she said, I desire one small petition of thee: I pray thee say
me not nay. And the king said unto her, Ask on, my mother: for I
will not say thee nay.'   (VI, ch. 4)[27]

This might amount to little more than self-gratifying fantasy if
Hardy did not make it quite clear that there is deadly error in
Clym's idealized devotion, that both Mrs Yeobright's possessiveness
and Clym's attachment to her are pernicious. He does this by
making Mrs Yeobright the chief cause of the tragic mischief of the
novel. Two years before Clym's arrival, she had opposed Venn's
courtship of Thomasin on the grounds that as a farmer's son he was
unworthy of her. She then offended Wildeve by publicly opposing
his marriage to Thomasin, and Wildeve, a moody, sensitive man,
gradually drifted into a 'revengeful intention' toward her – an
intention that results in his ruthless appropriation of the Yeobright
guineas from Christian. Venn's retrieval and misapplication of the
same guineas leads directly to tragic misunderstanding and to Mrs
Yeobright's death. Even more important, Mrs Yeobright offends
Eustacia by regarding her as a voluptuary and a witch. This angers
Clym, and prepares the way for the break between Clym and Mrs
Yeobright that culminates in her death, in Clym's break with
Eustacia, in Eustacia's and Wildeve's deaths, and in Clym's
inconsolable guilt and grief. In sum, Clym is blindly loyal to a
destructively jealous mother who denies her children the freedom to
grow toward independence. Though Mrs Yeobright is portrayed
with some sympathy, the terrible results of her intrusiveness are not
to be denied.

Hardy depicted the abnormality in Clym's attachment to his
mother obliquely, through the personalities and circumstances of
the other 'children' of the novel: Johnny Nunsuch, Susan Nunsuch's
weirdly precocious son; and Christian Cantle, Grandfer Cantle's
timid, childish son. Even the presence of Eustacia Clementine, the
infant daughter of Thomasin and Wildeve, can be seen to be a
comment on Clym's prolongation of childhood. Like Clym, Johnny
is fatherless (at least, we hear nothing of a Mr Nunsuch) and the
victim of jealous maternal attention; and, again like Clym, he comes
under the direct influence of Eustacia. Susan Nunsuch, like Mrs
Yeobright, believes Eustacia a witch and hates her for afflicting her
son. Susan's revenge, with needle and wax effigy, is savage; Mrs
Yeobright's, with slander, merely more subtle.

Hardy's purpose in likening Clym to Johnny is suggested by the nature of the two episodes in which Johnny is most prominent: the one in which he stokes the fire that Eustacia uses to signal Wildeve (I, ch. 6); the other in which he watches over Mrs Yeobright during her last moments of life (IV, ch. 6). Childhood, as represented in Johnny, is not a time of radiant, innocent joyfulness, but of fear, sadness, and even terror. In the episode with Eustacia he is the 'little slave' who feeds her signal fire: 'he seemed a mere automaton galvanized into moving and speaking by the wayward Eustacia's will'. Rewarded for his strange labours with a crooked sixpence, he traipses off across the dark heath, 'singing in an old voice a little song' to keep up his courage, only to meet the devilish-looking Venn, 'a sublimation of all the horrid dreams which had afflicted the juvenile spirit since imagination began' (I, ch. 9). Similarly, in his encounter with Mrs Yeobright we find him something other than a fearful naïf. There is childlike naiveté only in his first questions to her: 'What have made you so down? Have you seen an ooser?' (IV, ch. 6). Once aware that she is weaker than he, he becomes objective and even censorious in a cruelly precocious way. To her reply to his two questions – 'I have seen what's worse, a woman's face looking at me through a window pane' – he responds,

> 'You must be a very curious woman to talk like that.'
> 'O no, not at all. . . . Most people who grow up and have children talk as I do. When you grow up your mother will talk as I do too.'
> [He replies] 'I hope she won't; because 'tis very bad to talk nonsense'   (IV, ch. 6)

The boldness in Johnny's remarks seems hardly childlike. Nor does his third question, which suggests that he takes some pleasure in her pain:

> 'Why do you, every time you take a step, go like this?' The child in speaking gave to his motion the jerk and limp of an invalid.
> 'Because I have a burden that is more than I can bear.' . . .
> When she had seated herself he looked long in her face and said, 'How funny you draw your breath – like a lamb when you drive him till he's nearly done for. Do you always draw your breath like that?'   (IV, ch. 6)

First a naive curiosity, then a mildly accusatory contempt, and finally an oddly detached observation and imitation of her suffering – but not a trace of instinctive sympathy and tenderness in this sad boy of the heath. It is as if Johnny were acting on vengeful behalf of all the other 'children' of the novel whom this mother has injured. Though frightened at 'beholding misery in adult quarters hitherto deemed impregnable', Johnny finds Mrs Yeobright's suffering somehow attractive. After bringing her a drink of water – in 'an old-fashioned teacup . . . which she had preserved since her childhood, and had brought with her today as a small present for Clym and Eustacia' – he abandons her.

Why would Hardy have his reader look through the eyes of this sad and at times unfeeling boy in his circumstances much like Clym on these two important occasions? In other words, why is the boy exposed to the working of Eustacia's passionate nature, then to the anguish in death of Mrs Yeobright, the second experience making him the bearer to Clym of Mrs Yeobright's bitter last words? There seem to be several answers to this. Johnny is made the common element in the encounter with Eustacia and with Mrs Yeobright because Clym is suspended between the two women. To have the boy see and speak at these crucial moments is to convey, to some degree, the incurable boyishness in Clym, his older counterpart. In this way the reader can come to see that, just as Johnny responds to Eustacia and Mrs Yeobright, so the inextinguishable boy in Clym, that part of him that cannot grow to manhood, responds to them. Clym seems to understand Eustacia, especially the passionate Eustacia whose fire Johnny feeds in the dark of Mistover, as little as Johnny does. Johnny's fearfulness is in some ways Clym's. Johnny as representative of Clym's problematic relation to his mother is somewhat different. Johnny both censures Mrs Yeobright and ministers to her, and his ambivalence is the apt embodiment of Clym's mixed feelings about a mother who wants him to return to Paris, yet wants him to remain at home, though under her, not Eustacia's, influence. This complication of feelings is familiar to Johnny because it is *his* mother's as well. He has been well-groomed by the jealously protective Susan to play this strange part in Clym's story.

The chief function of this oblique portraiture – and it is central to what has been called the self-censuring impulse in the novel – is to point up Clym's folly in trying to regain the conditions of his boyhood at Bloom's End. Johnny's circumstances illustrate Hardy's deterioristic assumption in the novel, an assumption revealed in the remark that 'a long line of disillusive centuries' had permanently displaced the Hellenic 'zest for existence':

> What the Greeks only suspected we know well; what their Aeschylus imagined our nursery children feel. The old-fashioned revelling in the general situation grows less and less possible as we uncover the defects of natural laws, and see the quandary that man is in by their operation. (III, ch. 1)

Though the contours of Clym's face bear witness to this 'new recognition', he does not see what it means for his attempt to find happiness by trying to recover the conditions of childhood. 'The old-fashioned revelling' – whether in the childhood of the race or in the childhood of the individual – is gone forever. Like Little Father Time in *Jude the Obscure*, Johnny is 'Age masquerading as Juvenility'; and, just as Father Time takes from Sue the hint of despair that leads to murder and suicide, Johnny echoes his mother's jealous hatred for Eustacia when he shatters Clym by repeating before him Mrs Yeobright's last words: 'She said I was to say that I had seed her, and she was a broken-hearted woman and cast off by her son . . .' (IV, ch. 8; cf. V, ch. 2).

Christian Cantle, the second of Clym's childish foils, is a mixture of timid piety, fetishism and sexual impotency. As fearful as Johnny of Diggory Venn, as bewildered as Johnny by Eustacia, Christian is in several ways as boyish as Johnny is 'aged', as bad a case of arrested development as Johnny is of premature growth. And, like Johnny, he is associated with Clym. Like Clym, Christian has lost one parent and is somewhat at odds with the other. The lusty Granfer Cantle has as little regard for his son's fearfulness as Mrs Yeobright for Clym's loss of ambition. Christian works at Bloom's End as a factotum and seems a stepson of sorts to Mrs Yeobright, who entrusts him with the delivery to Clym and Thomasin of the family guineas, and with results as disastrous (for her) as in the case of her entrusting to Clym the future of the Yeobrights. Christian's superstitious beliefs suggest Clym's secularized faith: both are unstable mixtures of belief and impiety. Christian's childish fears of injury and of the dark, his constant concern for his own safety, suggest Clym's yearning for the security of childhood. Most striking, however, is the connection between Clym's asceticism – he reminds Eustacia of the Apostle Paul (IV, ch. 6) – and Christian's sexual impotency. Christian is 'the man no woman would marry, a faltering man, with reedy hair, no shoulders, and a great quantity of wrist and ankle beyond his clothes' (I, ch. 3). He is pathetically hopeful that he will find a mate, but women scorn him as a 'slack-twisted, slim-looking, maphrotight fool' (I, ch. 3). By his own admission, he is 'only the rames of a man, and no good for my race at all' (I, ch. 3). Biologically, he is apparently no man at all, for he is described as a 'wether', that is, as a male sheep castrated before it has reached sexual maturity. During the lively dancing of the rustics atop Rainbarrow in the novel's opening scenes, Christian – like Clym at the Christmas party and at the May Day proceedings – does not participate. Dancing – as can be seen in the description of the May dance in which Eustacia and Wildeve join at one point (IV, ch. 3) – is a highly charged event in this novel (see pp. 139–40 below). Christian refrains from dancing because he believes ' 'tis tempting the Wicked One' to dance (I, ch. 3). It seems more likely that he is emotionally unequal to dancing, for as a close look at the episode involving the transfer of the guineas suggests, Christian is neither a mere fool nor an expression of Hardy's anti-Christian attitudes.[28] He is the instrument of Hardy's carefully contrived attempt to show that sexual immaturity, perhaps even sexual impotency, is an important element in Clym's character.

Christian, already identified as 'no man', as a 'maphrotight [hermaphrodite] fool', and as a 'wether', is entrusted by Mrs Yeobright with the delivery of the Yeobright family guineas to Clym and Thomasin during the wedding celebration at Mistover, which Mrs Yeobright refuses to attend. On the way to Mistover, Christian meets Fairway and the others and is persuaded to go with them to the raffling of a woman's gown-piece. Christian joins in even though, as Fairway says, he's 'got no young woman nor wife . . . to give a gown-piece to' (III, ch. 7). Christian rolls the dice and wins the gown-piece:

'Mine?' asked Christian. '. . . What shall I do wi' a woman's clothes in my bedroom!' 'Keep 'em, to be sure', said Fairway. '. . . Perhaps 'twill tempt some woman that thy poor carcase had no power over when standing empty-handed.' (III, ch. 7)

Pleased with the thought of attracting a woman, Christian handles the lucky dice 'fondly', and marvels at the possible 'power that's in me of multiplying money'. He asks to be allowed to keep 'them wonderful little things that carry my luck inside 'em', and leaves the raffle with Wildeve, shaking the dice in his pocket as he walks. When he loses the Yeobright family guineas to Wildeve he cries, 'The devil will toss me into the flames of his three-pronged fork for this night's work, I know! But perhaps I shall win yet, and then I'll get a wife to sit up with me o' nights, and I won't be afeard, I won't.' Christian's excitement at winning the frock-piece, his feeling that virility can somehow be secured in the form of a pair of dice, is surely related to the earlier description of him as a wether, a creature deprived of testes and therefore of the 'power . . . of multiplying'. And the intense concern with the family guineas to be delivered to Clym at his wedding celebration may be a broadly humorous reference to the phrase the 'family jewels', slang for a man's, particularly a husband's, testes, called jewels because they have inherent value as the source of new life and the guarantee of the family's future. This possibility is not contradicted by the fact that, after Christian loses the guineas to Wildeve, it is Wildeve and Diggory who vie for the guineas, just as they vie for the hand of Thomasin. It is in them, Thomasin's husbands, that the future of the Yeobrights lies. They, not Clym, who will lose Eustacia to Wildeve, and certainly not Christian, are the active, successful males in this veiled sexual combat.

Something like Christian's deprivation – more psychic than physical, perhaps – seems to be at the root of the trouble between Clym and Eustacia. It is important to note that Clym's blindness, described as the result of hard study, occurs soon after Clym learns from Eustacia that she and his mother have quarrelled and cannot be reconciled. To that point, a loving Clym and his passionate wife had lived in something like perfect reciprocity (IV, ch. I). But Eustacia's insistence that they must move to Paris because she can never see Mrs Yeobright again is soon followed by Clym's blindness, 'an acute inflammation induced by . . . night studies'. Clym's affliction may well be taken to suggest an emotional paralysis brought on by the thought of separation from his mother and the heath, for shortly after this we find Eustacia depressed and apathetic, so hungry for gaiety that she visits a village dance, where she meets Wildeve and dances with him to 'the lusty music of the East Egdon band':

Through the length of five-and-twenty couples they threaded

their giddy way, and a new vitality entered her form. . . . There is a certain degree and tone of light which tends to disturb the equilibrium of the senses, and to promote dangerously the tenderer moods . . . and this light now fell upon these two from the disc of the moon. All the dancing girls felt the symptoms, but Eustacia most of all. . . . Eustacia floated round and round on Wildeve's arm, her face rapt and statuesque. . . . Her beginning to dance had been like a change of atmosphere; outside, she had been steeped in arctic frigidity by comparison with the tropical sensations here. She had entered the dance from the troubled hours of her late life as one might enter a brilliant chamber after a night walk in a wood.   (IV, ch. 3)

The language and tone of this passage can hardly be intended to convey only Eustacia's relief from her disappointment with Clym's refusal to take her to Paris. Dancing with Wildeve, in all likelihood a partner in earlier sexual liaisons, is for her a ritualized form of intercourse, just as it is for many of the other dancers (enjoying 'impassioned but temporary embraces'), and she seeks it here and with Wildeve because 'the full flush of her love for Clym' is no longer reciprocated. By flanking Clym with the immature Christian and the 'mature' Johnny and showing something of him in both, Hardy subtly and effectively conveys the sexual incompleteness of Clym, the failure in him of psychological and perhaps physical development that is in part the emotional cause of his desire to return to heath, home and mother. Clym is tragically suspended between mother and wife because he is emotionally suspended between manhood and boyhood. That this may reflect in some ways Hardy's sense of his own physical and psychological make-up can be inferred from the remark in the *Life* (p. 32) that 'a clue to much of his character and action throughout his life is afforded by his lateness of development in virility, while mentally precocious'.[29]

The birth to Thomasin of Wildeve's child (named Eustacia Clementine) at the moment of Clym's break with Eustacia (v, ch. 3) suggests – given the stability and purposiveness that follows for Thomasin – that a child might have brought peace and harmony to Eustacia, to Clym, and even to Mrs Yeobright. Perhaps Eustacia could have found in a child some of the promise of her dreams, Clym some of the glory and gleam of his lost childhood, Mrs Yeobright a new focus for her powerful maternal instincts. Certainly a great point is made of Thomasin's intense and tender love for the infant, which is seen as a fragile, vulnerable thing to be protected and cuddled. The description of it as a precious object protected by many layers of blankets – making it appear 'as the kernel to the husks' (v, ch. 8) – suggests again Hardy's view that infancy is to maturity as life is to death. During the frenzied activity around the weir, with such deadly results for Clym, Eustacia and Wildeve, the infant Eustacia Clementine is present, but held tenderly and lovingly (aloft at one memorable point) as if she were an emblem of the promises never kept, the hopes never realized by the frantic adults who thrash about in darkness and confusion.

In Thomasin, however, in Wildeve's wife and the mother of the child, is enshrined something like normality. Hardy's first description of her – as she returns in despair from her botched marriage to Wildeve – tells all:

> *Captain Vye*: 'You have a child there, my man?'
> *Diggory*: 'No, sir, I have a woman.'   (I, ch. 2)

Thomasin is a woman, a mature person, and not a child, because, though she returns in Venn's cart in near-disgrace, she does not, like Clym, attempt to remedy her misfortune by turning back the clock. It should be noted that her return to Egdon and Bloom's End precedes Clym's in the novel; she too is a returning native, and her stoic acceptance of change and determination to make the best of a bad thing is a silent comment on Clym's confused nostalgia. Thomasin accepts Wildeve's grim and self-serving (but in Hardy's view sound) opinion that life in actuality is never so 'pretty and sweet' as it is hoped it will be (I, ch. 5). And most important, in a novel filled with vengeful acts, Thomasin alone works persistently to make amends – by marrying Wildeve in spite of the first embarrassing error, by urging Mrs Yeobright to settle her differences with Clym and Eustacia, and, finally, by marrying Venn. She counsels Clym against excessive remorse over his mother's death and urges him to make it up with Eustacia. She is 'a practical woman' because – like Cytherea Graye, like Gabriel Oak, and like Ethelberta Petherwin – she can set aside self-interest and regret. 'I don't believe in hearts at all', she cries when, having swallowed her offended feelings, she returns to the moody Wildeve (II, ch. 8). Because she is not governed, like Clym, by a dream of lost felicity, or, like Eustacia, by a vision of future gaiety, a purity and sweetness of spirit are somehow always visible beneath her sadness (IV, ch. 3).

By acceding to the law of change-as-decay, by countering it with forgiveness, she keeps a firm hold on the fading ideal and in a way recaptures it in the form of her child, named, ironically, after two frustrated idealists. Because Thomasin accepts what she cannot alter, sad experience rubs off 'nothing of the bloom' (IV, ch. 3). She leaves the house named Bloom's End when Clym takes up residence there. The epitomy of womanhood and maturity, she is the novel's chief symbol of renewal, a living rebuke to all truncated myths of regeneration, and a clear contrast with Clym's uncertain waverings between juvenility and age. But her place is not at the novel's tragic centre; she is the heroine of the novel's comic subplot, belatedly elevated.[30]

If *The Return* is in any way a penetrating portrait of the artist or a profound criticism of life, it is because it is, as suggested earlier, a trenchant self-criticism. Clym is the victim of Hardy's irony. In both the first and the second conclusion of the novel, he is portrayed as a failure. He has failed in his ostensible purpose for returning – to improve the Egdonites and restore himself to a simpler, more joyous life. He has failed to see in marriage to Eustacia the opportunity to rediscover and renew, in a form appropriate to a man of thirty-three, the happiness he knew as a boy. His plight is complicated, of course, by Eustacia's being as desperate a dreamer as he, a dreamer moreover (of future rather than past dreams) who looks to him to fulfil her yearning. His willingness to defy his mother for a time proves that his love for Eustacia is genuine, and even after his mother's death, when he knows that Eustacia has erred, he has it in his power to forgive her and thus to preserve in their love a higher version of his lost childhood joy. But character (his guilt and nostalgia) and chance (the misdirected letter to Eustacia, the circumstances that prevent his mother's entering at Alderworth) block forgiveness and reconciliation. This is perhaps the bitterest fact of all – that forces beyond his control *both* within and without himself prevent him from forgiving Eustacia and thus from somehow countering the mutative process that blocks his attempt to go home again. To have forgiven Eustacia would have been, in a moral sense, to have granted her the foretime, to have reinstated her and himself to a semblance of that blissful time – a time of higher innocence and re-enactment of original innocence – before the door closed against Mrs Yeobright, the time of the Alderworth idyll (IV, ch. 1). But Clym cannot forgive because he cannot temper or uproot his fierce devotion to his mother and his boyhood home. And Mrs Yeobright's quarrel with Eustacia and her sudden death only serve to convince him that his deepest devotion is to his mother. This fatal fixity is the target of the novel's second conclusion, in which all – Diggory's transformation from devilish reddleman to respectable farmer, Thomasin's girlish enthusiasm, the May festivities, the budding child, the marriage ceremony – suggests that for them at least an earlier, happier time has been recovered, even if only illusively. 'Illusively' because this is truly an image of higher innocence, in which there is no denial that things are *not* as they were. The second ending of *The Return* offers an image of restoration amidst decay, but not for or through Clym Yeobright, whose virulent nostalgia blinds him to 'the inevitable movement onward' and makes him a moral failure, a man unable to forgive.

ANOTHER VERSION OF THE SAME: *THE WOODLANDERS* (1887)

Clym fails to find redemption through return because character and circumstances combine to thwart him. All his means of retrieval – his religious faith, his good sense, his affection for mother, wife and cousin – are lost to him. But he is not, we feel, wholly bereft. He clearly, if somewhat perversely, prefers unhappiness on Egdon to unhappiness in Paris. And in the end he still has one great resource, the physical presence of his old home and of Egdon Heath, that maternal, majestic and unchanging place of his earliest sensations. For Clym, this is probably enough. *The Woodlanders*, begun several years before *The Return*, but not completed until almost ten years after it, and strikingly similar to it in structure, seems designed to demolish the last two stays available to Clym – life-loyalties and nurturing nature – and thus to show not the tragedy but the ironic reality of the return of a narrative and any attempt to recover first things. Grace Melbury is loyal to the past only up to a point; and nature – well, the idea of nature in *The Woodlanders* is simply not the idea of nature in *The Return*, and in that lies much of the important difference between the two novels. The same plot used in *The Return* (and in *Under the Greenwood Tree*) to convey a tragic (and comic) vision based on a dualistic, anthropocentric view of nature is used in *The Woodlanders* to embody an ironic, monistic view of nature in which man is by no means at the centre of things. In *The Return* and *Greenwood Tree* human nature (nature-as-art) is seen as ultimately dependent on non-human nature and yet separate from and superior to it. Nature-as-law and as-impulse is that upon which humanity works its will, though not always with success (cf. pp. 98). The heath-folk make their living from the hide of Egdon, though it is probably impossible, as Wildeve and his predecessors on 'Wildeve's Patch' learn, entirely to domesticate Egdon. In *The Woodlanders*, in sharp contrast, human and non-human nature are viewed as coextensive aspects of the Will, as 'modulat[ing] into each other, one nature and law operating throughout' (*Life*, pp. 451–2).[31] In *The Woodlanders*, as in *Far from the Madding Crowd*, which it was to have followed hard on the heels of in the 1870s, we are again in the presence of an idea like Mill's idea that nature is 'everything that is, including man'. What is missing, of course, is the confidence that men and women can effectively impose their wills on nature.

This shift in outlook can be seen in the changing fates, throughout the three novels of return, of the characters I have labelled the Native and Alien Lovers (see note 2 to this chapter). In *Greenwood Tree* Dick Dewey wins Fancy Day; Thomasin, in the amended conclusion of *The Return*, marries Diggory Venn; but in *The Woodlanders* Giles Winterborne relinquishes Grace and never returns Marty's devotion. The fates of the Aliens form a significant contrast to this. Maybold swallows his bitter disappointment at losing Fancy and does the noble thing by releasing her from her promise; Eustacia and Wildeve meet dark, watery deaths; Fitzpiers survives Giles and Felice (who persecutes both Marty and Giles) and reunites with Grace. Patience, self-denial, simplicity – the chief strengths of Thomasin and Venn – are in Marty and Giles virtues all but useless in the struggle for survival. This helps to explain the different views of return and regeneration that emerge through the three novels. Fancy returned, married a native, and was reinstated by a still traditional community. Clym returned to stay, but at the terrible price of being a stranger at home. Grace returns, sees that the Hintocks cannot be her home, nor Giles her lover, any longer, and then turns back to Fitzpiers and a life of refinement. If we wished to draw the course of Clym's (or Fancy's) career, we might inscribe a circle; if we trace Grace's career, however, we must describe, in Comtean phrase, 'a looped orbit', an image that particularly appealed to Hardy because it preserved the inevitable movement onward that always for him underlay the illusion of return.[32] By adopting a monistic view of nature in *The Woodlanders* – nature as 'everything that is, including man' – Hardy effectively argues an essential and ironic unity between human and non-human nature, and in social terms, between urban and rural culture. In asserting this Hardy is denying that there can be anything simpler, happier, or better to which to return. In *The Woodlanders* Hardy pressed the search for regeneration through return into a philosophical blind alley.

One result of this fundamental shift of outlook can be seen in the language of *The Woodlanders*, especially its inverted use of the pathetic fallacy to objectify the view that human and non-human lives are co-extensive.[33] Of greater interest here, however, is the reflection of this shift in the novel's structure, especially as that structure is governed by the career of Grace Melbury, whose return to her father, to her childhood lover, and to her native woodland home is made to take its ironic final meaning from the series of 'minor' returns to the woods that recur insistently within this major one. All of Grace's returns to nature – major and minor – turn out to be head-on collisions with culture.

Before examining Grace's career, however, one other important difference between *The Return* and *The Woodlanders* can be noted – the way that Hardy in the later novel enlarged and brought to centre-stage the figure of the Intrusive Parent. In *The Woodlanders*, Grace's return shares the centre of the story with George Melbury's compelling and mischievous need to make reparation to one person from the past and to gain revenge on another. In this Melbury is a far more complex figure than either Mrs Yeobright or Keeper Day, his counterparts in the earlier novels of return. His conflicting motives – to atone for an old injury he had committed against Giles's father by marrying Grace to Giles, and to avenge an old insult against his humble station by giving her to Fitzpiers – intensify the novel's focus on the irreparability and irretrievability of things. It is most significant that Melbury's wish for revenge prevails over his wish to atone, a moral reality wholly compatible with Grace's discovery that she cannot go home again. No return for Grace, no reparation for Melbury: the social impossibility is at one with the moral impossibility. In an odd way this justifies revenge on natural grounds, for Melbury's desire for revenge becomes more consistent with the mutative nature of things than his wish to make reparation. To give Grace to Giles in order to make amends to the dead John Winterborne would be to try to fashion a semblance of things as they were, to create a fragile illusion of atonement and redemption. This is the stuff of the ending of *Under the Greenwood Tree* and of the second ending of *The Return*, but Hardy will have none of it here. And so Grace's union and reunion with Fitzpiers is 'right', for, even if it is heartless in some ways and dangerously sentimental in others, it is at least consistent with the law of change-as-decay that rules both human and non-human nature. Reunion with Giles would be retrogressive. The possible dignity and moral worth, the human value, of such a choice is unimportant. As Robert Schweik has said so well, *The Woodlanders* 'amounts to a study in the practical futility of moral struggle in a Darwinian universe'.[34]

Giles's great merit, and his folly, lies in his understanding the irreversibility of things and its consequences. He wants Grace with all his heart and soul, but he withdraws from her because he sees with terrible clarity her and her father's folly in trying to 'repair the almost irreparable error of dividing two whom nature had striven to join together in earlier days' (*W*, ch. 38):

> He was not versatile, but one in whom a hope of belief which had once had its rise, meridian, and decline seldom again exactly occurred, as in the breasts of more sanguine mortals. He had once worshipped her, laid out his life to suit her, wooed her, and lost her. Though it was almost the same zest, it was not quite with the same hope that he had begun to tread the old tracks again, and had allowed himself to be so charmed with her that day. Move another step toward her he could not. He would even repulse her – as a tribute to conscience. It would be sheer sin to let her prepare a pitfall for her happiness not much smaller than the first by inveigling her into a union with such as he. Her poor father was now blind to these subtleties, which he had formerly beheld in a noontide light. It was his own duty to declare them – for her own dear sake. (ch. 41)

Winterborne knows the terrible difficulty, for him the near-impossibility, of making reparation. This is a tragic knowledge whose truth and beauty go deeper than even the forgiveness that Grace will extend to Felice Charmond and Suke Damson in the late chapters of the novel. Grace seeks reunion with Giles. She forgives Suke and Felice for their indiscretions with Fitzpiers. Finally, she forgives the erring Fitzpiers and rejoins him in marriage. But in doing these things she has merely enacted, quite uncomprehendingly, the knowledge that Giles possesses from the beginning – that there is no undoing the done, no treading old tracks again.

Grace's unwitting discovery of this sad truth is conveyed through the series of eight retreats to the woods that define her stay in the Hintocks. These almost incidental returns to nature, like the larger return they reflect and re-enact, prove to be, paradoxically, encounters with culture; they thereby affirm the unity of the human and non-human worlds conveyed in the novel's language. The first of these returns occurs when Grace, shortly after arrival, visits a wood-auction 'in the densest quarter of the wood', there meets and then rebuffs the homely Giles and tries to ingratiate herself with the cosmopolitan Mrs Charmond (ch. 7). On the second excursion, a leisurely walk in the forest with her father, she is insulted by a hunter who mistakes her for a common girl. This social insult so angers Melbury that he there and then makes the bitter vow that she will never marry Giles (ch. 12). On the third retreat, to a bark and timber harvest deep in the woods, Grace meets Fitzpiers for the first time and is much attracted by his refinement and intellect (ch. 19). Her fourth journey, to join in the traditional Midsummer Eve festival, results in 'new relations' with Fitzpiers and in a final rebuff to Giles (ch. 20). On her next journey, to the top of High Stoy Hill, she is 'tempted' by Melbury with the prospect of Fitzpiers's extensive (and defunct) ancestral holdings (ch. 23). Thus far, all her ventures into 'nature' have resulted in meetings with forms or agents of culture – the auction, Mrs Charmond, the hunter and Fitzpiers.

Grace's sixth journey, again to the top of the High Stoy Hill (which watches over the Hintocks much as Rainbarrow broods over Egdon), occurs shortly after her return from her wedding journey. Doubtful now that Fitzpiers is faithful to her, she for the first time sees a likeness between her degenerating marriage and the decay of the woodlands: in 'the gorgeous autumn landscape . . . surrounded by orchards lustrous with the reds of apples, crops, berries and foliage . . . some kernels were unsound as her own situation and she wondered if there were one world in the universe where the fruit had no worm, and marriage no sorrow' (ch. 28). Out of this sense of personal failure and general decay comes a violent resurgence of admiration for Giles and the simple virtues she thinks he represents:

He looked and smelt like Autumn's very brother, his face being sunburnt to wheat-colour, his eyes blue as corn-flowers, his sleeves and leggings dyed with fruit-stains, his hands clammy with the sweet juice of apples, his hat sprinkled with pips, and everywhere about him that atmosphere of cider which at its first return each season has such an indescribable fascination for those who have been born and bred among orchards. Her heart rose from its late sadness like a released bough; her senses revelled in the sudden lapse back to Nature unadorned. The consciousness of having to be genteel because of her husband's profession, the veneer of artificiality which she had acquired at the fashionable schools, were thrown off, and she became the crude country girl of her latent early instincts. Nature was bountiful, she thought. No sooner had she been cast aside by Edred Fitzpiers than another being, impersonating chivalrous and undiluted manliness, had arisen out of the earth ready to her hand.   (ch. 28)

Grace courts delusion when, in a 'passionate desire for primitive life' and a belief that 'honesty, goodness, manliness, tenderness, devotion . . . only existed in their purity . . . in the breasts of unvarnished men' (ch. 30), she looks to Giles to restore her to the country girl she once was. She can no more realize this dream of return and restoration than her father can realize his dream of restitution. She is here as deluded by nostalgia as he is by his belief that a new divorce law will undo the damage of her entanglement with Fitzpiers. The woodlands can provide neither refuge nor renewal for Grace, as her last two journeys into their depths (to Mrs Charmond in ch. 33, to Giles in chs 40–2) make unequivocally clear.

Grace's seventh excursion brings her face to face with Felice Charmond, whom she approaches like 'a wild animal on first confronting a mirror or some other product of civilization' (ch. 33). They walk together into 'the deepest recesses of the wood' and, after a bitter quarrel (in which Grace clings 'like a limpet' to her belief that Felice loves Fitzpiers) they abandon each other amidst thick 'umbrageous surroundings'. 'Wild animal' and 'limpet' are Hardy's most striking uses of a brute–human analogy in the novel; and he is quick to drop them for the more congenial plant–human analogy: ' "I question if you will refuse to see him [Fitzpiers] again", said Grace dryly, as she bent a sapling back. "But I am not incensed against you as you are against me," she added, abandoning the tree to its natural perpendicular.' After wandering for a time through the gloomy wood, Grace and Felice meet again. They huddle together for warmth against the trunk of a tree: 'Mrs. Charmond's furs consoled Grace's cold face; and each one's body, as she breathed, alternately heaved against that of her companion; while the funereal trees rocked and chanted dirges unceasingly.' The heave of the bodies, the sway of the trees; in this almost symbiotic state of co-operation, when Grace has realized that she is in the wildest part of the wood for the first time since childhood – and when it might be thought she is on the verge of retrieving a long-lost simplicity – she is thrown suddenly into a state of cultivated, self-righteous horror by Felice's admission to sexual intimacy with Fitzpiers: 'O, my great God! . . . He's had you! Can it be – can it be!' Grace can no more become a daughter of nature than she can turn to the Hintocks; the would-be child of the soil is in fact a nervous daughter of St Paul. She abandons Felice momentarily, then softens and returns to her when she hears the sound of the older woman's sobbing. Though this sudden change of mind is not explained, its meaning is suggested by Grace's immediate and decisive turn toward culture. With Felice in tow, Grace gropes her way through the dark woods and unto 'the deserted highway where the Sherton man [Barber Percomb] had waited for Mrs. Dollery's van' – on page 1 of the novel. This formal hint at a second beginning – with Grace rather than Marty at the centre of the narrative – is thematically justified. Grace's move out of the forest and unto the path of civilized culture is a movement toward self-discovery. She has experienced, like Clym Yeobright, her 'bare equality with other living things' (*RN*, III, ch. 5); but she will not persist in going backward, as Clym does, into the old anthropocentrism. Nor will she, like Marty South, subside into a morbid and somewhat vindictive, if eloquent, loneliness. Though she does not say it, she is on the verge of demonstrating that she is of the 'one family of all organic life'.[35]

Grace may seem to contradict this new involvement of hers soon after, upon Suke and Felice's embarrassed visit to Melbury's house on the occasion of Fitzpiers's injury at the hands of the vengeful Melbury. Rising above instinct and self-interest, she will restrain her impulse to rebuke and humiliate her successful rivals in 'the wife's regulation terms of virtuous sarcasm, as woman, creature, or thing'. For 'life, what was it, after all? She had, like the singer of the Song of Asaph, been plagued and chastened all the day long; but could she, by retributive words, in order to please herself, the individual, "offend against the generation", as that singer would not?' (ch. 35). This allusion (to Psalm 73) helps to define the nature of Grace's turn toward civilization from the forest, where her responses to Felice were, at least momentarily, cruel and selfish. It is a turn from egotism to altruism, from instinctive to imaginative reasoning. 'A tenderness spread over Grace like a dew', tenderness the source of which is an awareness of pain shared with 'these fellow women'. Grace has indeed learned sympathy, and yet her education is by no means complete. She must now experience the moral inflexibility of Giles, whom she reveres as a 'natural', and therefore a good, man. In the limitations of her nostalgia lie also the limitations of her forgiveness. Living, without fully understanding it, the truth that the natural is not necessarily the good, she will be moving beyond nostalgia and forgiveness – beyond conventional sentiment and traditional morality – toward realization of the unregenerateness of things.

Grace's sojourn with Giles at One-Chimney Hut in 'the depths of the woods' occurs in the course of her flight from Fitzpiers and from the gossip of her neighbours. She goes to Giles in the deepest part of the forest prepared to act honestly, for she believes that in him she will find human nature unblemished by culture. In Giles, however, she finds precisely the thing from which she has fled – civilized constraint. Grace is eager to take him as her mate, but Giles is eager only to atone for his treachery in kissing her while knowing her to be Fitzpiers's wife – some six months earlier! Grace puts his hut in order, prepares his meals and is willing to share his bed: '*Come to me dearest! I don't mind what they say or what they think of us any more*' (ch. 41). Though she says this safely out of his hearing, her willingness to ignore her marriage vows, like her willingness later to allow Fitzpiers to draw 'the extremest inference' about her visit to Giles at One-Chimney-Hut, suggests that she is wholly sincere in her turn to Giles (ch. 43). But Giles's homely morality is inflexible. In a manner somewhat like Clym Yeobright's in recoiling from Eustacia at the death of his mother – even like Sue Bridehead's in turning from Jude at the death of their children, and like Angel Clare's in turning from Tess at learning of her impure state – the scrupulous Giles, 'as a tribute to conscience', withdraws from Grace (ch. 42). This entire episode at One-Chimney Hut is made to parallel – to Giles' discredit – that earlier episode at Hintock House in which Felice Charmond lovingly aids Fitzpiers after his fall from a horse. The passionate, cultivated Felice welcomed and cared for the errant Fitzpiers; the precise, rustic Giles keeps an ardent Grace at a distance. The cultivated woman responded with loving-kindness, the natural man with a suicidal discretion. What are we to make of this critique of pastoralism?

This critique of Giles's natural morality is another expression of the monistic view of things at work in the novel. As suggested above, in *The Woodlanders* Hardy discarded the dualism of nature versus culture he had exhibited in *The Return*. *The Woodlanders* does not open upon a 'vast tract of unenclosed wild', as does *The Return*, but amidst a 'wood-environed community' (*RN*, I, ch. 1; *W*, ch. 1). To this potent natural setting, Grace, like Clym, returns to play a part in a drama of 'grandeur and unity truly Sophoclean' (*W*, ch. 1). But Grace's drama, unlike Clym's, is to be 'enacted in the real' (*W*, ch. 1) and not the high tragic manner. The basis of this realism is the assumption throughout of a 'closely knit interdependence' between human and non-human lives (*W*, ch. 1). Nature in *The Woodlanders* is 'the Unfulfilled Intention, which makes life [human and non-human life] what it is' (ch. 7). Nature in *The Return*, as embodied in the humanized form of Egdon, is a vital, enduring force superior to culture for its longevity. Though Clym, midway through the novel, expresses a sense of humanity's 'bare equality with, and no superiority to, a single living thing under the sun' (*RN*, III, ch. 5), he cannot sustain this unflattering view of man's place in nature. He withdraws from it to a position, close to his mother's, in which man is viewed as the epitome of a higher order of life, the product of a special creation, and thus in no essential way akin to plants or to those 'maggoty shapes' that Mrs Yeobright observes 'heaving and wallowing with enjoyment' in the mud of the pools along the path of her fatal journey to Alderworth (IV, ch. 5). In sum, and this is the romanticism of *The Return*, Egdon Heath stands for permanence in a world of decay; to return to it, to be in harmony with it, 'and to know that everything around and underneath had been from prehistoric times as unaltered as the stars overhead, gave ballast to the mind adrift on change, and harrassed by the irrepressible New. The great inviolate place had an ancient permanence which the sea cannot claim' (I, ch. 2).

> Here, away from comparisons, shut in by the stable hills, among which mere walking had the novelty of pageantry, . . . *any man could imagine himself to be Adam without the least difficulty* . . . .
> (II, ch. 1; emphasis added)

Clym's unattainable destination is a permanent, stable place 'perfectly accordant with man's nature' (I, ch. I) though essentially different from it; in Egdon, therefore, is food for the imagination and therefore the possibility of regeneration, even though Clym can achieve neither. In profound contrast, the people of *The Woodlanders* (the irony of the title here becomes apparent) have no comparable non-human resource. All the woodlanders – human, animal and vegetal lives – are caught up in a fight for survival. Owls and stoats feed on mice and rabbits, mice and rabbits on seeds and greens; and men and women prey on these other lives as well as on one another. The human struggle for economic, sexual and social dominance is an extension of the struggle for survival to be seen among animals and plants. Not even Grace's generous forgiveness and her willing-ness to again take up old ways can turn the course of change-as-decay. If Clym could forgive Eustacia, we feel, a modicum of happiness, a happiness like Thomasin's, might be possible. But Grace's forgiving Mrs Charmond and Suke brings no change for the better, and her turn to Giles is but a turn to another form of the culture she thinks she can flee.

If human and non-human nature are one, and if the course of this one nature is down toward disorder, then where lies the possibility for amelioration? The art of a Gabriel Oak or the patience of Thomasin, like the loving-kindness of a Grace Melbury, would seem to count for little in the Hintocks. The answer is that amelioration, what there can be of it, lies with humanity's stubborn desire and its persistence, against all odds, to return, to redeem, to restore, to repair, to reinstate, to amend, to forgive – to somehow stem or even reverse time's destructive flow. Hardy does not deny the existence of a regenerative instinct in men and women, but he has taken its measure.

It can succeed only intermittently, only within the limits set by luck and the deathward tendency of things. Because this is so, the magnificent close of *The Woodlanders*, Marty's heart-rending utter-ance over Giles's grave, need not be read, as it usually has been, as a hymn in praise of natural humanity, as a pastoral prayer of a kind. Instead, it can be seen as yet another expression of the regenerative instinct, in this case the instinct of an untutored poetess for whom memory is a way of honouring a dead man, if not of raising him:

'Now, my own, own love,' she whispered, 'you are mine, and only mine; for she [Grace] has forgot 'ee at last, although for her you died! But I – whenever I get up I'll think of 'ee, and whenever I lie down I'll think of 'ee again. Whenever I plant the young larches I'll think that none can plant as you planted; and whenever I split a gad, and whenever I turn the cider wring, I'll say none could do it like you. If ever I forget your name let me forget home and heaven! . . . But no, no, my love, I never can forget 'ee; for you was a good man, and did good things!'

In one sense, such loyalty to the dead, however noble, is pure folly. Here, however, as not in the case of Clym's loyalty to the dead, the heart of the novelist goes out to the folly, as the rhythms and accents of the prose reveal. But the clear, cold eye of the novelist is, at the same time, on the rote, unfeeling process that spawns life only to consume it. Grace, as Marty says, forgets. But in this Grace is merely the obedient daughter of nature as unconscious, mutative, deteriorative process. Though her future with Fitzpiers seems gloomy, in turning to him and away from Giles and return and nostalgia she is wise in the way of the Will. It is as right, therefore, that Grace should turn to Fitzpiers and a life beyond Wessex as it is that Marty should tend Giles's grave – and as wrong. There is simply no way to reconcile the conflict between loving loyalty to the past and obedience to the heartless ongoingness of things. What the novel invites in its powerful close is that the reader contemplate the beauty of the sad truth that things decay.

THE 'NATIVE OF NATIVES': JOCELYN PIERSTON OF *THE WELL-BELOVED*

Grace's prospects with Fitzpiers are dim because her philosophic physician, in his patently erotic idealism, as in his practice of medicine, is largely indifferent to the claims of the individual. This 'subtlist in emotions' (*W*, ch. 40) is like the pure artist of whom Hardy would write in 'Memories of Church Restoration' (1906), 'The true architect, who is first of all an artist and not an antiquary, is naturally most influenced by the aesthetic sense, his desire being, like Nature's, to retain, recover, or recreate the idea which has become damaged, without much concern about the associations of the material that idea may have been displayed in.'[36] Fitzpiers is blind to what Hardy, on several occasions, spoke of admiringly as a beauty of old association. In *The Woodlanders* (ch. 17) he called it 'an almost exhaustive biographical or historical acquaintance with every object, animate and inanimate, within the observer's horizon'.

> He must know all about these invisible ones of the days gone by, whose feet have traversed the fields which look so grey from his windows; recall whose creaking plough has turned those sods from time to time; whose hands planted the trees that form a crest to the opposite hill; whose horse and hounds have torn through that underwood; what birds affect what particular breaks; what bygone domestic dramas of love, jealousy, revenge, or disappointment have been enacted in the cottages, the mansion, the street or on the green. The spot may have beauty, grandeur, salubrity, convenience; but if it lack memories it will ultimately pall upon him who settles there without opportunity of intercourse with his kind.

Because he lacks memories, such an artist unreflectingly obeys, to quote from 'Memories' again, 'the actual process of organic nature herself, which is one continuous substitution. She is always discarding the matter, while retaining the form'. Grace, by forgetting Giles and turning to Fitzpiers before eight months have passed, is truly at one with her husband, an idealist by temperament whose studies in Shelley, Spinoza, and Schleiermacher have taught him that love is a fleeting, a 'subjective thing':

> [It is] the essence itself of man . . . it is joy accompanied by an idea which we project against any suitable object in the line of our vision. . . . So that if any other young lady [than Grace] had appeared instead . . . I should have felt the same interest in her. . . . Such miserable creatures of circumstances are we all! . . . I am in love with something in my own head, and no thing-in-itself at all.   (ch. 16)

In Grace, however, Fitzpiers believes he has found the Ideal Incarnate: 'The design is for once carried out. Nature has at last recovered her lost union with the Idea' (ch. 18). Of course, it is difficult to take Fitzpiers with complete seriousness; his restless movement between Felice, Suke and Grace are as much an exercise in lust as in thought. In this, as in his heartless way of bargaining for Grammer Oliver's head, he is more the deluded hedonist than the detached thinker. But one thing is clear: in love, as in work, he subordinates the individual to the idea which for him it temporarily represents.

This becomes especially interesting when it is noted that in this respect the dissolute Fitzpiers is Hardy's rehearsal for his last, and in some ways his most intimately autobiographical, hero of return – Jocelyn Pierston of *The Well-Beloved*. Pierston, like Fitzpiers (there is a kinship in name), has a taste for Shelley and a passion for the Ideal in its feminine embodiment. Fitzpiers's restless lovemaking with Felice, with Suke and with Grace has its counterpart in Pierston's pursuit of the Caros, of Marcia Bencomb and of Nicola Pine-Avon. Robert Gittings has called *The Well-Beloved* a 'personal allegory carried to near-absurd lengths', a thinly-disguised expression of Hardy's own 'search from one woman to another for ideal beauty'. Its origin, according to Gittings, may lie with Hardy's successive fascinations for Martha, Mary, Rebecca and Tryphena Sparks, maternal first cousins who all bore some resemblance to his mother: 'More than most mother-fixed youths, Hardy was falling in love with his own mother over and over again, in a physical and consistent way that was a typical part of his own almost literal-minded nature.' Another critic, calling *The Well-Beloved* 'arguably the most autobiographical' of the novels, claims that in it Hardy refrains from a candid self-portrait 'in his desire to pursue something he cannot have, . . . in his tragic loss of love for what he already possesses, and bitter regret for that loss when the once possessed is his no more'.[37]

If regarded wholly as a phenomenon of the 1890s, *The Well-Beloved* is bound to remain something of an anomaly. But Hardy himself said it had been sketched 'many years' before 1892, 'when I was comparatively a young man, and interested in the Platonic idea' (*Life*, p. 286). Indeed, as early as 1871 the Platonic idea was in his mind, for he had written in *Desperate Remedies*, his first published novel, of 'the beautiful things of the earth [that] become more dear as they elude pursuit' and of 'some natures [for whom] utter elusion is the one special event which will make a passing love permanent for ever' (I, ch. 2). Like *Under the Greenwood Tree*, *The Return of the Native* and *The Woodlanders*, *The Well-Beloved* is a product of the 1870s – in conception, if not in composition. Pierston, like Clym, Grace and Fancy, comes back to his native place after long absence. His natal spot, the Isle of Slingers, is as magnetic for him as Egdon Heath is for Clym; and like Clym he falls in love upon return. But here the two homecomers part ways, for Pierston, as artist and as lover, is obsessed with pursuit of ideal love and truth. He is the true nympholept, the 'native of natives' as Hardy called him in the preface to the novel, the embodiment of the nostalgic idealism that moves, in different ways, a Clym and a Grace.[38] Pierston does not seek a substitute for the Ideal – a heath, a mother, a lover. He seeks the elusive Form itself, 'the essence and epitomy of all that is desirable in this existence' (*WB*, ii, ch. 9). He has been moved since his boyhood by longing for a 'migratory, elusive idealization he called his love who . . . had flitted from human shell to human shell an indefinite number of times' (ii, ch. 1).

Upon returning after some four years in London, Pierston meets Avice Caro, an eighteen-year old native of the Isle of Slingers; in Avice he thinks the elusive Ideal makes its home. He asks her to marry him but she refuses because she senses that he looks to her for something more than ordinary love. Her fear is well-founded, for he soon comes to believe that 'the idol of his fancy was [not] an integral part of the personality in which it had sojourned' (i, ch. 2). He then turns to another woman, 'a very Juno' named Marcia Bencombe, in whom 'the spirit, emanation, idealism which called itself his love' has, he is certain, taken up residence (i, ch. 5). He proposes marriage to her as well, but a quarrel soon parts them, and they are not reunited for forty years. Frustrated, Pierston turns avidly to his sculpture; and his art flourishes because it takes on the impress of his elusive Ideal. Nicola Pine-Avon is his next incarnation of 'the One', but she turns from him because she suspects he may be married. All this occurs in twenty years. Then, at age forty, the retrospective artist looks at an old photograph of Avice, now long dead, and sees her once more 'as she had appeared during the summer month or two which he had spent with her on the island twenty years before. . . . Now the times of youthful friendship with her, in which he had learnt every note of her innocent nature, flamed up into a yearning and passionate attachment, embittered by regret beyond words' (ii, ch. 3). Because she is dead and beyond reach he loves her as he had never loved her while she was alive. When he returns to the isle to visit her grave he meets there her daughter, also named Avice. A hope that the Ideal resides in Avice the second vanishes when he learns that she is secretly married and with child. He departs again, only to return again after another twenty years have passed, a 'young man' of sixty, to meet yet a third Avice Caro, the granddaughter of the simple girl he had deserted for Marcia Bencombe, forty years before. He of course proposes to her, but she is in love with another man, the stepson of Marcia Bencombe, with whom Pierston is soon reunited.

This almost gratuitous symmetry of *The Well-Beloved*'s plot, appropriate to the allegory, is shattered by its realistic ending. Having failed to embrace the essence of all that is desirable in life, Pierston grows ill and, though nursed by the faded Marcia, loses his youthful looks, his desire to pursue the Ideal, and his creative genius. Both the 1892 and the 1897 endings depict this failure, though in significantly different ways. The first version ended with a bitter sense of 'the grotesqueness of things'. The once-beautiful Marcia has become 'a wrinkled crone, with a pointed chin, her figure bowed, her hair as white as snow. To this the once handsome face had been brought by the raspings, chisellings, stewings, bakings and freezings of forty years. The Juno of that day was the Witch of Endor of this'. Pierston's hysterical laughter closes this version: 'O – no, no! I – I – it is too droll – this ending of my would-be romantic history! Ho–Ho–Ho!' But in the 1897 version, the aged Pierston, faced with a similar decline in his well-beloved, is resigned, philosophical, and practical-minded. Finding the artistic sense dead in himself, he is grateful for the loss because it means the end of many years of sexual and intellectual restlessness. The sight of his pale, withered Marcia causes not bitter regret but a desire to return with her to the Isle of Slingers, there to resume life 'always in a homely suit of local make, and of the fashion of thirty years before'. He even cultivates a beard to make himself look older than his sixty years. He marries his faded Juno and becomes a peculiar kind of local philanthropist: he alters old buildings to meet modern needs. He rebuilds old cottages, he closes old wells to prevent contamination. In all this he reminds one of Goethe's ideopraxic Faust seeking to reclaim land from the sea for the benefit of an ordinary humanity he had spurned during a life spent in pursuit of the unattainable. In short, Pierston submits to time's destructive flow in a way that benefits mankind.

The two conclusions of *The Well-Beloved* remind us that the conclusions of *The Return* and *The Woodlanders* also posed problems for Hardy. Hardy's 1912 changes in the ending of *The Return* (see note 30 to this chapter) were designed to rescue Diggory and Thomasin from utter loss. He had faced the same problem with Grace Melbury and the ending of *The Woodlanders*. He could not accentuate the unhappy ending he had in mind for Grace ('an unhappy life with an inconstant husband'), because the 'conventions of the libraries' forbade such an ending (*Life*, p. 220). Hardy's objection to a happy ending for Thomasin or Grace was not an objection to happiness, which his people from Bathsheba to Tess seek instinctively. It was rather an objection to the assumption that something lost could be regained, or that something ruined could be repaired or restored. In the original ending of *The Return*, for example, Diggory was to have retained his 'isolated and weird' character and disappeared from Egdon. To have to show him regaining his former occupation, manner and hue violated Hardy's sense of the irretrievability of things. Grace is 'doomed' to a miserable life with a philandering husband; to suggest that Fitzpiers will improve is, in Hardy's view, untrue to Fitzpiers's character and perhaps to the capacities of human beings in general. To suggest new beginnings in the reunion of lovers or mates is to create the illusion that things can somehow be as they were. As the bitter laughter of the first and the sad resignation of the second ending of *The Well-Beloved* suggest, things can never – except in fleeting moments of illusion – be as they were.

Pierston's discovery of this truth occurs as he sits beside the corpse of the second Avice:

> As he sat darkling here the ghostly outlines of former shapes taken by his love came round their sister the unconscious corpse, confronting him from the wall in sad array, like the pictured Trojan women beheld by Aeneas on the walls of Carthage. Many of them he had idealized in bust and figure from time to time, but it was not as such that he remembered and reanimated them now; rather was it in all their natural circumstances, weaknesses, and stains. And then as he came to himself their voices grew fainter; they had all gone off on their different careers, and he was left here alone.   (*WB*, III, ch. 7)

The quality of feeling in this passage may be called Virgilian for sounding the note *sunt lacrimae rerum*, or Shelleian or even Swinburnean for showing the misery of a nympholept. But it is Hardian in mingling both, as well as a bit of Miltonic gloom, with guilt and bitter regret. Pierston's search for the Ideal, wedded to his sense of having sinned against Aphrodite, becomes – soon after his rejection of the first Avice – a 'desire to make reparation' to the first Avice by marrying and enriching the second (I, ch. 2). But he is thwarted in his reparative effort 'as if by set intention of his destiny' (II, ch. 9).

> [Upon meeting Avice the second] Pierston . . . felt that his old trouble, his doom – his curse, indeed, he had sometimes called it – was come back again. His divinity was not yet propitiated for that original sin against her image in the person of Avice the First, and now, at the age of one-and-sixty, he was urged on like the Jew Ahasuerus – or, in the phrase of the islanders themselves, like a blind ram. (III, ch. 2)

Is deepening guilt or is brute sexuality the moving force in Pierston? The image of a sightless ram thrusting hither and yon in its urge to rut should remind us that Pierston's near kinsman is Edred Fitzpiers, a Shelleian idealist who is more a philanderer than a philosopher. To place at the centre of *The Well-Beloved* a figure who is both a self-portrait and a brother to an earlier figure of questionable conduct may explain Hardy's wish, in the words of one critic, 'to sidestep the issue and . . . leave himself out of the finished product'.[39] It may also be yet another example of Hardy's capacity for critical self-portraiture.

We can recognize in Pierston that mingling of guilt and idealism that characterizes Ethelberta Petherwin and Clym Yeobright. At the same time that Pierston offends the One, Aphrodite, by loving her incarnation in Avice the first, he offends Avice the first by pursuing the One in Avice the second, in Nicola, in Marcia, and in Avice the third. Falling in love with a real woman is a sin against Ideal Truth; pursuit of Ideal Truth is a sin against human loyalties. Ethelberta chose humanity; Clym could not extricate himself from devotion to the One in its maternal embodiment. Fitzpiers settled on Grace, though we are surely not expected to take with complete seriousness a reunion involving a vow to give up German philosophy, French romances and English cigars. Pierston, the only native whose pursuit of the Ideal we follow from youth to old age, submits to time-as-decay, to the deathward tendency in things. Such are the expressions of Hardy's divided allegiance – as architect and as writer – to the Ideal or the Design on the one hand and to the human embodiments of the Ideal and their 'old associations' on the other. In spite of a highly symmetrical structure the intent of which may be to screen self-portraiture, *The Well-Beloved*, seen in the context of the earlier narratives of return, is a revealing depiction of

Hardy's guilt-tinged longing for an original, a prime, a pure state of being forever lost to 'change and chancefulness'.

THE 'POEMS OF 1912–13': HARDY'S POETIC NARRATIVE OF RETURN

Just how personal a depiction is perhaps best judged by turning briefly to the 'Poems of 1912–13', in which the poet husband of the dead Emma Hardy replaces author-figures such as Yeobright and Pierston as the one who labours under a guilty and futile wish to retrieve a lost happiness and to make amends for old offences. In Yeobright, in Pierston and in the lonely elegist of the 'Poems of 1912–13' we have three men, variant portraits of the artist, who with like intensity and futility seek reinstatement and amendment through return. The poet husband of 1912–13 bears some interesting similarities to Clym and Pierston. Like Clym, he returns to a spot associated with an earlier joy in order to recover that joy. Like Pierston, he seeks in that spot – also a coastal haven – a reincarnation of a lost joy; and like Pierston with Marcia he must acknowledge the triumph of time. Like both Pierston and Yeobright, the poet husband of the 'Poems of 1912–13' seeks to make amends to a woman he has wronged. Dampening this desire to atone, however, is a stubborn, even an outraged, idealism that joins the elegist, Clym and Jocelyn with nostalgic idealists such as Angel Clare and Henry Knight. Evidence that a similar idealism actually affected Hardy's attitude toward Emma can be found in a letter Hardy wrote to Florence Henniker in July 1914, twenty months after Emma's death. He was reluctant, he said, to print some poems about Emma, 'those I wrote just after Emma died, *when I looked back at her as she had originally been*, and when I felt miserable lest I had not treated her considerately in her later life. However, I shall publish them as the only amends I can make, if it were so' (emphasis added).[40] It seems appropriate then to discuss the 'Poems of 1912–13' alongside the novels of return, because the poet husband of the 'Poems' bears strong resemblance to several important figures in the novels. Even more significant, perhaps, is the fact that the twenty-one poems form a return cycle, making them akin in structure, as well as in theme, to the novels of homecoming.

Hardy's sudden loss on 27 November 1912 of his wife of

nearly forty years confronted him with what in another context he had called a 'precipice in Time', an unbridgeable division from an earlier, happier period of his life. Hardy had known such breaks before – in 1862, when he left Bockhampton for London; in 1874, when he married out of his class – but the break of 1912 was final in a way the others had not been. Both of the others had been bridged, at least partially, by his returns to Dorset in the late 1860s and in the early 1880s. The death of his father in 1892 seems to have brought, as only death and mourning can, a renewal of intimacies among members of the Hardy family. But Emma's death, so sudden and unexpected after many years of acrimony, left no opportunity for reconciliation. The 'swan-necked one' with whom he had known life's 'very best' during the enchanting 'seventies had declined into the silent one: 'Why, then, latterly did we not speak / Did we not think of those days long dead / And ere your vanishing strive to seek / That time's renewal?' ('The Going', *CP*, pp. 338–9). The repentant husband who wrote the 'Poems of 1912–13' sought to make amends by revisiting Cornwall and somehow recovering in his poems the qualities of that earlier, happier place and time. In March 1913, the forty-third anniversary of their first meeting in the vicarage of St Juliot, he returned to St Juliot and other of their old haunts in Cornwall. Making amends to Emma, like making amends to those he had left behind in Higher Bockhampton in 1862, required that he return to spots associated with the deserted one and with the happiness known there.[41] To return to old places he had frequented with Emma might raise a ghost, as he says in 'Old Excursions': 'Her phantasm may flit out there, and may greet me anywhere / In those haunts we knew' (*CP*, pp. 550–1).

Because he hoped that return might raise a ghost, he went back to St Juliot, to Tintagel, Beeny Cliff and Bossiney, to Camelford and Pentargon Bay, to Launceston and Boscastle. He revisited Emma's birthplace in Plymouth (Devon), to which Emma had much wished to return to live in the 1880s, when it was decided that Max Gate would be the Hardys' permanent home. Hardy seems to have written a poem to honour every shrine he visited. Three years later, in the summer of 1916, he again visited Cornwall, this time to erect a memorial brass to Emma at St Juliot's Church, whose restoration he had supervised forty-six years before. On 22 August 1920, 'fifty years . . . to the hour' after he had visited Beeny Cliff with Emma in August 1870, he went to Stinsford churchyard to lay roses on her grave. On 27 November 1922, ten years after her death, he recorded another visit to the grave. On 7 March 1924 he noted the fifty-fourth anniversary of their first meeting. And, as is well known, after writing the twenty-one 'Poems of 1912–13', he continued to pore over his memories of her. Over half of the more than one hundred poems to Emma in *The Complete Poems* were published *after* 1914.

The twenty-one 'Poems of 1912–13', with their Virgilian epigraph from Dido's confession to her sister Anna that Aeneas has wakened her long-dormant passions,[42] are arranged so as to form a return. The first eleven are either set in or were written in Dorset, probably in December 1912 or January 1913. Poem 12 ('A Dream or No'), dated February 1913, marks the decision to return to the cherished spot in the west of England. Poems 13–18 and 20 are set at various spots in Cornwall, or in Devon ('Places'). These seven poems seem to have been written in March 1913, perhaps during the visit to Cornwall; and all revive moments from the courtship in the 1870s, more than forty years before. Poem 19, 'The Spell of the Rose', is a highly ironic monologue in which a woman recounts her futile attempt to renew a lost love by planting a rose-bush. The twenty-first and last poem in the cycle, 'Where the Picnic Was', seems to treat an incident that occurred in Dorset in 1911 or 1912. So we take a journey as we read these poems, from 1912–13 to 1870 and back again, from Dorset to Cornwall and back again. It is a journey of return whose chief meaning – as in the novels of return – is that regeneration through return is impossible, though brief, ecstatic moments of renewal through memory can occur.

The first three poems ('The Going', 'Your Last Drive', 'The Walk') establish the pervasive mood of self-reproach and regret and announce the cycle's main theme: 'All's past amend / Unchangeable' ('The Going', *CP*, p. 339). They also identify the speaker as a lonely, remorseful visitor to memory-laden places. Poems 4, 5, 8, 9 and 10 ('Rain on a Grave', 'I Found Her Out There', 'The Haunter', 'The Voice', 'His Visitor'), depict Emma's spectral returns to Cornwall, to the elements and to Max Gate. These first ten poems establish Emma as a difficult and reproachful presence, even something of an antagonist. More important, they clearly reveal – as the letter to Florence Henniker in July 1914 states – that Hardy's return to Cornwall and Devon was a return in pursuit of his well-beloved, of his 'original' Emma, the vivacious, living woman of 'The Voice' who tells the poet, to his intense satisfaction, that she is as she was before her change, probably in the late seventies:

> Woman much missed, how you call to me, call to me,
> Saying that now you are not as you were
> When you had changed from the one who was all to me,
> But as at first, when our day was fair.
>
> Can it be you that I hear? Let me view you, then,
> Standing as when I drew near to the town
> Where you would wait for me: yes, as I knew you then,
> Even to the original air-blue gown!
>
> (*CP*, p. 346)

The voice of Emma heard by the poet here, surely a projection of his nostalgic wish to hear the voice of the girl of forty years before, calls to him to tell him that in death she has become 'as at first'. The 'you' of the second stanza is this first Emma, perhaps the historical Emma of 1870 to 1876, before the occurrence of the family crisis that probably influenced *The Return of the Native*. The 'you' of the first stanza is the eccentric, often jealous, Emma of later years. It is difficult not to deplore Hardy's apparent devotion to the 'first', the original, Emma, and difficult not to regret the failure of sympathy that banished to Mellstock Churchyard the later Emma, the figure in 'His Visitor', slightly indignant at changes in her house and garden, the querulous, scolding Emma suffering perhaps from 'painful delusions'.[43] Like his own Pierston, Knight, Clare and Yeobright, Hardy seems to have possessed a stubborn devotion to the pure and unblemished; and like them he could not forgive his well-beloved for failing to embody the Ideal, the One. From this perspective, the moment in January 1879, preserved in the poem 'A January Night' (*CP*, p. 466) looms large, for as has been noted it was then that Hardy, like his own Henry Knight, felt 'that there had passed away a glory from the earth' (*Life*, p. 124).

'A Dream or No', the twelfth poem of the cycle and the first of its second movement, conveys the futility of Hardy's attempt, thirty-four years after that rainy January night in 1879, to recapture that same lost glory:

Why go to Saint-Juliot? What's Juliot to me?
    Some strange necromancy
    But charmed me to fancy
That much of my life claims that spot as its key.

Yes. I have had dreams of that place in the West,
    And a maiden abiding
    Thereat as in hiding;
Fair-eyed and white-shouldered, broad-browed and brown-tressed.

And of how, coastward bound on a night long ago,
    There lonely I found her,
    The sea-birds around her,
And other than nigh things uncaring to know.

So sweet her life there (in my thought has it seemed)
    That quickly she drew me
    To take her unto me,
And lodge her long years with me. Such have I dreamed.

(*CP*, p. 348)

In Hardy's poems the radiant vision of the dream is almost always violated by the sights and sounds of drab reality. In 'The Voice', for example, the image and utterance of the 'original' Emma turns out to be merely the wind and an accompanying optical illusion, both image and voice having been willed into existence by their remorseful survivor, 'faltering forward' (*CP*, p. 346). Something similar happens in 'A Dream or No': the last two stanzas darken the hope of the first four by expressing doubt that either the fair maid of St Juliot or St Juliot itself ever existed:

        But nought of that maid from Saint-Juliot I see;
            Can she ever have been here,
            And shed her life's sheen here,
        The woman I thought a long housemate with me?

        Does there even a place like Saint-Juliot exist?
            Or a Valancy Valley
            With stream and leafed alley,
        Or Beeny, or Bos with its flounce flinging mist?

The shining maid from St Juliot has faded into the troubled woman and drab housemate of later years.

This painful self-probing in 'A Dream or No' and the eleven poems that precede it leaves us wholly unprepared for the joyful cry of restoration-achieved in 'After the Journey', the thirteenth poem of the cycle. In 'After the Journey' the poet has reached Emma's 'olden haunts' and is looking eagerly for the image of the maid of St Juliot, with her 'nut-coloured hair / And gray eyes, and rose-flush coming and going'. He seems to find her, for in the second stanza he asks the maid, whom he has tracked 'through the years . . . and dead scenes', to speak of 'our past– / Scanned across the dark space wherein I have lacked you'. She (the maiden Emma) now looks forward from the past across the dark terrain of the marriage in which maiden glow died early, and her reply takes the form of her poet husband's bitterly sad questions: 'Summer gave us sweets, but autumn wrought division? / Things were not lastly as firstly well / With us twain . . . ?' Is the poet's tone here one of rebuke or of tenderness? Has a note of bitterness caused by Emma's 'change' crept into this ghostly conversation? She does not, it seems, want to discuss it; nor he: 'all's closed now'. He (somewhat shamefacedly?) submits to the will of his ghost-wife, and because he does he sees her silent intention for him:

> I see what you are doing: you are leading me on
>   To the spots we knew when we haunted here together,
> The waterfall, above which the mist-bow shone
>   At the then fair hour in the then fair weather,
> And the cave just under, with a voice so hollow
>   That it seems to call out to me from forty years ago,
> When you were all aglow,
>   And not the thin ghost that I now frailly follow

(CP, p. 349)

The Emma of the poem prefers to visit old haunts rather than to speak of the past. And so he follows his silent guide to the old familiar spots – the waterfall, the cave whose voice seems to speak just as it did forty years before (in contrast to Emma's). Neither the indifference of the birds, like-sounding descendants of those they had heard, nor the coming of the dawn, when the spectre must return to the land of the dead, disturbs what can only be called a moment of complete transport:

> Trust me, I mind not, though Life lours,
>   The bringing me here; nay, bring me here again!
>   I am just the same as when
> Our days were a joy, and our paths through flowers.

This is an extraordinary moment in 'The Poems of 1912–13', and in fact in the poetry as a whole. 'I am just the same' challenges the ground-note established in 'The Going', the hopeless 'All's past amend. Unchangeable'. The only comparable moment in the novels is, significantly enough, Clym Yeobright's discovery of his dying mother and the kiss that joins boyhood and manhood for a moment:

> 'O, what is it! Mother, are you ill – you are not dying?' he cried, pressing his lips to her face. 'I am your Clym. How did you come here? What does it all mean?' At that moment the chasm in their lives which his love for Eustacia had caused was not remembered by Yeobright, and to him the present joined continuously with that friendly past that had been their experience before the division.   (*RN*, IV, ch. 7)

The last phrase echoes the poem's 'autumn wrought division'. Even the Virgilian mood of the 'Poems of 1912–13 is present at this moment in the novel of 1878. 'Like Aeneas with his father', Clym carries his mother to shelter. In both instances, the destructive flow of time has for a moment been reversed. And in *The Return of the Native*, as in 'At Castle Boterel', 'Places' and 'The Phantom Horsewoman' (the sixteenth, seventeenth, and eighteenth poems), Hardy is contemplating a lesser consolation – preservation of the 'phantom figure' in thought or in memory. Though he, the rememberer,

>   Withers daily
>   Time touches her not
>   But she still rides gaily
>   In his rapt thought
>   On that shagged and shaly
>   Atlantic spot
>   And as *when first eyed*
> Draws rein and sings to the swing of the tide.

('Phantom Horsewoman', *CP*, p. 354; emphasis added)

Clym's (and Marty South's) fleeting consolation, the consolation of memory, is also Hardy's in his time of irrecoverable loss.

But if the thirteenth and eighteenth poems of the cycle offer renewal through memoried vision, 'A Death-Day Recalled', 'Beeny Cliff' and 'St Launce's Revisited' (the fourteenth, fifteenth and twentieth poems) reassert the main theme that carried, even for the tentativist Hardy, the weight of unassailable truth: the beloved places of Cornwall know nothing of Emma, she herself is now insensible of them, and so thoughts and memories of her are but flimsy things because she is 'vanished / Under earth; yea, banished / Ever into nought' ('St Launce's Revisited', *CP*, p. 357). 'The Spell of the Rose' and 'Where the Picnic Was', poems 19 and 21, formally advance this view by bringing us back from Cornwall and the idyllic past to Dorset and the real present. In 'The Spell', a wife we may take to be Emma speaks sorrowfully of her husband's failure to plant a rose, the flower of love, in their garden, and of her futile attempt to mend their severed lives by herself planting the flower. She died before it could bloom, and she wonders if 'he, as of old / Gave me his heart anew'. Perhaps, she wistfully concludes, 'he sees me as I was, though sees / Too late to tell me so!' (*CP*, pp. 356–7). Here 'Emma' is portrayed as one who shares her husband's view that days of incurable blight followed their days of joy, and that his loyalty should be to her 'first' self. Emma Hardy apparently made more than one attempt at reconciliation with her husband. The steady self-reproach in the 'Poems of 1912–13' in part stems from Hardy's regret that he successfully ignored her. His poems to her must be, as the Virgilian epigraph suggests, only 'marks of an old fire'.

Perhaps Hardy's reasons for choosing this particular phrase from Dido's words to Anna in Book IV of *The Aeneid* now become clearer. Dido's first loyalty was to Sychaeus, dead through the insane jealousy of her brother Pygmalion. Aeneas is her second great love, but he will prove to be treacherous. Is Hardy simply expressing, in his choice of phrase, a sense that remnants of his old affection for Emma are still alive in him? Undoubtedly this was one intention. And yet, as suggested by his sense that there were almost literally two Emmas – a blooming first Emma of the seventies, and a faded, eccentric second Emma of the thirty years after – the epigraph may also convey Hardy's lingering sense – first explored in the portraits of Eustacia in *The Return* and Marcia in *The Well-Beloved* – that Emma had proved to be a treacherous substitute for the object of his first love, whether maternal or ideal. Both intentions are present, I think, in Hardy's resonant choice of epigraph.

'Where the Picnic Was', the last poem of the cycle, completes the suggestion of the epigraph by turning our attention to the dead ashes of a picnic fire kindled probably in 1911 or 1912 – fit image for the finality of loss and the futility of return. The return to the magical land of Lyonesse and the haloed past – like the returns to Egdon, to the Hintocks, and to the Isle of Slingers – ends in a real land (Dorset) and the 'cold' and 'gray' present:

> Yes, I am here
> Just as last year,
> And the sea breathes brine
> From its strange straight line
> Up hither, the same
> As when we four came.
>
> – But two have wandered far
> From this grassy rise . . .
> And one – has shut her eyes
> For evermore.
>
> (*CP*, pp. 357–8)

In the 'Poems of 1912–13', as in the novels of homecoming, the turn to the past prompted by nostalgic idealism proves to be futile and destructive. But because both the return and its failure are inevitable and irremediable – return forced by unalterable traits of character, failure caused by the deteriorative tendency in things – an all-encompassing sense of pity, even a moral heroism, is possible. In a writer who is so often intimately self-exploratory, universal sympathy could easily crumble into self-pity; or the truth of inevitable decay could be sacrificed to comedic strategies for renewal like those that disturb the tragic order in *The Return* and *The Woodlanders*. As noted earlier in this chapter, such compromises derive from Hardy's divided loyalty – on the one hand to a 'beauty of association' deriving from a thing's human associations, on the other to the truth that all things decay. This second, the expression of an inexorable, impersonal process, had its own appeal for him, a simplicity of design and purpose that he could trace in himself and in the world around him and that as artist he felt bound to represent. The beauty of the sad truth that all things decay – this seems to have been one of the fruits of the novels of return. With this observation we enter on discussion of Hardy's tragic vision, the vision of *The Mayor of Casterbridge, Tess of the d'Urbervilles* and *Jude the Obscure*, the vision that grew up out of, and alongside of, the drama of return that he wrote and rewrote from the early 1870s to the end of his career as a novelist.

4 'Twice-Over Cannot Be': the Futility of Restoration in *The Mayor of Casterbridge, Tess of the d'Urbervilles* and *Jude the Obscure*

In turning now from Hardy's novels of return to his novels of restoration, two things may be reiterated. First, Hardy's view that return, in all its social and psychological aspects, is devilishly difficult is preserved and transformed in the analogous view that restoration, the reinstatement of a thing to its primal state, is wholly futile. Attempting to go home again was for Hardy as hopeless an undertaking as trying to bring a thing back to its original condition. Second, Hardy's way of depicting the drama of restoration in novels between 1871 and 1895 repeats his way of depicting the drama of return in novels between 1872 and 1897. In both cycles he moved from romantic comedy, through tragedy or near-tragedy, to tragic realism. His progress from *Desperate Remedies, A Pair of Blue Eyes, Far from the Madding Crowd* and *The Trumpet-Major* through *A Laodicean* and *Two on a Tower*, to *The Mayor, Tess* and *Jude* retraces his progress through *Under the Greenwood Tree, The Return of the Native, The Woodlanders* and *The Well-Beloved*. This second fact especially should suggest the incautiousness of describing Hardy as an artist who persistently failed 'to learn from his own past experiences'.[1] In some ways it would seem that he did little else.

If one reflects for a moment on *The Mayor of Casterbridge* (1886), *Tess* (1891) and *Jude* (1895), as well as on *Far from the Madding Crowd* and *A Pair of Blue Eyes*, their chief predecessors of the 1870s, he finds that in all Hardy has traced the career of an irreparably flawed protagonist. Elfride, Bathsheba, Henchard, Tess and Jude all have this in common – they are incurably flawed. Beside each of these unregenerates Hardy placed a physicianly figure – a Knight, an Oak, a Farfrae, an Angel Clare, a Sue Bridehead – who takes on, or tries to take on, the cure of the ailing protagonist. Only Oak succeeds, because only Oak is lucky. He is sustained by inborn virtues just as surely as Bathsheba is plagued by inborn vices. Farfrae succumbs to impatience, to ambition, and to the inexorable process of change that uses him to displace Henchard. Angel, like Henry Knight, is temperamentally unfit to forgive and thereby heal his erring beloved. Sue is as deeply flawed as the wretched Jude, who looks to her, of all persons, for a curative love. At the centre of each of these novels, then, is an image of the irremediable. Tragedy is averted in *Far from the Madding Crowd* because human remedies suffice; tragedy (as irreparable defect or error) prevails in *The Mayor*, in *Tess* and in *Jude*, because Farfrae, Angel and Sue are limited and ailing healers. Henchard's irremediably flawed character is his fate; much the same can be said of Jude and of Tess, though Tess, as shall be seen, is granted a limited kind of justice and transcendence, if not a cure.

Henchard, Jude and, to a lesser extent, Tess have defects that no natural, divine or human agency can eradicate. Their careers describe a similar pattern – sin (inherited or actual), attempted atonement, failure, and death. Henchard, determined to make a new start after a ruinous first marriage, sells his wife and daughter for five guineas, then rises, full of remorse, to the office of Mayor of Casterbridge. He tumbles from that eminence when the truth about his past is revealed. His life after the sale at Weydon-Priors is a futile attempt to atone for his desperate act, an act designed, it is too seldom noted, to mend the misfortunes of his life before Weydon-Priors. He cannot escape or atone because he is unalterably set in his moody, impulsive ways. Like Bathsheba Everdene, he is incurably infirm – though he is not viewed as being typical of his sex in this, as Bathsheba is of hers. Donald Farfrae, like the ministering Gabriel Oak, can manage the defects of non-human nature, as when he almost completely restores the blighted grain; but, again like Oak, he is nearly helpless before the defects of human nature. Henchard's impulses are as far beyond his humane intelligence as Boldwood's are beyond Oak's. Tess Durbeyfield, inhabitant of a blighted planet, heir to a certain incautiousness of character, but also an unintending sinner, is ruined by Alec d'Urberville, who then repents and seeks, without success, to mend his ways and to make reparation to Tess. Tess's fierce devotion to Angel is in part the result of her desire to find forgiveness and redemption in the love of a good man. But Clare, though himself guilty of a lapse similar to Tess's, rejects Tess; for he, ironically, had been looking to her, as she to him, as the means by which to recover a lost purity of spirit. Though Tess suffers and dies, her essential innocence, her intuitive kindness, and her unconscious harmony with nature constitute a genuine heroism, just as her taking revenge on Alec constitutes a real, if rudimentary, justice. Jude Fawley does not punish his tormentors, for Jude, even more clearly than Tess, is of bad seed; worse, he is an incorrigible idealist and dreamer of impossible dreams of amendment and reform. The flaw in his make-up coexists – and this is the chilling brilliance in Hardy's conception of him – with a compulsive need to imagine and to seek remedies for the evils of the world. Thus his restless progress from education, to love, to religion. But all to no avail; for in Jude's world, as in the world of Henchard and to a lesser extent of Tess, there is no way to mend the radical defect in things. For the reader, the experience of tragedy in these novels is the recognition of this grim fact *and* the perception of the strange beauty with which Hardy graces it.

A second similarity between the three great tragedies and *A Pair of Blue Eyes* and *Far from the Madding Crowd* is Hardy's use in all of architecture – Endelstow Church, the great Shearing Barn, Weatherbury House, the inns and houses of Casterbridge, the d'Urberville tomb and the pillars of Stonehenge, Alex's red brick manor house, Wintoncester, the razed church at Marygreen and the colleges of Christminster – to convey his deterioristic view of things. This use of architectural settings in the novels of restoration is a notable departure from the use of natural settings – the Mellstock and the Hintock woodlands, Egdon Heath, the Isle of Slingers and the sea surging round it – in the novels of return. The drama of return is always in one important sense a thwarted attempt to return to nature, that symbol of power and endurance against which men and women are measured. Why then the turn to architecture in the novels of restoration? There are at least two explanations.

The first is that an architectural element had been present in the novels and poems from the very beginning. Though a pronounced and distinctive use of architectural settings and themes is discernible for the first time in the novels of the 1880s, the theme of restoration and the analogy between persons and buildings was alive in the earliest novels and poems. In 'Heiress and Architect' the naive heiress learns from an architect-sage both to design her house and live her life in accord with a law of decay. The dying man in 'Her Dilemma' begs for the love of a woman, and he does so in a 'mildewed', 'wasted', 'wormy' church. She grants her love, regretting all the time that nature should devise such dilemmas for human beings (*CP*, pp. 13–14). In *A Pair of Blue Eyes*, the efforts of the architect hero (Smith) to restore Endelstow Church parallels his attempt to return to his native Endelstow and, more important, is made to comment on Henry Knight's futile attempt to recover through Elfride the lost glory and gleam of boyhood. In *Far from the Madding Crowd*, over against the complex and shifting workings of nature, Hardy placed the long-lived Shearing Barn, with its shining oaken floor, and its human counterpart in the resourceful and durable Gabriel Oak. Even Troy's selfish villainy is given an architectural slant when, in conversation with Oak, he heartlessly proposes a a thorough renovation of the old farmhouse at Weatherbury Farm. For Troy (as for Hardy, interestingly enough) architectural 'creation and preservation don't go well together (*FMC*, ch. 35). In *The Hand of Ethelberta* we find a humorous analogy between 'a man and his mansion' – that is, between the deceitful Lord Mountclere and his marble-veneered brick manor, Enckworth House (*HE*, ch. 38).[2]

But, even with these precedents, it comes as something of a surprise to find that *The Trumpet-Major*, *A Laodicean* and *Two on a Tower* have, each of them, a building at its centre – Overcombe Mill, Stancy Castle and Ring's Hill Speer, respectively – and that these buildings, like the heath in *The Return* and the woodlands in *The Woodlanders*, constitute a symbolic setting through which Hardy comments on the human lives in the novels. Similarly, in *The Mayor*, and in *Tess* and *Jude* in a strikingly antithetical way, ancient buildings and their human associations loom large. As Douglas Brown has said so well, 'the singularities and visible strange histories of ancient buildings impressed on [Hardy] . . . the analogous unexpectedness and incongruity of the fabric of human affairs'.[3]

A second answer to our question – Why the turn from nature to architecture in the novels of restoration? – is suggested in chapter 40 of *The Mayor of Casterbridge*. There we find Henchard plunged into deepest despair because he has just been rebuffed by Farfrae. Only a short time before, he had nearly killed his former friend in a struggle in a hayloft; now, repentant, as always, in the afterthought, he has sought out Farfrae to tell him that Lucetta is near death, the victim of the skimmity ride. But Farfrae, suspicious and fearful, ignores Henchard and drives on. Of Henchard's gloom at this critical point Hardy wrote, 'To this he had come after a time of emotional darkness of which the adjoining woodland afforded inadequate illustration.' This negative comparison might be intended simply to suggest the intensity of Henchard's dejection at being unable to make amends to Farfrae. But it has another point as well – and it is that an analogue from nature *cannot* illustrate the moral consciousness of Michael Henchard, because Henchard, unlike nature, is unregenerate, is without an innate capacity for restoration. This is borne out, not long after, when Henchard, shocked to find Newson dancing merrily at Elizabeth and Farfrae's wedding, is described as 'a dark ruin, obscured by "the shade from his own soul upthrown" ' (ch. 44).[4] 'The shade from his own soul' is, of course, the shade cast by the indelible blemish in the character of the man whose character is his fate. The appropriate symbol of his character and fate is the architectural ruin, the decayed human creation that, unlike a tree, lacks inherent powers of regeneration.

Thus Hardy's turn from nature to culture in his turn from the narrative of return to the narrative of restoration is, implicitly, a turn from hope in non-human means of redemption or restoration. It suggests in him a deepening conviction, from about 1880 on, that the destiny of man is entirely in the hands of imperfect men and women. There is no natural ideal to be regained or to be recalled; there is no supernatural reward to which to look forward. For Henchard, a healing return to nature is no more possible than a belief in a merciful God or a renewal of childhood simplicities. Between *Tess*, with its heavy reliance on natural settings, and *Jude*, with its equally heavy use of architectural settings, this question is in sharp symbolic debate. But throughout the three tragedies one thing is consistent – regeneration for the protagonist lies almost wholly with fallible human agents. Henchard must rely on Elizabeth-Jane and Farfrae, Tess on Angel, Jude on Sue. And all these would-be redeemers fail because they, like their practitioners, are victims of the unregenerateness of things. And so the image of a ruined or rotting building – so familiar to the eye and the hand of a writer who was also a restorer of Gothic churches – becomes an apt symbol for a human life.

THREE 'ARCHITECTURAL' NOVELS: *A LAODICEAN*, *THE TRUMPET-MAJOR* AND *TWO ON A TOWER*

As has been noted, each of the novels of the eighties written before *The Mayor* – *The Trumpet-Major* (1880), *A Laodicean* (1881) and *Two on a Tower* (1882) – has a building at its centre. And it may be said that Overcombe Mill is to *The Trumpet-Major*, Stancy Castle to *A Laodicean*, and Ring's Hill Speer to *Two on a Tower* what Egdon Heath is to *The Return* and the Hintock Woodlands to *The Woodlanders* – the central symbolic setting, the chief internal source of commentary on human destiny in the narrative. Behind all these novels, and behind *The Mayor*, is a favourite architectural question of Hardy's: how to reconcile the desire to preserve the old with the need to create anew? Or, as Troy put it in the episode from *Far from the Madding Crowd* mentioned a few pages ago,

> A philosopher once said in my hearing that the old builders, who worked when art was a living thing, had no respect for the work of builders who went before them, but pulled down and altered as they thought fit; and why shouldn't we? 'Creation and preservation don't do well together,' says he, 'and a million of antiquarians can't invent a style.' My mind exactly. I am for making this place [Weatherbury farmhouse] more modern, that we may cheerful whilst we can. (ch. 35)

Should the old simply be thrust aside to make room for the new? The antiquarian in Hardy (and in Oak in this episode) said no. It would be a pity, Oak thinks, to alter the ancient farmhouse by installing sash-windows, by brightening up or removing the old oak wainscoting and papering the walls; and yet no one knows better than Oak (a shepherd on his way to becoming an independent farmer) that change is not only inevitable but also at times welcome. The same division is apparent in Hardy himself in 'Memories of Church Restoration' (1906), where he calls for 'the protection of an ancient edifice against renewal in fresh materials', then sadly admits that the 'original' must be sacrificed to the needs of the present. A similar dichotomy of thought and feeling shaped the four novels written between 1880 and 1886. In the *Trumpet-Major* Hardy fancifully depicted the reinstatement, through forgiveness and self-sacrifice, of an earlier, happier phase in the lives of Bob Loveday and Anne

Garland. In *A Laodicean* he explored the possibility of juxtaposing old and new and of walking a *via media* between preservation and creation. In *Two on a Tower* he exhibited the ruthless and inevitable displacement of old by new, but tempered that by showing the growth of moral consciousness in his hero and heroine. In *The Mayor*, the great culmination of these 'architectural' experiments, he set aside all compromise for the illumination of a tragic knowledge, the knowledge that character is fate, and fate – for men and for buildings – a matter of unavoidable decay. Restoration is delusion. In the remarks that follow, I shall try to show how in *The Mayor* and the three novels that precede it Hardy used architectural settings to exhibit his increasingly gloomy view of human possibilities.

The Trumpet-Major depicts the restoration of things past. The roving Bob Loveday, something of a nineteenth century Odysseus, returns to marry his boyhood sweetheart and to live happily on his native isle after a heroic role in the Napoleonic struggle. His return is possible for several reasons: because he is granted the command of a coastal vessel, a situation that offers him a compromise between the roving and the home life; because his beloved Anne Garland can forgive and forget his vagaries of the heart; and, most important, because his loyal brother John, the Trumpet-Major of the novel's title, can set aside his own love for Anne in order that Bob may reunite with her. One is reminded by this of the conclusion of *Under the Greenwood Tree*, where Parson Maybold steps aside in order that Dick Dewey and Fancy Day might marry. There is even a similar touch of grim reality to temper the happiness: John's going off to die in the Peninsula Campaign is like the secret that Fancy will never tell Dick. But this is not all. Bob Loveday's restoration through good fortune, Anne's forgiveness, and John's self-sacrifice have a fitting symbol, an objective correlative, as it were, in Overcombe Mill. Upon returning home after many years in foreign lands, John finds the ancient mill to be the same as it was in his boyhood:

> The panes of the grinding-room, now as heretofore clouded with flour as with stale hoar-frost; the meal lodged in the corners of the window-sills, forming a soil in which lichens grew without ever getting any bigger, as they had done since his dimmest infancy; the mosses on the plinth toward the river, reaching as high as the capillary powers of the wall would fetch up moisture for their nourishment, and the penned millpond, now as ever to the point

of overflowing into the garden. Everything was the same.
(ch. 15)

The mill endures while dynasties falter because it combines utility
with beauty of human association. It is at once a source of 'food for
the body' (*Life*, p. 151) and a record of past lives – a standing symbol
of community, of the solidarity and continuity of feeling expressed
in the generosity of John and Anne.

In *A Laodicean*, the novel Hardy began to write while the early
instalments of *The Trumpet-Major* were appearing in *Good Words*,
neither Captain de Stancy nor Sir William de Stancy, penniless
aristocrats seeking to restore their ancient family to its former glory,
is so prominent as Stancy Castle, once the de Stancy stronghold, or
as Paula Power, the heiress and *parvenue* who has purchased the
castle in order to restore it to its former splendour.[5] Because Captain
de Stancy, after many years in India, returns to try to reclaim his
patrimony by marrying the wealthy newcomer, *A Laodicean*, like
The Trumpet-Major, is a story of love and of homecoming with a
building at its centre. But it differs fundamentally from its idyllic
predecessor because it is not a romantic account of what Hardy in
the preface to it called 'a change back to the original order' (p. vii).
Instead, it is a depiction of an inevitable movement forward into a
new one.

Paula Power is a Laodicean because she cannot choose between
conflicting attitudes toward the past. De Stancy, who wishes to
marry her in order to restore his family's lost glory and to somehow
undo an indiscretion that produced an illegitimate son, appeals to
her romantic regard for the antique. George Somerset, the young
architect and religious agnostic who is to direct the restoration of
the castle, knows that it is impossible to restore the old building and
offers a somewhat whimsical compromise. He does not seek to
restore the medieval edifice; he instead advises Paula to leave
Stancy Castle (burnt to the ground by Captain de Stancy's son) in
ruins and to build a new house alongside. He would solve the
creation–preservation problem by adapting an 'old building to the
wants of a new civilization. He had placed his erection beside it as a
slightly attached structure, harmonizing with the old, heightening
and beautifying rather than subduing it' (*L*, VI, ch. 5). The
romantic vision of *The Trumpet-Major*, in which Bob Loveday can
live in the present and yet turn back the clock, has given way here to
the realistic view that consciousness and history are parts of a linear,

unreturning process of change.[6] And there seems to be little doubt that the general tendency of this change is downward. The political theme of the novel, which urges that an orderly and dignified medievalism is being displaced by a vulgar and anarchical democratic system, suggests as much. The best to be hoped for, in architecture if not in politics, is the harmonious but temporary coexistence of the old and the new, a hope that will be contemplated then discarded in *The Mayor*.

There is yet a third view of the past put before Paula, for, even before she meets the pragmatic Somerset or the romantic de Stancy, she is instructed in the possibility of supernatural regeneration by a Baptist clergyman, Pastor Woodwell, who urges her to be baptized and thus 'born again'. For his trouble, Woodwell is trounced by Somerset in a hot debate on the authority for infant baptism (*L*, I, chs 6–7). Usually dismissed by critics as an autobiographical vagary, the baptismal question, which dominates the opening of the novel and produces some of its best writing, has a logical place in the novel's argument against the possibility of restoration or regeneration.

Through Woodwell Hardy for the first time took up in his ongoing exploration of the question of regeneration the traditional theological idea of spiritual renewal through a supernatural agency. This traditional view provided an answer to the question of regeneration, an answer Hardy had known from the time of his earliest religious experience, the doctrine of the Resurrection of Christ and the redemption of man that follows from it. Hardy's interest in this ancient Christian teaching lingers on in Swithin St Cleeve's inner debate on Confirmation in *Two on a Tower*, in Michael Henchard's fetishistic longing for 'transsubstantiation' in *The Mayor*, in the harrowing baptismal ceremony conducted by Tess and in Angel's rejection of the Resurrection in *Tess*, and in Sue's wish to reconstruct parts of the New Testament in *Jude*.[7] Paula's eventual rejection of adult baptism with the aid of Somerset is a rejection of the possibility of a supernatural source of regeneration, just as her rejection of de Stancy is a rejection of nostalgia. Her choice, the Laodicean one of compromise and coexistence, parallels Somerset's architectural philosophy of juxtaposing the old and the new.

If Overcombe Mill represents an ideal and reattainable early nineteenth century past, and Stancy Castle a lost but partially preservable thirteenth century order, then Ring's Hill Speer, the war monument that dominates the setting of *Two on a Tower*, suggests yet a third possibility, the adaptation of the old to an entirely new use – modern wine in medieval bottles. The original purpose of the Speer, to memorialize a hero of the American Revolution, has been forgotten by the time, less than a century later, that Swithin St Cleeve makes it over into an astronomer's observatory and workshop. The war memorial has become a citadel of science, and this suggests what Hardy is about in this novel – a near-tragic view of history. In *Two on a Tower* Hardy exhibits not the juxtaposition of old and new, not the reinstatement of the old, and certainly not the miraculous renewal of former things. Instead, he shows the inevitable displacement of the old by the new – the view that will govern the tragedy of *The Mayor of Casterbridge* – but here tempers tragedy by offering, much as in *The Trumpet-Major*, a secularized version of the theological concept of redemption. Just as science takes up residence in a building designed for heroic and memorial purposes, so ethical humanism moves into the house vacated by theology. To manage this, Hardy used elements of the enticement story he had used a decade earlier in *Desperate Remedies*.

In *Two on a Tower* Hardy wrought, with a significant twist, another version of Miss Aldclyffe's entrapment of Cytherea in *Desperate Remedies*. Viviette Constantine is a love-starved widow of twenty-nine seeking to recover the bliss of first love, a bliss denied her in an unhappy marriage. She seeks it in marriage to Swithin St Cleeve, a handsome, well-educated nineteen-year old of mixed parentage (his father was a parson, his mother the daughter of a farmer) wholly devoted to the study of astronomy. Swithin carries on his sightings and calculations from atop Ring's Hill Speer, a tower as isolated among fields and woodlands as Robinson Crusoe's island on the lonely sea. To Swithin, the Speer is not a memorial but an instrument of study, a vessel for lofty intellectual voyaging. It suggests a 'primitive Eden of consciousness' in which he, in his total devotion to physics, can dwell free from intrusion:

His heaven at present was truly in the skies, and not in that only other place where they say it can be found, in the eyes of some daughter of Eve. Would any Circe or Calypso . . . ever check this pale-haired scientist's sailings into the interminable spaces overhead, and hurl his mighty calculations on cosmic force and stellar fire into limbo? (*TT*, ch. 5)

Swithin (–Adam–Odysseus) is enticed from his paradise of pure thought by Viviette (–Eve–Circe), who is, however, not at all happy with her role as enchantress. She has pangs 'of conscience, like a person who had entrapped an innocent youth into marriage for her own gratification, till she remembered that she had raised his social position thereby' (ibid.). For Viviette, Ring's Hill Speer is a symbol of possible sexual fulfilment, a phallic presence to which she, in her burning loneliness, turns and returns until she achieves both maternity and death within it. 'The lessenings and increasings of speed with which she proceeded in the direction of the pillar', writes Hardy, 'could be accounted for only by a motive much more disturbing than an intention to look through a telescope' (ch. 4).

This pattern, if entirely that of *Desperate Remedies*, would be a simple one – innocence tempted by experience, youth by age from 'the secluded fir-tree island to the wide world beyond' (ch. 18). But there is, as noted above, a twist. If Viviette initiates Swithin into the mysteries of love, Swithin, 'a curious juxtaposition of youthful ardour and old despair' (ch. 4), introduces Viviette to the terrifying vastnesses of cosmic space and time. She introduces him to the mysteries of the flesh; he shows her the 'Immeasurable' mind:

> Whatever the stars are made for, they were not made to please our eyes. It is just the same in everything; nothing is made for man.
>
> The actual sky is a horror. . . . Impersonal monsters [exist there], namely, immensities . . . monsters of magnitude without known shape.
>
> And to add a new weirdness to what the sky possesses in its size and formlessness, *there is involved the quality of decay*. For all the wonder of these everlasting stars, eternal spheres . . . they are not everlasting.   (ch. 4)

'It is not worthwhile to live,' cries Viviette; 'it quite annihilates me' (ibid.). Adam, it seems, is having his revenge.

This simultaneous 'fall' of hero and heroine into a state of new knowledge works to save both: Swithin from an unfeeling dedication to science, and Viviette from an unthinking devotion to love or religion. Swithin's intellect is strengthened by the rousing of his affections. Both his refusal to give up Viviette for an annuity (offered him by a woman-hating uncle) that would enable him to visit the southern hemisphere, and his loyalty to her upon his return from later travels reveal in him a growth of sympathy. The counterpart of this is the awakening of unselfish love in Viviette. When she discovers that their marriage contract is void, because her first husband, Sir Blount Constantine, was still alive at the time she married Swithin, she refuses to urge that the ceremony be repeated because she knows now it will jeopardize Swithin's studies.

> She in her experience had sought out him in his inexperience, and had led him like a child. . . . Love between man and woman, which in Homer, Moses, and other early exhibitors of life, is mere desire, had for centuries past so far broadened as to include sympathy and friendship; surely it should in this advanced stage of the world include benevolence also. If so, it was her duty to set her young man free.   (ch. 35)

Taught by Swithin of her insignificance within the vast reaches of time and space, she can reason altruistically and grant him the freedom to pursue his studies. Though life is brief and without an eternal consolation, human sympathy and intelligence can ennoble and perhaps redeem it. It is never blissful or easy, as Viviette's death will show, but it need not be mean or ignoble. In this way, Hardy indeed suggests that between the contrasting magnitudes of the 'infinitesimal' human universe and the 'stupendous' stellar one, 'the smaller might be the greater' (*TT*, 'Preface').

The novel's drift toward ethical humanism, perhaps even a 'religion of humanity', is underlined by its attack on traditional Christianity. The satire on the Bishop, Swithin's reluctance to be confirmed and Viviette's attendance at a Commination service (a recital of God's anger and judgement against sinners) are all used to suggest that Christianity is a quaint, outmoded faith. The Bishop of Melchester is made ridiculous in being, on the one hand, the stern preceptor who lectures Swithin on the dangers of the flesh and, on the other, the ardent pursuer of the lovely and lonely Viviette. His hypocrisy is punished in a way that shocked many of Hardy's readers: Viviette, pregnant by Swithin but unable to recall him from his travels in time to marry, weds the Bishop without revealing her condition. Less humorous than the cuckolding of a clergyman is Hardy's treatment of the Confirmation and Commination services.

Viviette insists that Swithin be confirmed because she wishes to justify her secret marriage to him (ch. 21). At first, Swithin refuses the sacrament, because he regards traditional religious doctrines,

like certain old books on astronomy in the library of Welland House,
as 'hulls and husks, whose human kernels had long ago perished'
(ch. 21). He is merely amused by Viviette's superstitious fear of the
dead and of the ordinances of the Church: 'Nothing is ominous in
serene philosophy. . . . There are either causes, or there are not
causes' (ch. 23). But he finally agrees to be confirmed, that is, to
renew the promise and vow made in his name at his baptism. And
so, we presume, this devotee of science studies the Creed, the Lord's
Prayer, the Ten Commandments, the Catechism, and renews the
vow to renounce the devil, the world and the flesh; to believe in
God, Christ, the Holy Saints, the Remission of Sins, the Resurrection of the Flesh, the Life Everlasting – all in order that the Old
Adam in him may be buried and the new man raised up.
Swithin's submission in the face of his doubt suggests that he has
emotional needs never satisfied by his 'ardent desire to bring down
the immeasurable to human comprehension'. And in fact his
religion of science ('that sublime mystery on whose threshold he
stood as priest') does not serve him well when trouble comes. When
he accidently shatters a telescopic lense, he imagines that the world
is his enemy: 'When the world has accidents on its side in addition to
its natural strength, what chance for me!' (ch. 5). Upon learning
that his great discovery has been anticipated by an American's, he
throws himself recklessly upon the wet, cold ground and, like some
primitive superstitionist, thinks himself a victim of 'the impishness of
circumstances' (ch. 9).

However inadequate it may be in times of trouble, Swithin's
scientific humanism is viewed by Hardy as superior to the
redemptive faith of his forefathers. What the novel gropes toward is
a non-theological scheme of redemption. And this seems to be
Hardy's point when he juxtaposes the Commination service, with its
condemnation of sinners, and Swithin's announcement to Viviette
that a new discovery has made him 'the Copernicus of the stellar
universe' (ch. 9). Swithin's new knowledge places him among those
who, in the words of the denunciatory service, are cursed because
they put their trust in man, and take man for their defence, and in
their heart go from the Lord (ch. 9).[8] In the last phrases of the
Commination service in the Prayer Book, sinners are exhorted to
'return unto Him, who is the merciful receiver of all true penitent
sinners' for renewal of a right spirit. But for Swithin, and now for
Viviette, a religion centring upon the Resurrection and the
Redemption has been displaced, as if according to Comtean plan,[9]

by a religion of science and humanity whose end is a wholly human scheme of redemption. 'To think', cries Viviette, 'that the whole race of shepherds, since the beginning of the world, – even those immortal shepherds who watched near Bethlehem, – should have gone into their graves without knowing that for one star that lighted them in their labours, there were a hundred as good behind trying to do so' (ch. 8). If a hundred stars, then, as suggested in such a poem as 'Unkept Good Fridays', a hundred redeemers, a hundred 'Christs of unwrit names' (*CP*, pp. 842–3). Viviette is one of them: 'By the extraordinary favour of a unique accident she had now an opportunity of redeeming Swithin's seriously compromised future, and restoring him to a state no worse than his first' (*TT*, ch. 35). Luck and an unusual capacity for self-sacrifice enable Viviette to be Swithin's redeemer, and make *Two on a Tower* Hardy's happiest, and last, vindication of a humanist credo.

THE ARCHITECTURAL MATRIX OF *THE MAYOR OF CASTERBRIDGE*

In *The Mayor of Casterbridge*, published some three years after *Two on a Tower*, Hardy seems to be mediating between the views of redemption he exhibited in *The Trumpet-Major*, *A Laodicean* and *Two on a Tower*. In setting for a time the old-fashioned Henchard and the reforming Farfrae side by side as friends and partners in the grain trade, Hardy flirted with the strategy of Somerset in *A Laodicean* to juxtapose an old, ruinous building and a new one. It might even be argued that *The Mayor*, in its pervasive use of some of the old buildings of Dorchester, memorializes and thus symbolically preserves Henchard and the old order, Casterbridge functioning in this in much the way Overcombe Mill functions in *The Trumpet-Major*. On the other hand, in showing Henchard's gradual displacement by Farfrae, Hardy seems to be repeating the view in *Two on a Tower* that the old must give way to the new – theology to science, Speer to observatory, Viviette to Tabitha. If in *The Mayor* Hardy flirts with each of these views but embraces none of them, it is because in each of them he had averted tragedy. In the three novels that precede *The Mayor*, the amending and restoring powers of intelligence, charity and self-sacrifice are actively in play; the idea that change is decay seems to have been set aside. In *The Mayor*, however – in its conception of character as fate, in its fatalistic turn of plot, in its peculiar use of architectural setting – intelligence and love are found, finally, to be inadequate to the task of redemption or restoration. A deterioristic view of things prevails.

This – that restoration or redemption is impossible – is the tragedy, and Hardy is in full possession of his tragic concept in *The Mayor*. But at the same time he was incapable of displaying it without qualifying it, without expressing his anguish that it should be true that all is decay. And so the tragic vision in *The Mayor* contends with an antiquarian and commemorating attitude in the novel, an attitude that urges that if restoration is impossible it is yet powerfully appealing, an authentic and profound human need. In making this observation it is worth noting that Hardy wrote *The Mayor* during a flurry of architectural and antiquarian activity between 1880 and 1886. This included not only his writing three 'architectural' novels, but his joining the Society for the Protection of Ancient Buildings and the Dorset Natural History and Antiquarian Field Club, as well as his designing and building Max Gate. *The Mayor* is an intensely local novel at the same time that it is a tragedy of universal scope and significance. Henchard is associated with Faust, with Cain and with Saul; but important aspects of his character derive as well from 'local' personalities of Dorchester-past – not just a man who sold his wife, but also, as I shall show, from a Dorchester stonemason who refused to take part in the razing of a fine old Dorchester house called the Trenchard Mansion.

It might be said that in *The Mayor* Hardy's attitude toward Henchard and the old order he represents is deeply divided between an antiquarian and an aesthetic aim. On the one hand he is trying to memorialize old Dorchester (Casterbridge), to recall and thus preserve the picturesqueness and bustle of a county town before the intrusion of the railway, farm machines, and a new style of life. On the other, he is dedicated to showing, in all the beauty of its grim truth, the working of the law of decay, both in Henchard, whose defects of character are irremediable, and in the historical process itself, which replaces a Henchard with a Farfrae with ruthless inexorability. This latter impulse – to show the beauty of decay – Hardy would call 'the artist instinct'; the former – to preserve the beauty of former things – he would call 'the caretaking instinct'. Both phrases occur in a striking passage in 'Memories of Church Restoration', in which the dilemma of the Hardy who reluctantly and almost guiltily restored old churches can be seen to be much the same as that of the creator of the incorrigible but powerfully attractive Michael Henchard of *The Mayor*:

The artist instinct and the care-taking instinct part company over the disappearing creation [i.e. the ruinous church]. The true architect, who is first of all an artist and not an antiquary, is naturally most influenced by the aesthetic sense, his desire being, like Nature's, to retain, recover, or recreate the idea which has become damaged, without much concern about the associations of the material that idea may have been displayed in. Few occupations are more pleasant than that of endeavouring to recapture an old design from the elusive hand of annihilation. Thus if the architect have also an antiquarian bias he is pulled in two directions — in the one by his wish to hand on or to modify the abstract form, in the other by his reverence for the antiquity of its embodiment. . . . In short, the opposing tendencies excited in an architect by the distracting situation can find no satisfactory reconciliation. All that he can do is of the nature of compromise.[10]

In *The Mayor*, Hardy, as 'artist', tries to exhibit the working of the inexorable process that annihilates both churches and men; this is 'the idea that has become damaged', the law of decay that has been obscured by belief in various redemptive schemes, whether human or divine. At the same time, as 'antiquary', he seeks to commemorate the 'embodiments' of the tragic truth, 'the [human] associations of the material' in which the tragic idea found expression. In short, in *The Mayor* Hardy is a tragic artist with an 'antiquarian bias', a novelist torn between his obligation to show the deterioristic working of history, of circumstances, and of character and his duty to memorialize the victims of this, for him, fatal process.

Commentators on tragedy in *The Mayor*, interested mainly in character and plot, have generally ignored Hardy's use of architectural setting to define the terms of Henchard's tragedy.[11] On the other hand, critics interested in the architectural milieu of the novel have ignored the implications of that milieu for Hardy's concept of Henchard as a man both noble and depraved whose character is his fate. For Henchard's fate is reflected in Casterbridge just as surely as Clym Yeobright's, for example, is reflected in Egdon Heath. J. Hillis Miller has observed that 'in some way the houses and the landscape of Casterbridge objectify the relations of the characters' in *The Mayor*. C. J. P. Beatty has described a pervasive architectural element in the novel: a variety of architectural styles on display; the attribution of human qualities to buildings and of architectural terms to men; the association of different social groups of Casterbridge with different buildings of the town; the dramatic function of the competition between Henchard and Farfrae to build different kinds of fairing tents; the use of the Three Mariners and High Place Hall as nodal points in the novel; and, most important, the way in which Henchard's career 'can almost be measured architecturally'.[12] That is, Henchard begins as a wandering labourer seeking 'a house to let' at Weydon-Priors in a time when 'pulling down'[13] rather than building is the practice. The rise of the homeless labourer is marked by his occupancy of a large house, his control of barns and granaries, his heading a banquet at the stylish King's Arms, his occupancy of the Town Hall as a mayor and a magistrate. He himself is described as of 'heavy frame' (chs 5, 35) and as 'stately and vertical' (chs 6, 38). His decline is marked by his loss of his great house, by his move into a small cottage located near a ruined abbey, by his unsuccessful attempt to get a new start as a merchant in a seed shop, by his visit to Elizabeth-Jane's wedding through the back door of the large house that was once his but is now Farfrae's, and, finally, by his death in a crumbling hut on Egdon Heath.

What has not been noted in discussions of architecture in *The Mayor* is a fact, only recently come to light, that tends to confirm the importance of such discussions – the discovery that the name 'Henchard' and several traits of Henchard derive from the name and history of a particular building of old Dorchester, the Trenchard Mansion, a Renaissance-style house that looked out onto Dorchester's West High Street until it was pulled down in about 1850.

If one walks north from the West High Street into Glyde Path Road (formerly Shire Hall Lane) in Dorchester, it is still possible to see, on the east wall of the building (No. 56–7) on the northwest corner, a piece of balustrade that is obviously a remnant of an earlier structure. This bit of ornament is all that survives of a fine house that until about 1850 stood on the northwest corner of what was then Shire Hall Lane and West High Street. Directly behind it had stood Colliton House (the original for High Place Hall in *The Mayor*), as well as Hardy's residence (at 7, Glyde Path Road) from 1883 to 1885. Here Hardy wrote much if not all of *The Mayor*.[14]

A print (dated 1840) in the Dorset County Museum shows that the balustrade once surmounted a Renaissance building that looked out on the High Street through an imposing front with twelve windows.[15] The house was called the Trenchard Mansion because it was the town house of the Dorset branch of the Trenchard family, a once-flourishing Elizabethan clan with one of its estates at Wolfeton Manor, near Charminster, a village two miles north of Dorchester. In about 1800 Wolfeton was purchased by James Henning, Esq.[16] The Hennings lived at Wolfeton until about 1862, and it seems that Henning or another member of the family occupied the house at the corner of Shire Hall Lane until it was pulled down in the late 1840s.[17] In 1840, a William Lewis Henning, possibly a member of the same family, became the Mayor of Dorchester.[18] As has been mentioned, Hardy wrote *The Mayor* while living just north of the 'new' building (with its bit of balustrade from the razed Trenchard Mansion) then standing on the site of the old Mansion. He must have passed the balustrade daily on his way to the High Street and the centre of town. It seems altogether likely that he formed the surname of the hero of the novel he was then writing by combining the first syllable of the name 'Henning' with the last syllable, or the last seven letters, of the name 'Trenchard' to create 'Henchard', a compound that at once recalls a former mayor of the town and a fallen house and family.[19] The names Henning and Trenchard must have been closely associated in Hardy's mind from at least the 1850s, when, as an apprentice to John Hicks, a Dorchester architect and church-restorer, Hardy had not only worked at the restoration of old buildings of Dorchester and surrounding communities but had also written up accounts of some of this work for the *Dorset County Chronicle*. Though we have long known that Hardy drew heavily on buildings and other features of Dorchester, as well as on aspects of local history, for the setting of *The Mayor*, the discovery that the name 'Henchard' combines the name of a fallen house with the name of a former mayor of Dorchester suggests that Hardy fused the human with the architectural, a man with a mansion, in a peculiarly significant way.

Just how he fused them is suggested in some remarks he made about *The Mayor* and old Dorchester in a speech to a Dorchester audience in November 1910, when he was granted the Freedom of the Borough of Dorchester. The subject of his talk at that time was the preservation of the old houses of Dorchester, many of which (including one he called 'the fine mansion of the Trenchards') had been demolished long before 1910. Hardy was divided in this talk – just as he had been in *The Mayor* – between a comic and a tragic view of the matter, between a desire to preserve the town's 'ancient

features' and a desire to show that 'the power to preserve is largely
an illusion'. His paraphrase of a sentence from Ruskin at the end of
his talk ('comedy is tragedy if you only look deep enough') suggests
that his underlying intention was to describe, in veiled terms, the
irremediable tragedy of historical change. In this context, he
described the function of *The Mayor* as a memorial one:

> When I consider the liberties I have taken with its [Dorchester's]
> ancient walls, streets and precincts through the medium of the
> printing press, I feel that I have treated its external features with
> the hand of freedom indeed. True, it might be urged that my
> Casterbridge . . . is not Dorchester – not even the Dorchester as
> it existed sixty years ago, but a dream-place that never was
> outside an irresponsible book. Nevertheless, when somebody said
> to me that 'Casterbridge' is a sort of essence of the town as it used
> to be, 'a place more Dorchester than Dorchester itself', I could
> not absolutely contradict him, though I could not quite perceive
> it. At any rate, it is not a photograph in words, . . . particularly
> in respect of personages.   (*Life*, p. 351)

Hardy was allowing here, in a tentative way, that in *The Mayor* he
may have recovered and symbolically preserved the kernel of
Dorchester-past. And he allowed further on in the talk that
something like preservation can occur when old houses are saved
from demolition by 'the education of . . . owners of temporary
trustees, or . . . by Government guardianship' (*Life*, p. 351).
However, he soon qualified this for him comedic view of things-past
when, in his concluding sentences, he expressed, in highly charged
language, his strong sense that old Dorchester was, to borrow a
phrase of Elizabeth-Jane's in *The Mayor*, 'gone for good':

> When all has been said on the desirability of preserving as much
> as can be preserved, our power to preserve is largely an illusion.
> Where is the Dorchester of my early recollections – I mean the
> human Dorchester – the kernel – of which the houses were but the
> shell? Of the shops as I first recall them not a single owner
> remains; only in two or three instances does even the name
> remain. As a German author has said, 'Nothing is permanent but
> change.' Here in Dorchester, as elsewhere, I see the streets and
> the turnings not far different from those of my schoolboy time; but

the faces that used to be seen at the doors, the inhabitants, where are they? I turn up the Weymouth Road, cross the railway-bridge, enter an iron gate to a 'slope of green access', and there they are! There is the Dorchester that I knew best; there are names on white stones one after the other, names that recall the voices, cheerful and sad, anxious and indifferent, that are missed from the dwellings and pavements. Those who are old enough to have had that experience may feel that after all the permanence or otherwise of inanimate Dorchester concerns but the perma-nence of what is minor and accessory. . . . Dorchester's future will not be like its past; we may be sure of that. Like all other provincial towns, it will lose its individuality – has lost much of it already. We have become almost a London suburb owing to the quickened locomotion, and though some of us may regret this, it has to be. I will detain you no longer from Mr. Evans's comedy that is about to be played downstairs. Ruskin says somewhere that comedy is tragedy if you only look deep enough. Well, that is a thought to remember; but to-night, at any rate, we will all be young and not look too deeply. (*Life*, pp. 352–3)

This is a sombre note to sound on a festive occasion, and it is full of meaning for *The Mayor*, which exhibits that encroachment by the modern that 'has to be' and is therefore not simply the memorial work that Hardy's 'someone' would have it be. Hardy's underlying view in the speech, as in the novel he wrote a quarter-century before, is that any attempt to preserve or restore the old buildings of Dorchester is delusive because their dead occupants, whose faces and voices haunt Hardy's memory, are gone forever. And for him the 'human interest' of an edifice, as he had said just four years earlier in 'Memories of Church Restoration', always ranked higher than its 'architectural interest, however great the latter may be'. He made the point again in the address of 1910 to his fellow citizens: 'Milton's "Almost as well kill a man as kill a good book" – applies not a little to a good old building; which is not only a book but a unique manuscript that has no fellow' (*Life*, p. 352). The unique, unreturning process called history was for Hardy a tragic process whose victims he wished somehow to redeem. In fashioning from the names 'Henning' and 'Trenchard' the name 'Henchard', in wedding in a single central figure both the human and the architectural realities of old Dorchester, he created a powerful image of both the 'kernel' and the 'shell', of both the enduring and the transient elements, of Dorchester-past. In doing this he was being faithful to both the 'artist' and the 'care-taking' impulses at work in the 'architectural' novels of the 1880s.

Interestingly enough, Hardy discovered the human kernel associated with the Trenchard Mansion and preserved in Michael Henchard not among the noble Trenchards, who built the Mansion, nor among the middle-class Hennings, who occupied it for many years, but rather, as suggested in the poem 'A Man (In Memory of H. of M.)', in the career of a humble stonemason who refused to participate in the destruction of the Mansion. Some aspects of Henchard may well derive from this Dorchester working man, who in the poem refuses to wreck 'what our age cannot replace / To save its tasteless soul'

> In Casterbridge there stood a noble pile,
> Wrought with pilaster, bay, and balustrade,
> In tactful times when shrewd Eliza swayed. –
> On burgher, squire, and clown
> It smiled the long street down for near a mile.

> But evil days beset that domicile;
> The stately beauties of its roof and wall
> Passed into sordid hands. Condemned to fall
> Were cornice, quoin, and cove,
> And all that art had wove in antique style.

Dismissed for his stubborn refusal to take part in the razing of the noble house, H. of M. 'backed his tools and went / And wandered workless' until his lonely death. In the last two stanzas of the poem, Hardy set side by side the death of the man and the fall of the mansion:

> Years whiled. He aged, sank, sickened; and was not;
> And it was said, 'A Man intractable
> And curst is gone.' None sighed to hear his knell,
> None sought his churchyard-place;
> His name, his rugged face, were soon forgot.

> The stones of that fair hall lie far and wide
> And but a few recall its ancient mould;
> Yet when I pass the spot I long to hold
> As truth what fancy saith;
> 'His protest lives where deathless things abide!'[20]

H. of M. and Michael Henchard are strongly similar in several ways. The description of H. of M. as rugged, intractable, and curst recalls, respectively, the appearance, character, and fate of Henchard. H. of M.'s lonely death recalls Henchard's death in a ruined hut on Egdon Heath. The description of him wandering 'workless' with tools 'backed' recalls Henchard both at the beginning and at the end of his story. Even more important is the fact, never before mentioned, I think, that in the early pages of the manuscript of *The Mayor* Michael Henchard is by occupation not a haytrusser but, like H. of M., a stonemason.[21]

Could it have been one of Hardy's early intentions that Henchard, an itinerant mason who sells his wife and daughter, would become a leading Casterbridge builder, as Henchard the haytrusser becomes the town's leading grain merchant? And would it be this Henchard's sad realization that restoring old buildings, like making amends for selling a wife and child or restoring blighted grain, is more than nature will allow? This seems more than mere speculation if we consider that Hardy probably derived the name and some of the qualities of his hero from the history of the Trenchard Mansion, that he kept the theme of restoration – of the 'growed' wheat, of the unregenerate Henchard, of the erring Lucetta – at the centre of his story. For Hardy in *The Mayor*, the 'growed' wheat, the crumbling buildings of Casterbridge, and the flawed Henchard are analogous phenomena because they cannot, any of them, be restored to their original condition. Nor do they contain within them the seeds of their own renewal. The wheat's primal freshness, the buildings' pristine appearances and early human associations, and Henchard's innocence can none of them be recovered. The power to restore or redeem the past, like the power to preserve the old, is 'largely an illusion'. Farfrae can bring back the mouldy wheat only so far, for nature will not allow complete restoration. Henchard can for a time conceal the truth of the past and repress the urgings of his nature in order to be a 'new' man as mayor and merchant, but because his character cannot change he is always, in his essence, what he was at Weydon-Priors. Lucetta's attempt to regain respectability is frustrated by chance and by the vindictiveness of Henchard. Underlying all illusions of restoration is a tragic reality, what Hardy in November 1887 called 'a state of things in the life of an individual which *unavoidably* causes some natural aim of his to end in a catastrophe when carried out' (*Life*, p. 176; emphasis added).

Unavoidable catastrophe dogs Henchard from the first. His natural aims and desires are perverted by his moody, violent temper: his defective character is his fate. The novel is a running argument against the possibility of his amendment and redemption. His career consists of a series of shocking affronts (against Susan and Elizabeth-Jane, against Farfrae, Jopp and Newson, even against a Royal Personage who visits Casterbridge) followed by unsuccessful attempts to make amends. One of his reasons for selling Susan and Elizabeth to Sailor Newson is that he hopes to make a fresh start after his early, improvident marriage to Susan. After the sale he swears off alcohol for twenty-one years because he believes that this penance will somehow purge him. Some twenty years later he remarries Susan, returning to her the five-guinea sale price, in the hope of making amends; and he would do the same on behalf of Lucetta, the woman he had compromised during the years of his penitence. He lies to Newson when the genial sailor returns Elizabeth-Jane, because he foolishly hopes to begin a new life with her, and this lie will destroy his best hope of redemption, her love and goodwill. He seeks out Farfrae with the news of Lucetta's fatal seizure in spite of having nearly killed Farfrae earlier in the same day; and he does this because he naively assumes that Farfrae can forgive or forget the incident and somehow trust him. Later, when Henchard returns to attend the wedding of Farfrae and Elizabeth-Jane – caged goldfinch in hand – he simply trusts that Elizabeth-Jane will forgive him for the lie that kept her from her natural father. In a crude, instinctive sort of way, Henchard is an optimist. His perverseness derives in part from his inability to extend to others the right to forgiveness or amendment that he bluntly and imperiously claims for himself. He is a pessimist when it comes to making amends to the protesting bakers and housewives of Casterbridge to whom he has sold faulty grain: 'It can't be done', he cries. And to Jopp, whom he first invites to apply for the position of bailiff then abruptly rejects, he says, 'It can't be helped'. And he cannot forgive poor Abel Whittle the error of coming late to work.

Henchard's optimism begins to collapse when he discovers in a letter written by the dead Susan that Elizabeth-Jane is not his but Newson's daughter and that his own daughter by Susan, *his* Elizabeth-Jane, is long dead. This is his first lesson in the irreparable: his true daughter is forever beyond him, gone for good, and there is no making amends to her. It is this realization that plunges him into the fetishistic belief that he is the victim of 'some sinister intelligence bent on punishing him' and leaves him in a state of mind that Hardy objectifies by sending him off on a gloomy ramble through the mists and ruins of the north-eastern precincts of Casterbridge (*MC*, ch. 19). There the ruins of a Franciscan priory and mill, the looming figure of the county gaol and the gallows, and the cottage of the hangman impress him deeply: a 'lugubrious harmony' exists between the locale and 'his domestic situation'. He will return to this same locale after his exposure by the furmity woman (ch. 31).[22] His scheme of 'reinstation' has been reduced to 'dust and ashes'; Elizabeth-Jane Newson can no more become the long-dead Elizabeth-Jane Henchard than Michael Henchard can become the man he was, the man innocent of selling wife and daughter, before Weydon-Priors. If, as advised by Farfrae, he had told Elizabeth-Jane the truth about his past upon her arrival in Casterbridge, she might now stand by him. But stubborn pride prevented him then, just as stubborn pride prevents him now from telling her that she is Newson's daughter. 'His daughter he had asserted her to be, and his daughter she should always think herself, no matter what hypocrisy it involved' (ch. 19). Henchard faces the evil of his past only when it explodes in his face (as when the furmity woman exposes him) or when it is too late to even attempt to remedy it (as when he returns to Weydon-Priors after Newson's return). Incapable of the self-knowledge that might lead to self-correction, he falls deeper and deeper into superstitious fear.

At times, Henchard's fear that he is the plaything of some impish god verges on the hope that the imp is an angel who watches over him. Hardy's interest in the possibility of a supernatural scheme of redemption, which produced the Baptism episode in *A Laodicean* and the Confirmation and Commination scenes in *Two on a Tower*, continues in *The Mayor*, though in altered form. From the beginning, Henchard, for all his waywardness, is portrayed as a sternly religious man of an Old Testament cast, one for whom something like sacrificial atonement is more congenial than the Christian belief in atonement through love and forgiveness. Thus the idea of 'an eye for an eye' that seems to lie behind his twenty-year vow of abstinence – one year of self-denial for each year of his life. He is 'as stern as the Lord upon the jovial Jews' with those of his workmen who drink. He shows little mercy to poor Abel Whittle, so much like him at Weydon-Priors in being but nineteen years old and 'flawed in his make'. Though a church-warden and therefore an observer of at least the externals of orthodoxy, he reverts quickly to a grim religion of fear and retribution when he learns that Elizabeth-Jane is not his daughter. Later, when heavy buying of grain (at the advice of a conjurer) brings him to bankruptcy, it becomes clear that his religion, like his fate, is the creation of his character: 'If Henchard had only waited long enough he might at least have avoided loss though he had not made a profit. But the momentum of his character knew no patience. At this turn of the scales he remained silent. The movements of his mind seemed to tend to the thought that some power was working against him' (ch. 27). That there is little room for forgiveness in this man of eerie misgivings about waxen images and unholy brews becomes clear when he forces the church choir to direct the comminatory Psalm 109 against Lucetta and Farfrae (ch. 33).

Hardy uses this devilish psalming in The Three Mariners to suggest that music might have brought Henchard to his senses. Like the Old Testament's Saul, Henchard is peculiarly susceptible to melody.[23] It was Farfrae's Orphean singing at The Three Mariners that first endeared him to Henchard ('How that fellow does draw me!'), and the Scotsman's whistling the same melody just moments before his struggle with Henchard in the loft nearly diverted Henchard from his murderous intent: 'Nothing moved Henchard like an old melody. He sank back. "No; I can't do it!"' (chs 8, 38). When Henchard is plunged in deepest gloom by the loss of Susan and Elizabeth-Jane, as well as of his wealth, his office and his good name, it is again suggested that music might restore him:

If he could have summoned music to his aid, his existence even now might have been borne; for with Henchard music was a regal power. The merest trumpet or organ tone was enough to move him, and high harmonies transsubstantiated him. But hard fate had ordained that he should be unable to call up this Divine Spirit in his need.   (ch. 42; cf. ch. 33)

A few hours later, we find that Henchard thinks himself in 'the actual presence of an appalling miracle' because he is prevented from drowning himself in Ten Hatches Weir by the chance appearance on the water of the effigy of him that had been displayed by the mob in the skimmity ride (ch. 41). Good luck brings it before him just in time to prevent his death. And unexpected good luck, like sudden bad luck, induces belief in the supernatural in this impressionable man. He questions Elizabeth-Jane with eager interest, but now in the hope that there is a kindly god at work on his behalf: 'Are miracles still worked, do ye think, Elizabeth? I am not a read man. I don't know so much as I could wish. I have tried to peruse and learn all my life; but the more I try to know the more ignorant I seem' (ch. 41).

But Elizabeth, the confirmed sceptic who earlier had declared to Farfrae that 'the romance of the sower is gone for good' (ch. 24), replies, 'I don't think there are any miracles nowadays'. Desperate for reassurance, Henchard persists: 'No interference in the case of desperate intentions, for instance? Well, perhaps not, in a direct way.' Henchard's tremulous hope that a benevolent spirit will intervene, like his terrible fear that a sinister spirit had intruded, has a simple explanation. Chance is the cause of both his good and his bad fortune, and he is more frequently its victim than most men because he lacks the patience, the humour, or the humility to accept its workings. If Henchard were patient in his dealings, if he were humble before the truth of his past, he might hold his future in his hands. But he is ruled by his moody, violent nature.

If Henchard cannot exorcise his demon, and if divine intervention is unlikely, then the redemption of this sinner might lie with his fellow men. As can be shown, luck sometimes places Hardy's flawed protagonists in the hands of the forgiving – of a Parson Maybold, a Gabriel Oak, or a John Loveday – but Henchard, like Tess and Jude after him, has no such luck, even though it seems for a time that in Farfrae and Elizabeth-Jane he has found his deliverers. Elizabeth-Jane, fearful lest he destroy himself after his failure in business, asks to live with him and to be allowed to care for him. He responds with all the eagerness of a drowning swimmer offered a life preserver:

> 'May you come to me?' he cried bitterly. 'Elizabeth, don't mock me! If you only would come!'
>
> 'I will,' said she.
>
> 'How will you forgive all my roughness in former days? You cannot!'
>
> 'I have forgotten it. Talk no more of that.'   (ch. 42)

Elizabeth does not promise forgiveness – she claims to have forgotten the past – because the idea of forgiveness, like the romance of the sower, is alien to a woman 'whose youth had seemed to teach that happiness was but the occasional episode in a general drama of pain' (ch. 45). In such a world, forgiveness is another word for resignation. One does not forgive the universe. Later, Elizabeth-Jane's refusal to forgive Henchard for keeping her identity from Newson will send him into exile and to his lonely death. This fact places Elizabeth-Jane, whom Hardy – somewhat unexpectedly – describes as a 'discerning silent witch' with an almost-vicious love of respectability and 'correctness of procedure' (chs 24, 30), alongside Knight, Yeobright and Clare as one whose inability to forgive damns a penitent. But for the moment she is Henchard's saviour: 'Then Henchard shaved for the first time during many days, and put on clean linen, and combed his hair; and was as a man resuscitated thenceforward' (ch. 41). The Biblical echoes in this sentence mock Henchard's optimistic state of mind. He thinks he sees a divine hand in the timely appearance of the effigy and in Elizabeth-Jane's goodwill: 'Who is such a reprobate as I! And yet it seems that even I be in Somebody's hand!' Elizabeth knows better, and her scepticism is shared by the narrator: 'The emotional conviction that he was in Somebody's hand began to die out of Henchard's breast as time slowly removed into distance the evening which had given that feeling birth. The apparition of Newson haunted him. He would surely return' (ch. 42).

Even more than Elizabeth-Jane, Donald Farfrae is cast as the agent of renewal and hope in the unregenerate world of the novel. He has the knowledge to restore almost completely the blighted wheat; his Orphean singing wakens the sympathies of the crusty denizens of The Three Mariners as well as a deeply buried brotherly feeling in Henchard; he works to rehabilitate Henchard after Henchard's fall from prosperity; he offers a second chance and a new life to Lucetta; and, eventually, he rescues Elizabeth-Jane from loneliness and neglect. But even Farfrae, for all his sympathy and intelligence, must submit to the fact that human powers for amelioration are, at best, minimal. 'Nature won't stand so much' as the complete restoration of the 'growed' wheat (ch. 7). His efforts to raise the fallen Henchard are thwarted by Henchard's incurable pride. Chance, working through a Jopp angered by Henchard, destroys the happiness that Lucetta has found in Farfrae's love. And Farfrae himself, in the course of the novel, degenerates from a joyful, open-handed, and compassionate man of business into an unfeeling, merely practical man of affairs. His early hopefulness gives way to a sober acceptance of things as they unchangeably are that stops just short of inhumaneness. Confronted with Henchard's self-obliterating last Will, the once resourceful and tender-hearted Scot can only echo the dead man's fatalism and ask, 'What are we to do?' (ch. 45). In *Jude the Obscure*, Phillotson, under the influence of Arabella Donn, will suffer a similar decline from altruism into egotism.

Nothing alters Henchard's fate – not supposed divine intervention, not music, not the kindly ministrations of step-daughter and friend, not self-knowledge – because nothing can alter 'that idiosyncracy . . . which had ruled his courses from the beginning and had mainly made him what he was' (ch. 42).

> Externally there was nothing to hinder his making another start on the upward slope and by his new lights achieving higher things than his soul in its half-formed state had been able to accomplish. But the ingenious machinery contrived by the Gods for reducing human possibilities of amelioration to a minimum – which arranges that wisdom to do shall come *pari passu* with the departure of zest for doing – stood in the way of all that. (ch. 44)

In the face of an irremediable defect in things 'contrived by the Gods', wise men see that, in the words of Elizabeth-Jane, 'there's no altering – so it must be' (ch. 45).

A discussion of the relation of Henchard's character to his fate could end here, with Henchard's obliteration, his desire 'that no man remember me' (ibid.). Whether one views him as 'a man guilty of having violated a moral order who brings upon himself a retribution for his crime' or as an 'essentially good man . . . destroyed by the chance forces of a morally indifferent world', it is difficult not to feel – with Elizabeth-Jane, with Farfrae and with the novel's narrator – that there is no altering his fate.[24] In fact, however, Hardy quietly qualified this view of the matter in the closing pages of the novel. Like Hardy the architect torn between aesthetic and memorial duties, Hardy the novelist was 'pulled in two directions – in one by [a] wish to hand on or to modify the abstract form, in the other by [a] reverence for the antiquity of the embodiment'. He was determined, it seems, to honour both impulses, to show the relentless working of time-as-decay and to preserve the uniqueness of the individual caught up in the deteriorative process. He manages this in the last chapter of the novel through the simple eloquence of Abel Whittle, in whose language Hardy found it possible to exhibit a regenerative power he had previously denied both men and gods, the regenerative power of poetic utterance. Though a victim like the others of Henchard's violent temper, Whittle has forgiven his tormentor and succours him when others reject and shun him. His eloquence, like Marty South's at the end of *The Woodlanders*, is the eloquence of a generous and forgiving love.

> Yes, ma'am, he's gone! . . . I seen en go down street on the day of your worshipful's wedding to the lady at your side, and I thought he looked low and faltering. And I followed en over Grey's Bridge, and he turned and seed me, and said, 'You go back!' But I followed, and he turned again, and said, 'Do you hear, sir? Go back!' But I zeed that he was low, and I followed on still. Then a' said, 'Whittle, what do ye follow me for when I've told ye to go back all these times!' And I said, 'Because, sir, I see things be bad with 'ee, and ye wer kind-like to mother if ye were rough to me, and I would fain be kind-like to you.' Then he walked on, and I followed; and he never complained at me no more. We walked on like that all night; and in the blue o' the morning, when 'twas hardly day, I looked ahead o' me, and I zeed that he wambled, and could hardly drag along. By that time we had got past here, but I had seen that this house was empty as I went by, and I got him to come back; and I took down the boards from the windows, and helped him inside. 'What Whittle,' he said, 'and can ye really be such a poor fond fool as to care for such a wretch as I!'
>
> (ch. 45)

Only a short time before, when 'like a dark ruin' he had appeared before Elizabeth-Jane to beg forgiveness and had been rejected, Henchard seemed beyond reclaim. The dark deeds of his past, the fruits of his violent nature, had returned to haunt him. But here a good deed out of the past – his having provided coals for Whittle's mother during a cold winter – has returned to console him. Whittle has forgiven Henchard's public humiliation of him, and his forgiveness and sympathy, because conveyed in the language of poetry, effect forgiveness and sympathy in the minds of Elizabeth-Jane, Farfrae and the reader. Henchard, like some ruinous ancient edifice, has been pulled down; but now he is transformed, preserved, raised up as it were by the poetry – the harmonious sound – of Whittle's utterance.[25] The conflict inherent in an art that is both aesthetic and memorial in its aim is reconciled in language that exhibits the beauty of the grim truth that decay is king. But this may be saying too much, for where the simple Whittle can forgive Henchard, the more reflective pair to whom he speaks can only accept Henchard's fate. The reader is left suspended between two responses to the tragedy of Michael Henchard: Whittle's forgiving love, and Elizabeth-Jane's fatalistic 'there's no altering – so it must be'.

TESS VERSUS JUDE

This division between a 'care-taking' and an 'artist' instinct in Hardy, between a desire to preserve and regenerate and an urge to show the unregenerateness of things, assumed monumental proportions both in and between *Tess of the d'Urbervilles* (1891) and *Jude the Obscure* (1895), sibling novels in which Hardy brought to a vigorously dialectical end (in the fiction) his deep concern with the question of regeneration. That *Tess* and *Jude* stand apart from the earlier novels in setting, theme, and tone has long been noted; but their striking interrelationships have for the most part been ignored.[26] Perhaps the best way to approach them in their connectedness is to imagine oneself studying an unusual kind of diptych, a picture painted or engraved on two hinged tablets between which certain shared elements have been reversed. Suppose that men do in the second (the right) half what women do in the first; that a lush natural setting on the left is countered by an arid urban setting on the right; that the bright greens, reds and other basic colours of the first contend with greys and washes in the second; that the first is rendered in powerful, flowing strokes, the second with an almost intrusive geometric concern for line, balance and antithesis. I offer this admittedly crude analogy because *Tess* and *Jude*, as much as *The Return*, *The Woodlanders* and *Under the Greenwood Tree*, and even more than *The Mayor* and the three novels that precede it, demand to be read together, side by side. In *The Mayor* and its three predecessors Hardy probed different views of restoration. In the novels of return, he explored different possible results of the attempt to turn back the personal or the cultural past. In *Tess* and *Jude* he used the story of seduction (of a woman and of a man, respectively) to give two radically different answers to the question of regeneration. In *Tess* he exhibited the regenerative power of nature for a tragic life lived in harmony with nature. In

Jude he in a sense rewrote *Tess* to show both the destructiveness of
nature and the absurdity of tragic values. *Jude* proceeds out of *Tess*
by imitating its structure while rejecting its tragic and heroic
consolations.

D. H. Lawrence was perhaps the first reader to note the terms of
the dialogue between *Tess* and *Jude* when he wrote as follows: '*Jude*
is only *Tess* turned round about. Instead of the heroine containing
the two principles, male and female, at strife within her one being, it
is Jude who contains them both, whilst the two women with him
take the place of the two men to Tess. Arabella is Alec d'Urberville,
Sue is Angel Clare. These represent the same pair of principles'.[27]
Lawrence's identification of Tess with Jude, Alec with Arabella,
and Angel with Sue suggests an almost mechanical repetition of
narrative elements between the two novels. But nothing could be
further from the truth. Albert Guerard could have been speaking of
Jude when he said that though 'a novel may be in direct reaction
against the preceding one . . . it nearly always proceeds out of it in
some discernible way – especially since a true novelist can hardly
exhaust his intentions in a single book'.[28] This is a useful idea with
which to approach *Tess* and *Jude*, because only in these two novels,
as Guerard goes on to say, did Hardy face 'the characteristic
nightmares of the late Victorian Age: the problem of ethics without
dogma and the problem of the restless and isolated modern ego'.
More specifically, in *Tess* and then again in *Jude* Hardy explored
the minimal opportunities for regeneration in a world that Tess calls
a 'blighted' star (*TD*, 1, ch. 4) and that Jude thinks of as a flawed
'terrestrial scheme' (*JO*, 1, ch. 2). But *Jude* is not merely a male *Tess*.

In *Tess* Hardy showed the regenerative power of tragic
experience, the moral and spiritual triumph of Tess in death, the
enlargement of her limited powers by association of them with the
vast powers of nature. Tess's ruin is not fatal because she sins
without intending to sin and because she is, finally, one with nature
and therefore not subject to a merely social morality. As Hardy
explained in his 1892 Preface to *Tess*, Tess's story was one 'wherein
the great campaign of the heroine begins after an event in her
experience which has usually been treated as fatal to her part of
protagonist, or at least as the virtual ending of her enterprises and
hopes (*TD*, p. xvii). Tess's death is not the end, we feel, because she
has struggled valiantly to live; and because nature, represented as
surely in the pagan monuments at Stonehenge and the prospective
union of Angel and Liza-Lu as in the 'sporting' of the President of

the Immortals, will endure and prevail. In striking contrast, *Jude*, as Hardy said in his Preface of 1895 to that novel, is an attempt to depict 'the fret and the fever, derision and disaster, that may press in the wake of the strongest passion known to humanity; to tell, without a mincing of words, of a deadly war waged between flesh and spirit; and to point the tragedy of unfulfilled aims' (*JO*, p. viii). If Hardy seems more contemptuous of Arabella than of her counterpart, Alec, it is not just because, as Lawrence slyly remarked, Hardy 'is something of an Angel Clare'. All the people of *Jude* suffer more than their counterparts in *Tess*. Critics from Edmund Gosse to Michael Millgate have complained about an element of gratuitous suffering in *Jude*. But the suffering in *Jude* is not gratuitous if we see *Jude* as being by design a repudiation of the severe but ultimately hopeful vision of *Tess*.[29]

Tess is 'a pure woman', Jude a tainted man with 'the taint of grossness always dragging him down'.[30] Angel is a fastidious fool but is at least capable of regaining his senses; Sue is epicene, psychopathic, cruel to herself, to her lovers and to her children. Alec is a rake, Arabella a monster. Tess is allowed to punish her seducer and to reunite, if only briefly, with her beloved Angel; Jude is ever the victim. The victory of Tess's will to love and live becomes in *Jude* the victory of Arabella's will to power. Tess 'suffers her tragedy, Jude deliberately courts his'.[31] As Lascelles Abercrombie observed some years ago, in *Tess* Hardy gives us the 'general tragedy, the tragic situation of which all others are specializations', and in *Jude* 'the special case of this essential tragedy':

> [Tess is punished for] the sin of personal existence; but Jude, with the more rebellious consciousness of masculine nature, adds to this the further sin of aspiration – he being thus typical of his sex, as Tess is of hers. . . . Without absurdly forcing sexual differences, it seems justifiable to take these two novels as giving a typically feminine and a typically masculine embodiment to the same tragic conflict of personal against impersonal.[32]

Abercrombie's awareness of Hardy's emphasis on sexual differences is correct but incomplete. He fails to mention that Hardy combined his shift from a female to a male protagonist with a shift from a male to a female antagonist. Hardy did this, it seems, in the interest of completeness, and perhaps out of a certain masculine defensiveness. He wished to show that lads fall as easily as maids, that women are as predatory as men in matters of sex. 'It has never struck me', he wrote in 1894, 'that the spider is invariably male and the fly invariable female'.[33] Even more important, he wished to show that, though the female and general tragedy is in some ways remediable, the male tragedy, the tragedy of blocked aspiration, is beyond remedy. Hardy repeated in *Jude* the assault on innocence in *Tess* because he found the seduction of a maid too crude a vehicle for the particular kind of tragic loss he wished to depict. Whatever is lost to physical assault seems to differ in his view from what is lost to that subtler assailant, enticement into sexual activity. It is one thing, he seems to say, for a maid to be ravished and yet to be able to plead innocence of intention; it is quite another for a lad who wished never to grow up to be enticed into sexual aggression, and thus to be guilty in act *and* intention. Seduction of a male is here a metaphor for self-willed corruption, better described as self-rape; it carries with it all the sneaking dubieties of suicide, which happens to be an inherited tendency of Jude Fawley. Rape is violent intrusion, a kind of murder; enticement requires self-violation and is therefore akin to suicide. A man, Hardy seems to suggest, must always be a willing accomplice to his sexual ruin. Thus *Jude* is something more than *Tess* 'turned round about' in a merely mechanical way; but we cannot ignore the deep imprint of *Tess* on *Jude*, which was in gestation while *Tess* was being written and was completed while the reviews of *Tess* were jangling in Hardy's sensitive ears. A brief outline will suggest some of the basic structural relationships (see the chart on p. 203).

Several things may be noted by way of beginning. First, there are some basic structural correspondences. *Tess* I and II corresponds to *Jude* I, *Tess* III to *Jude* II, *Tess* IV to *Jude* III, *Tess* V to *Jude* IV, V and VI. There is no counterpart to *Tess* VI and VII in *Jude*, for *Tess* ends with its heroine's fulfilment in death, *Jude* with its hero's annihilation by death. Second, Hardy arranged the story of Tess's 'campaign' in seven 'phases', each phase corresponding to a stage in Tess's development from an innocent maid to a mature woman of tragic understanding. He arranged Jude's story in six 'parts' and connected each part with a place – Marygreen, Christminster, Melchester, Shaston, Aldbrickham and Stoke-Barehills, and Christminster again. This contrast between a linear, phasal and developmental movement in *Tess* and a spatial, cyclical pattern in *Jude* is of basic importance; it reveals that Hardy thought of Tess as a

	Tess		*Jude*
Phase I	The Maiden (chs 1–11) [At Marlott][34]	Part I	At Marygreen (chs 1–11) [The Innocent and Innocent No More][34]
Phase II	Maiden No More (chs 12–15) [At Trantridge]		
Phase III	The Rally (chs 16–24) [At Talbothays]	Part II	At Christminster (chs 1–7) [The Rally]
Phase IV	The Consequence (chs 25–34) [At Flintcomb]	Part III	At Melchester (chs 1–10) [The Consequence]
Phase V	The Woman Pays (chs 35–44) [At Flintcomb and Elsewhere]	Part IV	At Shaston (chs 1–6) [The Man Pays]
		Part V	At Aldbrickham and Elsewhere (chs 1–8) [. . . and Pays]
		Part VI	At Christminster Again (chs 1–11) [. . . and Pays]
Phase VI	The Convert (chs 45–52) [At Flintcomb and Elsewhere]		
Phase VII	Fulfilment (chs 53–9) [At Stonehenge]		

figure developing toward fulfilment through adversity, but of Jude as a man entrapped and in decline (spiralling down) because always within the closed circle of his irremediable defects. The phases of Tess's career are, of course, also associated with places – Marlott, Trantridge, Talbothays, Flintcomb, Sandbourne, Stonehenge, Wintoncester – but they are made to represent stages in her growth toward understanding and acceptance. They are not, as in *Jude*, emblems of an environment that resists or mocks moral growth. If Jude moves in a descending spiral, Tess moves in an ascending one. Tess is somehow as untouched by the Slopes, Sandbourne, Flintcomb and Wintoncester as she was by Alec. Jude, the would-be restorer of rotting stone edifices, is never untainted.

Finally, structural differences are reinforced by fundamental differences between the settings of the two novels. *Tess* is a rural novel, *Jude* an urban one. Nature imagery marks Tess's progress from Marlott to Stonehenge; architectural images dot Jude's decline from Marygreen to Christminster. Hardy used architecture in *Tess* to symbolize the death of traditional medieval culture and the stubborn vitality of garish, vulgar modern culture. The Slopes, the estate of the spurious Stoke-d'Urbervilles, is a recently-built 'crimson brick lodge' set behind 'acres of glass-houses' (*TD*, I, ch. 5). Tess is hanged at Wintoncester in an 'ugly flat-topped octagonal tower' atop 'a large red-brick building' (VII, ch. 59). Her ancestral tomb, like the d'Urberville family itself, is in a state of advanced decay. But she, of course, is at home in neither these medieval nor these modern edifices; her true home, to which she finally returns, is among the seemingly eternal prehistoric stone pillars of Stonehenge on Salisbury Plain – 'a very Temple of the Winds', 'a forest of monoliths' older than the centuries, older than the d'Urbervilles (VII, ch. 58).

The vulgarity and decadence of Jude's world is conveyed not just by the rotten buildings of Christminster, Melchester and Shaston, and the 'new red brick suburb' of Stoke-Barehills, but also and even more by the ruthless means of restoration undertaken in ancient places such as Shaston and Marygreen. For example, the 'original church' in Jude's native Marygreen has been pulled down and 'either cracked up into heaps of road metal . . . or utilized as pig-sty walls, garden seats, guard-stones to fences, and rockeries in the flower-beds of the neighbourhood' (*JO*, I, ch. 1). Neither its original design nor its old associations have been retained in the building put in its place:

> A tall new building of modern Gothic design, unfamiliar to English eyes, had been erected on a new piece of ground by a certain obliterator of historic records who had run down from London and back in a day. The site whereon so long had stood the ancient temple to the Christian divinities was not even recorded on the green and level grassplot that had immemorially been the churchyard, the obliterated graves being commemorated by eighteenpenny cast-iron crosses warranted to last five years. (ibid.)

In *Jude*, as in *The Mayor*, the state of architectural affairs is a measure of the state of human affairs. And not the least of Jude's several follies is that he is an uncritical participant in the restoration of old buildings. His heart goes out to the rotting buildings of Christminster: 'The condition of several moved him as he would have been moved by maimed sentient beings. They were wounded, broken, sloughing off their outer shape in the deadly struggle against years, weather, and man' (II, ch. 2). Tess extends a similar sympathy to the dead and wounded game birds she finds in the course of her flight from Angel (*TD*, V, ch. 42), but, where she wrings the necks of the wounded and takes from their suffering and deaths a new determination to go on with her life, Jude fantasizes about the possibility of restoring the 'wounded, broken' buildings of Christminster. He thinks the workyard of the stonemason who employs him 'a little centre of regeneration' when it is in fact, as Hardy points out, only a place of 'copying, patching, and imitating'. Sue will have to inform Jude that the railway station has replaced the cathedral at the centre of civilized life; he is slow to see that 'medievalism was as dead as a fern-leaf in a lump of coal; that other developments were shaping the world around him' (*JO*, II, ch. 2). With these several basic differences in mind, we can compare the two novels in more detail.

In the opening segments of both novels an innocent is entrapped and ruined, Tess by Alec (and by the folly of her parents), Jude by Arabella. Jude differs from Tess in being orphaned, though he, like she, has inherited a family curse. The ominous legend of the d'Urberville coach and the supposed cruelty of Tess's noble ancestors are like the antipathy to marriage of Jude's father and paternal aunt (Sue's mother), an antipathy that years before resulted in the theft of a child and the execution of one member of the Fawley family. In short, both Tess and Jude, though free from actual sin when they meet their seducers, are burdened with inherited defects. Tess has inherited a 'slight incautiousness of character' that reveals itself in her pride and her quick temper, as well as in her sensuality (*TD*, II, ch. 14). Jude, in spite of his literary and religious interests, has strong appetites and suicidal inclinations. But Tess, as Hardy's sub-title reminds us, is 'a pure woman'. Jude is endowed with no comparable redeeming quality.

Phase II of *Tess* ('Maiden No More') has its counterpart not in the Part II of *Jude* ('At Christminster') but in *Jude* I, for Jude is both an innocent and an 'innocent no more' at Marygreen. Troutham's beating, his aunt's scoldings, and Vilbert's deception mark him as a victim even before Arabella dupes him into believing that she carries his child and that he must therefore marry her. Marriage to Arabella is his ruin not just because it destroys his plan to enter one of the colleges of Christminster but also because it plunges him into sensuality. We should note that Jude's ruin is brought about not by

an urban intruder on the countryside like Alec d'Urberville, but by
a country girl with strong animal instincts; in *Jude*, as not in *Tess*,
country ways are as vicious as urban ones. For the equivalent of *Tess*
II, in which Tess makes the agonizing return to Marlott, we must
look ahead in *Jude* to Parts V and VI, where Father Time, Jude's son
by Arabella, returns from Australia, lives for a time with Jude and
Sue, then hangs Jude's children by Sue and hangs himself along
with them. The irredeemable cruelty of Jude's world is conveyed
best in the fact that Father Time, unlike Tess's Baby Sorrow, had
not been baptized, because, as he himself explains, to be baptized is
to be put to the expense of a Christian burial. Tess's christening of
her child, like her acting the saviour of her family by becoming
Alec's mistress, is a heroic act suggestive of her still vital instinct to
seek human means of remedy in a world whose divine redeemer has
abandoned it. But even so feeble and futile a redemptive gesture as
this is beyond Jude, whose initial hopefulness gradually crumbles
before his growing conviction that a law of cruelty pervades human
and non-human nature. And Jude's deterioration is physical as well
as spiritual. He is as sickly as Tess is robust.

Jude II ('At Christminster') corresponds closely to *Tess* III ('The
Rally'), for Christminster is, potentially at least, Jude's Talbothays,
a place of possible recovery from his ruinous marriage to Arabella.
But the lush, fecund nature of Talbothays finds no corollary in the
corrupt and decadent culture of Christminster. Where Talbothays
is the vital setting and symbol of Tess's resurgence through work,
companionship and love (here she meets Angel), Christminster is
the moribund setting and symbol of all that opposes Jude's efforts to
rise in the world and to fulfil his dreams. This of course includes Sue,
whom he first meets in the city of learning. Jude goes to
Christminster to fulfil his boyhood dream of becoming a learned
man, a dream sullied by contact with Arabella and soon to be
shattered by his troubled devotion to Sue. Tess goes to Talbothays
in response to a strong, unconscious will to live; there she meets
Angel, and, though he will betray her trust, she at least conceives a
hope of union with a man whose love *can* confirm her in what she
knows is her essential purity. This contrast between Tess and Jude is
crucial, for it reveals how closely Hardy associated Tess, though not
Jude, with an enduring, perennial process in which growth toward
fulfilment could occur:

Almost at a leap Tess thus changed from simple girl to complex woman. Symbols of reflectiveness passed into her face, and a note of tragedy at times into her voice. Her eyes grew larger and more eloquent. She became what would have been called a fine creature; her aspect was fair and arresting; her soul that of a woman whom the turbulent experiences of the past year or two had quite failed to demoralize.   (II, ch. 15)

After the burial of her child, named Baby Sorrow, Tess will leave Marlott with 'the pulse of hopeful life within her', seeking to obliterate the past by going to a place where she is not known. She wonders about restoration: 'Was once lost always lost really true of chastity? she would ask herself. She might prove it false if she could veil bygones. The recuperative power which pervaded organic nature was surely not denied to maidenhood alone' (ibid.). She undergoes a natural transsubstantiation: the 'stir of germination' on a fine spring day 'moved her, as it moved the wild animals, and made her passionate to go' (ibid.). It was unexpended youth, surging up anew after a temporary check, and bringing with it hope and the invincible instinct for self-delight:

> The irresistible, universal, automatic tendency to find sweet pleasure somewhere, which pervades all life, from the meanest to the highest, had at length mastered Tess. Being even now only a young woman of twenty, one who mentally and sentimentally had not finished growing, it was impossible that any event should have left upon her an impression that was not in time capable of transmutation.   (II, ch. 16)[35]

In sharp contrast to this bright hopefulness at the beginning of Tess's 'Rally', is the gloomy fact that Jude's decision to go to Christminster is preceded by his attempt to kill himself. He tries, but fails, to plunge himself through the ice of a pond at Marygreen. He is puzzled by his failure.

> It was curious, he thought. What was he reserved for? He supposed he was not a sufficiently dignified person for suicide. Peaceful death abhorred him as a subject, and would not take him. What could he do of a lower kind than self-extermination; what was there less noble, more in keeping with his present degraded position? He could get drunk. Of course that was it; he

had forgotten. Drinking was the regular, stereotyped resource of
the despairing worthless.   (*JO*, I, ch. 11)

Jude's turn back to his boyhood dream of study at Christminster is
dictated not by the strength of instinctive life (in *Jude*, that strength
is Arabella's), but by nostalgia, for Hardy an attractive but usually
treacherous state of memory:

> On the evening following . . . [Arabella's] emigration, . . . he
> came out of doors after supper, and strolled in the star-light along
> the too-familiar road towards the upland whereon had been
> experienced the chief emotions of his life. It seemed to be his own
> again. He could not realize himself. On the old track he seemed to
> be a boy still, hardly a day older than when he had stood
> dreaming at the top of that hill, inwardly fired for the first time
> with ardours, for Christminster and scholarship. 'Yet I am a
> man,' he said. 'I have a wife. More, I have arrived at the still riper
> stage of having disagreed with her, disliked her, had a scuffle with
> her, and parted from her.' He remembered then that he was
> standing not far from the spot at which the parting between his
> mother and his father was said to have occurred.   (I, ch. 11)

His recognition that he has changed is not complete because it is not
sealed with the knowledge that the past is irretrievable. It is
countered and weakened by his recalling a milestone on which he
had long ago – 'in the first week of his apprenticeship, before he had
been diverted from his purpose by an unsuitable woman' – carved
his dream. He searches and finds the stone, and the sight of his old
words, 'Thither J. F.', concealed by grass and nettles but
'unimpaired', strikes in his soul a fine Virgilian sentiment, 'a spark
of the old fire':

> Surely his plan should be to move onward through good and ill –
> to avoid morbid sorrow even though he did see ugliness in the
> world. *Bene agere et laetari* – to do good cheerfully – which he had
> heard to be the philosophy of one Spinoza, might be his own even
> now. He might battle with his evil star, and follow out his original
> intention.   (I, ch. 11)

Driven toward self-destruction (as Tess is driven toward self-
renewal), Jude succumbs to one of the worst follies in Hardy's

world: he attempts to regain time-past, to recover the glory and the gleam, 'to follow out his original intention'. This is yet another version of the error of Henry Knight, of Grace Melbury, of Clym Yeobright, and, in a different way, of Michael Henchard, who tries to make a second beginning, as hopelessly as Jude at this point, with the tools of his trade on his back and a disastrous first marriage behind him. It is also, of course, the error of Angel Clare, who seeks through marriage with Tess to recover a purity he has forever lost. But compare to Jude Tess upon her return to Blakemore Vale after her fall at Trantridge. She does not see in Blakemore the spectre of a lost childhood and a glorious innocence that she must recover at all costs. She finds her native vale 'terribly beautiful', for since she had last seen it 'she had learnt that the serpent hisses where the sweet birds sing, and her views of life had been totally changed by the lesson. Verily another girl than the simple one she had been at home was she who, bowed by thought, stood still here, and turned to look behind her. She could not bear to look forward into the vale' (*TD*, II, ch. 12). She looks instead behind her, towards Trantridge and the sad events of the more recent past. She knows that her future must take its shape from the events at Trantridge; she refuses to delude herself by putting before herself the memories of Blakemore and her innocence. The beauty and innocence of Blakemore have been made terrible by the experiences at Trantridge; but though she wishes she had never been born, she cannot help but go on living. Tess rejects nostalgia; she does not, like Jude, turn back to an original intention. And it is precisely her unconscious identification with nature's regenerative ongoingness that causes her to reject also, in anger and scorn, the hell-fire belief of the painter of religious texts whom she soon meets – 'a hideous defacement', Hardy calls it, 'the last grotesque phase of a [redemptive] creed which had served mankind well in its time' (ibid.). Overflowing with the will to live, and firm in her knowledge that she sinned without intending to sin, Tess can say 'pooh' to the words 'THY, DAMNATION, SLUMBERETH, NOT.' Tess knows her mind, and her worth. At a comparable moment in his career, Jude, engulfed by nostalgia, falls asleep at the end of his first day at Christminster with Bishop Ken's 'familiar rhyme, endeared to him from earliest childhood', on his lips: 'Teach me to live, that I may dread / The grave as little as my bed' (*JO*, II, ch. 1).[36] Belief in the Resurrection is one aspect of Jude's disabling nostalgia.

Deprived, as Tess is not, of innate recuperative powers like nature's, Jude becomes the victim of the destructive powers of nature – that is, of the deathward tendency in things that is the necessary complement to the life-impulse that sustains Tess. Or better, in *Jude*, as noted above, the dominating will to live embodied in a Tess is replaced with a dominating will to destroy or control embodied in Arabella; and Jude is its ready victim. As a stonemason, as a would-be scholar and clergyman, and as a man of tender sympathies toward man and beast, Jude betrays a strong temperamental belief in redemption and renewal. This is the reason for the utter failure of all his efforts, and it is revealed early, in the contrast shown between his and Arabella's view of their untimely marriage. Jude wishes things had not gone so far, but he believes 'it is never too late to mend' (i, ch. 9). Arabella, upon informing Jude several months after the marriage that she is not pregnant (she believes) after all, is more realistic: 'Don't take on, dear. What's done can't be undone' (i, ch. 9). Tess's saving wisdom, her understanding of the pastness of the past, is here Arabella's cunning, and with predictably different results. Arabella not only understands the folly of belief in amendment (note how quickly her new-found religion gives way, in Part iv, to renewed ardour for Jude), she also knows how to use the pastness of the past to further her own ends. Tess, like Arabella in this, moves forward by setting the past behind her; Jude attempts to move forward by retaining his 'original intention'. And his virulent nostalgia, his fatal inability to adjust his original wish to his dream-shattering later experiences, is precisely what makes the restoration of old buildings attractive to him. When he finally sees the folly of looking backward, it will be too late, for by that time his children will be strangled, his ambitions smashed, and his once-sceptical, once-scintillating Sue a frightened, morbidly pious wreck of a woman.

Jude meets Sue at Chrisminster, as Tess meets Angel at Talbothays. Though Angel and Tess are not cousins, as is the case with Jude and Sue, the unions of both couples are foreshadowed – Jude's with Sue in the interest he shows in their aunt's picture of her in the cottage at Marygreen, Tess's with Angel in their brief encounter during the May dance at Marlott. Both Angel and Sue are fastidious, repressed personalities, and both are highly critical of Christianity. Angel cannot subscribe to 'an untenable redemptive theolatry' centred upon the Resurrection (*TD*, iii, ch. 18). Sue, whose favourite poet is Swinburne, fancies herself a neo-pagan and rejects Christian asceticism. When pressed, however, both Angel and Sue reveal a hidden puritanism. Angel cannot forgive Tess's ruin, although he himself had suffered a similar lapse. Sue is uneasy with Jude's previous marriage and downright distressed by his eager sexuality. In spite of her disdain for Christian doctrine, she cannot rid herself of the belief that Arabella's child killing her children is a sign of God's displeasure with her unconventional marriage to Jude. Her return to Phillotson's bed travesties the idea of penance as a prelude to amendment because it offers masochistic self-sacrifice instead of prayer or devotion of another kind as a means of satisfaction.

The difference between Angel and Sue – like the difference between Alec and Arabella – is the difference between pasteboard and reality. Almost all the secondary characters of *Jude* have a depth and complexity that their counterparts in *Tess* lack. Alongside Sue, Angel is little more than a foil to Alec, and Alec little more than the seducer of melodrama. Angel is often no more than a prig, but Sue, as Hardy himself explained in a letter of November 1895, was something more complicated – a study in 'abnormalism':

> There is nothing perverted or depraved in Sue's nature. The abnormalism consists in disproportion, not in inversion, her sexual instinct being healthy as far as it goes, but unusually weak and fastidious. . . . One point illustrating this I could not dwell upon: that though she has children, her intimacies with Jude have never been more than occasional, even when they were living together (I mention that they occupy separate rooms, except towards the end), and one of her reasons for fearing the marriage ceremony is that she fears it would be breaking faith with Jude to withhold herself at pleasure, or altogether, after it; though while uncontracted she feels at liberty to yield herself as seldom as she chooses. This has tended to keep his passion as hot at the end as at the beginning, and helps to break his heart. (*Life*, p. 273)

As Hardy guardedly suggests here, Sue is helplessly and self-gratifyingly cruel in her connections with men. Like Fancy Day and Bathsheba Everdene before her, she derives a degree of pleasure from the pain she is compelled to inflict on men. What Hardy calls the 'disproportion' in her sexual instinct makes her a sadistic sexual tease. For her sexual pleasure derives in part from observing the distress in men from whom she withholds herself while at the same time living with them in relative intimacy. Thus her fifteen months of unviolated cohabitation with a Christminster undergraduate (ending in his death). Thus her invitation to Jude, whom she knows to be passionately in love with her, first to play the part of groom in a mock wedding ceremony at Melchester, then to give her away to Phillotson at the ceremony itself. The pleasure she derives from Jude's pain is at least as great as her love for Phillotson, whom she soon subjects, not altogether willingly, to similar torments. The horrible logic of her self-torturing return to Phillotson grows from this. Only sexual intimacy with a man she despises can purge her of the sexual contact she so loathes.

Sue's 'abnormalism' explains, I think, the most sensational episode of the novel and the cruellest act of her tormented life, her half-conscious encouragement of Father Time's murderous remedy for the family's poverty. Her detached, self-pitying statements to him in the garret at Christminster where Jude had left them in temporary lodgings plunge the already morbid child into despair and turn him into a murderer and a suicide. Thoroughly frightened by Jude's failure to find lodgings for the family, Father Time (whom Sue now calls 'Judie') turns to Sue for reassurance, only to find evasiveness and rejection:

> 'Mother, *what* shall we do to-morrow!'
> 'I don't know!' said Sue despondently. 'I am afraid this will trouble your father.' . . .
> 'Can I do anything?'
> 'No! All is trouble, adversity, and suffering!'
> 'Father went away to give us children room, didn't he?'
> 'Partly.'
> 'It would be better to be out o' the world than in it, wouldn't it!'
> 'It would almost, dear.'
> ' 'Tis because of us children, too, isn't it, that you can't get a good lodging?'
> 'Well – people do object to children sometimes.'

Sue speaks for herself, not for rentors of lodgings, when she says this to the fearful boy. The troubled Father Time has led her to confess her own deepest aversion.

'Then if children make so much trouble, why do people have 'em?'

'O – because it is a law of nature.'

'But we don't ask to be born!'

'No indeed.' . . . .

'I wish I hadn't been born!'

'You couldn't help it, my dear.'

'I think that whenever children be born that are not wanted they should be killed directly, before their souls come to them, and not allowed to grow big and walk about.' (*JO*, vi, ch. 2)

Sue neither reproves nor discourages the boy's murderous remedy for unwelcome births; she allows him to entertain it because it expresses both her self-pitying sense of herself as a victim of nature and her wish to be rid of her children. This self-indulgence leads to her decision to inform 'Judie' that another child is soon to be born, a fact that drives the boy to tearful and bitter reproaches ('How ever could you, mother, be so wicked and cruel as this . . . .'). This reproach moves Sue to the most bizarre gesture of her bizarre career: she begs the boy to forgive her for the pregnancy. He, understandably, refuses. And to his ominous 'if we children was gone there'd be no trouble at all!' she replies, 'Don't think that, dear. . . . But go to sleep!' With that double-edged dismissal of a morbid child, Sue goes off elsewhere early next morning (without waking Father Time) to breakfast with Jude. Upon returning she finds her hanged innocents and their dead executioner and is thrown into agony by the 'awful conviction that her discourse with the boy had been the main cause of the tragedy' (ibid.).

Jude's explanation for Father Time's act reflects his nostalgia for a better past: it is, he says, an expression of 'the coming universal wish not to live'. Sue, quite rightly, sets aside such sentimentality: 'It was I who incited him really, though I didn't know I was doing it!' She almost sees here that her own yearning for innocence has destroyed innocence. She does see that an unconscious destructive force is at work in her, and this insight is a turning point for her. She now discards the view of nature that had guided her unconventional life up to this point: 'that it was Nature's intention . . . that we should be joyful in what instincts she afforded us' (ibid.). The name 'Bridehead', a combination perhaps of 'Bride', one who willingly relinquishes sexual innocence, and 'maidenhead', meaning hymen or virgin, suggests Sue's essential nature. She is the virgin bride and therefore, even more than Jude, the victim of longing for an innocence and purity she cannot retrieve. She bitterly resents the loss of maidenhood (and maidenhead) to Jude; and her children, the products and reminders of her irrecoverable loss, must suffer for it. What a departure all of this is from the career of Angel Clare, Sue's counterpart in *Tess*, who, after abandoning Tess to travel and work in Brazil, learns the folly of his ways from a wise fellow-traveller and returns to England eager (even if too late) to make amends to Tess. There is in *Tess* no corruption of a child, no massacre of innocents. There is in *Tess* no challenge to nature's will to joy, and no equivalent to Sue's return to a mate who disgusts her. But then there is no counterpart to Phillotson in *Tess*.

Phillotson represents a most striking and most significant departure from the pattern of *Tess*. Phillotson, one might say, begins as the Parson Tringham of *Jude* – that is, as the sower of a fatal seed of discontent in a naive mind. But Phillotson is much more than a patronizing antiquarian who by informing a tipsy man of his illustrious past sets in motion the events that lead to the ruin of a pure maid. Phillotson wakens Jude's dream of education and ordination by example as well as by words; he is Jude's model as well as his mentor. He is also a father-substitute who later becomes a sexual rival. Where Tringham dies quietly off-stage, Phillotson returns to the centre of the narrative when Jude seeks him out at Christminster and introduces him to Sue. From this point on, Phillotson's relationship with Sue parallels Arabella's connection with Jude; and by the end of the novel Phillotson's position as the husband of a chastened, self-torturing Sue corresponds with disturbing closeness to Arabella's position as the wife of subdued and dying Jude. Phillotson's imitation of Arabella is perhaps the most devastating irony of the novel.

This is so because Phillotson is an almost wholly sympathetic character, a moral and generous man. Like Jude he seeks education and fails, like Jude he marries Sue and fails, like Jude he opposes conventional morality and fails. When learning and love elude him, he somehow manages to preserve his compassion. He refuses to blame Sue or to seek amends from her, and with heroic self-denial he grants her request for freedom and even forgives her the ruin of his profession as a schoolmaster. His rejection of Gillingham's conventional advice to hold tight to Sue at any cost, his defence before his school's directors of her right to be free, his subsequent generosity to Jude and Sue – all constitute an effort to place loving-kindness before self-interest. As the Miltonic epigraph to Part IV implies, Phillotson, at least at that point in his career, seems designed to prove that Charity still lives: 'Whoso prefers Matrimony or other Ordinance before the Good of Man and the plain Exigence of Charity, let him profess Papist, or Protestant, or what he will, he is no better than a Pharisee.' But Phillotson's utter defeat shows that charity and the good of man are nothing before public opinion, the exigence of self-interest, and what Sue calls the 'horrid and cruel' nature of 'the universe . . . [and of] things in general' (IV, ch. 3). Phillotson's attempt to remedy things by forgiving Sue and denying himself is futile in such circumstances. The love his name ironically suggests – unlike the love of Cytherea Graye, Parson Maybold, Gabriel Oak, John Loveday, Viviette Constantine, Abel Whittle or Marty South, or for that matter of Tess Durbeyfield – does not somehow bring good out of evil or redeem grim reality. His generosity brings disgrace on his own head and misery to Sue and Jude.

And so the disturbing irony of the fact that Phillotson's social redemption begins when, at the instigation of Arabella, he exploits Sue's pathological guilt to take her back to him and restore her and himself to respectability. In short, he retrieves his place in society when he rejects moral sympathy for the sly, coercive ways of Arabella. From the moment she hurls the pig's pizzle, that blatant symbol of her designs, Arabella dominates and controls Jude, and she does so because she knows how to satisfy his basest appetites. She deceives him into marriage by feigning pregnancy, soon tires of him, then leaves him to go off to Australia. Upon her return from Australia years later, she hovers over him, mixes him exotic drinks at Christminster, invites him to her bed at Aldbrickham, visits him and Sue during their happy days together and manages to provoke Sue to sexual jealousy. This last achievement leads directly to Sue's downfall, for Sue does not give herself to Jude until Arabella's presence threatens her control of Jude. Arabella's influence is in part to blame then for the sexual self-hate that causes Sue to 'incite' Father Time to an act that spells the ruin of her union with Jude, a situation that Arabella is quick to exploit. In all of this, Arabella is something of a female Iago – not just brutal, as has often been asserted, but also cunning, tenacious, and even intelligent in her understanding of those whom she manipulates and destroys. Even after she has married a prosperous innkeeper, she has an eye for Jude. When she sees him at an agricultural show (V, ch. 5), she buys from Vilbert, Jude's first deceiver, a love-philtre with which to ensnare Jude again. At Kennetbridge Fair, where Arabella (a temporary convert, like Alec d'Urberville, to Evangelicalism) finds Sue and Father Time selling Christminster cakes of Jude's manufacture, Arabella throws off her newly found piety and declares that she will have Jude again.[37] She meets Phillotson, informs him that Sue was innocent of adultery when he divorced her, and upbraids him for not curbing and holding her (v, ch. 8). She in this way turns Phillotson back to Sue. Keeping a watchful eye on Jude after the death of the children, Arabella informs Phillotson that Sue has left Jude, that they had never married, and that Sue regards Phillotson as her husband in the eye of heaven and of the Church. This well-placed message moves Phillotson to seek out Sue, and Arabella is, of course, waiting watchfully when the guilt-ridden Sue urges Jude to return to Arabella. In a re-enactment of the events at the cottage near Marygreen many years before, Jude marries Arabella. She domineers him, neglects him during his fatal illness, and leaves him lying dead in order to take up with Jude's first deceiver, Vilbert, whom she has in the meantime tricked into swallowing some of his own love-philtre. Beside Arabella, Alec, her counterpart in *Tess*, is humane and sympathetic, if only in the afterthought. Arabella knows neither guilt nor remorse. By her sexual hold over Jude, by her provocation of jealousy in Sue, by the presence of her son in Sue's house, and by her manipulation of Phillotson, she effectively controls the fate of the two lovers. The last words of the novel are fittingly hers, for she, not a distant President of the Immortals, has ended her sport with Jude. Standing over Jude's corpse, she says of Sue: 'She may swear that [she has found peace] on her knees to the holy cross upon her necklace till she's hoarse, but it won't be true! . . . She's never found peace since she left his arms, and never will till she's as he is now' (vi, ch. 10).

Though all the kinships between *Tess* and *Jude* have by no means been described, perhaps enough has been said to show how *Jude* at once proceeds out of *Tess* and departs from it. As noted above, the events and phases of *Tess* i to iv are compressed into *Jude* i to iii, and the events comparable to those of *Tess* v ('The Woman Pays') occupy *Jude* iv, v and vi. But there is no counterpart in *Jude* to Tess's revenge and fulfilment in *Tess* vi and vii. This suggests that Jude was marked for a degree of suffering and humiliation that Tess was not. Angel torments Tess by his absence, and she is indifferent to the attentions of men like Alec and Farmer Groby; Sue tortures

Jude with her tantalizing presence, and marries Phillotson, Jude's mentor and friend, and with Jude present. Arabella reappears to plague Jude in Part III. Alec does not appear again until Phase VI ('The Convert'), and then his new-found faith is demolished by Tess. The result of compressing events comparable to those in *Tess* I and IV into *Jude* I to III was to allow three segments of *Jude* (Parts IV, V, and VI) for depiction of what is treated in one phase of *Tess* ('The Woman Pays'). Jude pays, and pays, and pays. This shift of emphasis is confirmed by the contrasting conclusions. *Tess* ends with the heroine's revenge upon her tormentor and her fulfilment in reunion with her lover. Tess lives on, both in the enduring natural order with which she is closely associated, and in the prospective union of Angel and Liza-Lu. In the ending of *Jude* we find not the hero's retaliation against his torturer and his fulfilment in reunion with his well-beloved, but his resubmission to Arabella and his final separation from Sue. Tess *is* ruined, but she rallies, pays the price, retaliates, and finds fulfilment. Jude is ruined, rallies briefly, then is obliterated.

The interrelationships of Hardy's last two major novels not only suggest the danger of offering any single statement about Hardy's view of the human condition; they also mark clearly the terms of his profound indecision. From *Tess* we have this. The triumph of Tess in death is the expression of Hardy's belief that self-sacrifice and the will to live can triumph over misfortune, stupidity, cruelty, and even heredity. The persistence of Tess and of the procreative natural order with which she is associated argues a progressive, if painful and severe, tendency in things. Angel's turnabout and Alec's attempted turnabout argue a possibility, however halting, for self-amendment. Tess's return to Stonehenge is a return to the home of her maternal ancestors and a reawakening of a strength, symbolized by the enduring stones of the pagan altar, that her paternal forebearers (and their rotten Gothic) have lost. Thus *Tess*, as tragic realism, exhibits the inexhaustibility of human means of redemption. For all its terrible severity, *Tess* is hopeful. From *Jude* we have this bitter reply to *Tess*. The triumph of Arabella shows that cruelty and cunning can triumph over love and enlightened intelligence. The degradation of Phillotson, of Jude, and of Father Time – a decline touching three generations – argues a deteriorative tendency in things, a tendency asserted in the recurring images of cultural decay and of ineffectual modes of repair. The dramatic turnabout of Sue exposes the vulnerability of the so-called liberated mind. Sue cannot live without the support of the traditional morality and social rituals she says she despises. Phillotson rises only when he sets aside kindness for self-interest.

Jude exhibits, without qualification by assertions of love for the venerable–antique or for the creative–natural orders, the utter futility of return, of forgiveness, and of restoration. Jude's return to Arabella, Sue's reunion with Phillotson, and Jude's return to his native Marygreen are as futile as attempts to recover a lost felicity as Jude's labours on the buildings of Christminster are hopeless as attempts to recover a lost architectural style. Jude's return to Christminster, his spiritual home, in Part VI – a significant departure from the pattern of *Tess* – is his complete undoing. *Jude* exhibits the exhaustibility of human means of redemption and thereby exposes the fatal weakness of any humanist system, such as Positivism, that promises, in the name of inevitable progress, the emergence of a world free from theological or metaphysical delusion. The individual mind unsupported by tradition must recapitulate the course of Comtean history, and often – as in the case of Sue and Jude – disaster is the result. If *Tess* is tragic realism, perhaps *Jude* is tragic reality. But the point is not to separate the two novels. We must refrain from speaking of them separately, for Hardy's view of things˙ is a truly dichotomous one; it rests somewhere inside the extraordinary dialogue he carried on through the two halves of the magnificent diptych with which he chose to end his career as a writer of novels.

Conclusion: 'One Man's Literary Purpose'

In the closing paragraphs of the General Preface to the novels and poems, which he wrote in 1911 for the Wessex Edition of his writings, Hardy, age seventy-one, looked back over his literary labours and defended them as an impressionist thinker's attempt to tell the truth about the nature of human existence in the only way his temperament and experience enabled him to tell it:

> Existence is either ordered in a certain way, or it is not so ordered, and conjectures which harmonize best with experience are removed above all comparison with other conjectures which do not so harmonize. . . . And there is another consideration. Differing natures find their tongue in the presence of different spectacles. Some natures become vocal at tragedy, some are made vocal by comedy, and it seems to me that to whichever of these aspects of life a writer's instinct for expression the more readily responds, to that he should allow it to respond. That before a contrasting side of things he remains undemonstrative need not be assumed to mean that he remains unperceiving. (*TD*, pp. xii–xiii)

What is most striking here is Hardy's portrait of himself as one acted upon by superior forces both without and within him ('Existence is . . . ordered . . . .' 'a writer's instinct . . . responds'). He views himself as one who *finds* his tongue, who *becomes* or *is made* vocal 'in the presence of differing spectacles'. He is one, in sum, who does what he must do, but who, as the last sentence suggests, knows there are things he cannot do. Hardy's use of passive and intransitive verbs conveys his sense of himself as one acted upon.

Hardy's view of himself here as a writer endowed, or as one deprived, but in either case as one compelled to write as he does, helps explain, I think, the patterning and repetition in his fiction. During an initial period of literary experimentation (from 1862 to about 1875) in which he came to see the meaning of his growth toward manhood and marriage, and of his experience of religion and architecture, he formed the deterioristic view of existence his nostalgic temperament and his situation within a dying traditional order exacted of him. This temperament, to paraphrase his account in the General Preface, found natural tongue in the presence of the deteriorative side of life – the unique, unreturning nature of time, history, and consciousness. That this was an impression of things rather than a conviction about them is argued by the way in which he went on to fashion different versions of the cognate stories – of return and restoration – that were for him private as well as universal in meaning. In *Under the Greenwood Tree* one finds a comic return or homecoming with tragic undertones, in *The Return of the Native* a tragic homecoming with a happy ending (later altered), in *The Woodlanders* an ironic homecoming with a tragi-comic ending (the comic element was later repudiated), in *The Pursuit of the Well-Beloved* an allegorical homecoming, tragi-comic in tone and later revised and republished as *The Well-Beloved*. Through *The Mayor of Casterbridge* and the three novels of the 1880s that precede it, one discovers an inconclusive probing of the question of restoration and renewal. Between *Tess* and *Jude* one finds an amazing set of polarities: male versus female, city versus country, culture versus nature. Here tragedy finds its antithesis not in comedy but in absurdity, in meaningless agony. One might even argue that the investigation into the order of existence begun in *Tess* finds antithetical reply not just in *Jude* but in *The Dynasts* as well. The evolutionary meliorism of *The Dynasts* (outlined and begun in the form we now know it in early 1897) is yet a third response to the question of regeneration under study in *Tess* and *Jude*. Three views of nature's working are embodied in these three great end-of-the-century works: nature as harmonizing and nurturing power in *Tess*; nature as destructive impulse in *Jude*; nature as indifferent, evolutionary force in *The Dynasts*. Napoleon, like Tess and Jude but with far greater historical consequences, is separated from an ideal of his early days.

The ultimate effect of Hardy's tentativist habit of working and reworking the same materials throughout his novels is not the mere inconclusiveness or aimless relativism that words such as 'tentative' or 'impressionistic' may imply. The effect is rather one of completeness and comprehensiveness. I have found it possible to make this point with university students with whom I have studied Hardy by using a particular example, the example of what I call 'the Yeobright circle'. Clym Yeobright, I propose to them, is an author-figure, a partial self-portrait who undoubtedly reflects something of Hardy's conflicting loyalties to his mother and his wife during the years of his courtship of Emma Gifford and the early years of his marriage. But for the 'full' meaning of Clym within the world of Hardy's fiction, I then suggest, we must consider the other members of Clym's 'circle': the sexually timid Henry Knight of *A Pair of Blue Eyes*, the repressed Farmer Boldwood of *Far from the Madding Crowd*, the fastidious Angel Clare of *Tess*, the fancifully erotic Jocelyn Pierston of *The Well-Beloved*, perhaps even the epicene Sue Bride-head of *Jude*, the philandering Edred Fitzpiers of *The Woodlanders*, and the remorseful poet husband of the 'Poems of 1912–13'. This circle, as noteworthy for the variety of sexual attitudes it contains as for anything else, defines Clym. He is less fastidious than Clare, more restrained than Fitzpiers, less the idealist than Pierston, less unsettled than Boldwood. The observations will vary with the reader, but the point to be made is that Clym's identity in *The Return* is in a sense incomplete until we consider his predecessors and successors in the novels (and perhaps some of the poems). Once we begin to contemplate Clym within his circle, we find it possible to discuss his character and circumstances in a way we could not before. If we learn to see him within this group of sexually troubled individuals – keeping in mind at the same time that in Fancy Day and Grace Melbury he has, to a point, female counterparts, and in Gabriel Oak a complete antithesis – we begin perhaps to see him within the 'circumscribed scene' in which Hardy imagined him. We move closer through him and his associates to the mystery of human existence as Hardy imagined and exhibited it. The universal dimension of Hardy's fiction has to be seen first, I think, in the created universe of his novels; only then can it be held up against 'our' universe. Clym's story is a perfectly credible one when we read it apart from its echoes and re-enactments throughout the fiction. But it comes alive in a powerful and complex way, in a way we might wish to call Hardian, when we learn to read it for its echoes and after-images, or when we learn to see Clym as but one in a series of partial, often highly unflattering, self-portraits. Recent views of Hardy as a perpetual adolescent, as one lacking in humanity, as a man somewhat shrivelled in soul might be corrected by study of his capacity for severe and accurate self-criticism. At the very least, Hardy must be credited with knowing his shortcomings and accepting them – capacities neither adolescent nor inhumane.

Something similar can be said, I think, of *Tess* and *Jude*. The effect of reading either *Tess* or *Jude* alone and without reference to the other is profoundly moving; it is the deeply moral and emotional experience of great art. But having done this, to then read them for the quarrel being conducted between them, to know as one reads *Tess* that *Jude* exhibits the negation of Tess's painful triumph, is to read quite differently; it is to read with a sense of other, magnificently realized, possibilities, and with a deepened sense of irony (the constant 'this may be so, but . . .'). Perhaps Hardy had this in mind when he wrote, again in the General Preface of 1911, of how human nature is exhibited on a restricted canvas:

> It has sometimes been conceived of novels that evolve their action on a circumscribed scene – as do many . . . of these – that they cannot be so inclusive in their exhibition of human nature as novels wherein the scenes cover large extents of country, in which events figure amid towns and cities, even wander over the four quarters of the globe. I am not concerned to argue this point further than to suggest that the conception is an untrue one in respect of the elementary passions. But I would state that the geographical limits of the stage here trodden were not absolutely forced upon the writer by circumstances; he forced them upon himself from judgment. I considered that our magnificent heritage from the Greeks in dramatic literature found sufficient room for a larger proportion of its action in an extent of their country not much larger than the half-dozen countries here reunited under the old name of Wessex, that the domestic emotions have throbbed in Wessex nooks with as much intensity as in the palaces of Europe, and that, anyhow, there was quite enough human nature in Wessex for one man's literary purpose.   (*TD*, pp. viii–ix)

Here, in striking contrast to his earlier description of his artistic stance as a passively receptive one ('Existence is . . . ordered . . .', the artist is 'made vocal'), Hardy strongly asserts his conscious control over geography. He 'forced' the 'geographical limits' of his stage 'upon himself from judgment'. The same might be said of his handling of character: the human limits of Hardy's stage were not forced upon him entirely by circumstances; he 'forced them upon himself from judgment' – that is, from invention and from observation of himself and others. Perhaps it was a judgement influenced by his early study of Greek drama and myth, in which the adventures of a small circle of heroes are told and retold. Perhaps Hardy took from the plays of Sophocles and Aeschylus, their antecedents in Homer and reverberations in Virgil, the first hint for the kind of fiction he was to write. But even if this were certain, his carefully delineated world and its people are intensely English, intensely West Country, and uniquely his at the same time they are universal. Not only do they reflect a nostalgic sensibility and a traditional upbringing violated by 'change and chancefulness'; they are the story of his experience of his own temperament at work on his surroundings and its people, the image of his mournful, many-sided sense of the beauty of the sad truth that 'what has gone has gone forever'.

Notes

NOTES FOR INTRODUCTION

1. Quoted by J. Hillis Miller in his Introduction to *The Well-Beloved*, New Wessex Edition (London: Macmillan, 1975) p. 15. See also Bruce F. Kawin, *Telling it Again and Again: Repetition in Literature and Film* (Ithaca, NY: Cornell University Press, 1972) esp. chs 1 and 2.
2. 'Study of Thomas Hardy', in *Phoenix*, ed. Edward D. McDonald (New York: Viking, 1936) p. 488.
3. Cf. the painful homecoming of Nicholas Long in 'The Waiting Supper' (1887), of Luke Holway in 'The Grave by the Handpost' (1897), of John Lackland in 'A Few Crusted Characters' (1891), and the 'home-woe' of Matthaus Tina of 'The Melancholy Hussar' (1889). The stories of thwarted restoration include 'Fellow-Townsman' (1880), 'Interlopers at the Knap' (1884), 'A Tryst at an Ancient Earthwork' (1885), 'A Mere Interlude' (1885), 'Alicia's Diary' (1887), 'The Withered Arm' (1888), 'The Son's Veto' (1891) and 'For Conscience' Sake' (1891). The poems of thwarted return and restoration include the following: 'Dance at the Phoenix', 'Souls of the Slain', 'The Revisitation', 'The Re-enactment', 'He Revisits his First School', 'The Two Houses', 'A Wife Comes Back', 'The Wanderer', 'She Revisits Alone the Church of her Marriage', 'In a Former Resort after Many Years', 'Rover Come Home', 'Whaler's Wife', 'The Second Visit', 'A Daughter Returns', 'The Peasant's Confession', 'A Trampwoman's Tragedy', 'A Sunday Morning Tragedy', 'The Two Rosalinds', 'The Flirt's Tragedy' and 'The Sacrilege'. The twenty-one 'Poems of 1912–13', taken together, form a return cycle the theme of which is that restoration of things past is futile (see pp. 160–8 below).
4. *The Woodlanders* (1887) was conceived and probably outlined in 1874 (*Life*, p. 102). *The Well-Beloved* (first published in 1892 as *The Pursuit of the Well-Beloved*) is first mentioned in entries in the *Life* for 1884 and 1889, but Hardy said he sketched it 'many years' before 1892, when he was 'comparatively a young man' (*Life*, pp. 164, 217, 286). *An Indiscretion in the Life of an Heiress*, a story of return salvaged from 'The Poor Man and the Lady' (1867), was first published in 1878.
5. *Under the Greenwood Tree, Far from the Madding Crowd* and *A Pair of Blue Eyes* were all written in Higher Bockhampton. The uncertain *Ethelberta* was produced in London and Swanage, the masterful *Return of the Native* at Sturminster Newton (Dorset). Upper Tooting 'produced' *The Trumpet-Major* and *A Laodicean*; Wimborne (Dorset) *Two on a Tower*. *The Mayor of Casterbridge, The Woodlanders, Tess, Jude, The Dynasts* and the great majority of the poems were written at Max Gate.

6. *Repetition: An Essay in Experimental Psychology*, trs. Walter Lowrie (Princeton, NJ: Princeton University Press, 1946) p. xxii. For a discussion of the return motif in Victorian literature, see John R. Reed, *Victorian Conventions* (Athens, Ohio: Ohio University Press, 1975) pp. 216–50.
7. *Anatomy of Criticism* (Princeton, NJ: Princeton University Press, 1957) esp. pp. 33–67.
8. In 'On the Modern Element in Modern Literature' (1961), where he writes, 'The questions asked by our literature are not about our culture but ourselves, if we are saved or damned – more than with anything else, our literature is concerned with salvation. No literature has ever been so intensely spiritual as ours. I do not venture to call it religious, but certainly it has the special intensity of concern with the spritual life which Hegel noted when he spoke of the great modern phenomenon of the secularization of spirituality' – from *The Idea of the Modern*, ed. Irving Howe (New York: Horizon Press, 1967) p. 64.
9. Roy Morrell, *Thomas Hardy: The Will and the Way* (Kuala Lumpur: University of Malaya Press, 1965) esp. pp. 1–28. Cf. F. R. Southerington, *Hardy's Vision of Man* (London: Chatto and Windus, 1971) p. 218: 'It was Hardy's purpose to find some area in which meaningful change might be caused by human endeavour'.
10. Morrell, *Thomas Hardy*, p. 15.

NOTES FOR CHAPTER I: HARDY'S DETERIORISTIC MODE OF REGARD

1. See Robert Gittings, *Young Thomas Hardy* (Boston, Mass.: Little, Brown, 1975) pp. 7–8. Hardy makes no mention of his illegitimacy in the *Life*.
2. See J. O. Bailey, *Poetry of Thomas Hardy: A Handbook and Commentary* (Chapel Hill, NC: University of North Carolina Press, 1970) p. 27; also Gittings (*Young Thomas Hardy*, p. 9), who describes Mary Hardy as her famous brother's 'lifelong companion and confidante'.
3. Bailey (p. 179) argues that Hardy himself is the fiddler in the poem, but see the *Life* (p. 15): 'He [Hardy] was of ecstatic temperament, extraordinarily sensitive to music, and among the endless jigs, hornpipes, reels, waltzes, and country-dances that his father played of an evening in his early married years, and to which the boy danced *pas seul* in the middle of the room, there were three or four that always moved the child to tears, though he strenuously tried to hide them. . . . He used to say in later life that . . . he danced at these times to conceal his weeping. He was not over four years of age at this date.'
4. See Wordsworth's Ode, lines 5, 17, 55–6, 83, 125, 177–8; also note 25 to ch. 2.
5. Typescript of *Early Years*, pp. 130–1 (Dorset County Museum).
6. Gittings (*Young Thomas Hardy*, p. 27) suggests that Jemima sent young Hardy along with her father in order to discourage possible flirtations on the part of her husband. Hardy seems to recall it as part of Jemima's campaign to get him off into the world.
7. In 'After the Last Breath (J. H. 1813–1904)', Hardy's elegy to his mother, he writes, 'Our well-beloved is prisoner in the cell / Of Time no more' (*CP*, p. 270).

8. 'In Tenebris, III' (*CP*, p. 169). Cf. in 'The Roman Road' (*CP*, pp. 264–5) the phrase, the 'mother's form . . . guiding my infant steps', and 'On One who Lived and Died where He Was Born' (*CP*, pp. 659–60), in which Hardy reveals his respect for his father's strong 'place-attachment', a quality he admired in William Barnes as well (see his obituary for Barnes, in *Personal Writings*, p. 105).

9. See Gittings, *Young Thomas Hardy*, pp. 25ff.

10. Passages from the typescript of the *Early Life* (p. 33a) in the Dorset County Museum make it clear that Hardy's love for Louisa was stronger than he suggests in the *Life* (p. 26). It lasted well into the 1860s, 'since he used to meet her down to his 23rd or 24th year on his visits from London to Dorset. Of Louisa's grave he wrote as follows in the typescript of *Early Years* (though not in the *Life*): 'and a nameless green mound in the corner of Mellstock Churchyard was visited more than once by one to whom a boyish dream had never lost its radiance'.

11. See Gittings, *Young Thomas Hardy*, pp. 28–9, 64 (see note 15 below), and *Thomas Hardy's Later Years* (Boston, Mass.: Little, Brown, 1978) esp. pp. 122ff. Cf. the poems 'Concerning Agnes' (*CP*, p. 878) and 'The Opportunity (For H. P.)' (*CP*, p. 621). In 1906 Hardy suggested in a letter to Edmund Gosse that Gosse seek out Helen Paterson (then the widowed Mrs William Allingham) and tell him 'what she looks like as an elderly woman' (Bailey, *The Poetry of Thomas Hardy*, p. 461).

12. Gittings, *Young Thomas Hardy*, p. 29. Hardy's sense of himself as one lacking in virility appears in the very first remark about him in the *Life* (p. 14), where it is stated that 'he showed not the physique of his father'. In 'In Tenebris, II' the poet seems to associate unbelief with impotency ('the blot'); the sceptical speaker of the poem forms a shrinking contrast to 'the many and strong' whose shouts are echoed by the 'swoln bosoms' of the clouds. These 'stout upstanders' are also 'the potent'; 'their dawns bring lusty joys . . . their evenings all that is sweet' (*CP*, p. 168).

13. *Young Thomas Hardy*, p. 217.

14. Gittings (ibid., p. 64) notes that in 1862, after his arrival in London, Hardy courted, perhaps fell deeply in love with, his cousin, Martha Mary Sparks, then a lady's maid in Paddington.

15. Gittings (ibid.) connects Hardy's strong familial sense with his unusual attachment to his mother: 'All the [Sparks] girls had the features of the Hand family, and therefore of Hardy's mother. More than most mother-fixed youths, Hardy was falling in love with his own mother over and over again, in a physical and consistent way that was a typical part of his almost literal-minded nature.'

16. From 'Prelude' in Swinburne's *Songs Before Sunrise*; Hardy used the same phrase as one of the epigraphs to Part II of *Jude the Obscure*.

17. Cf. Hardy's remark in a letter to Florence Henniker in January, 1897: 'The ordinary Dorset landowners only tolerate an author: they do not associate with him (especially when he is such a fearful wild fowl as this misunderstood man is supposed to be). Writing this recalls to mind Lady Waldegrave's answer to Browning, when he proposed to her. "We dine our poets, Mr. Browning, but we do not marry them." *Mutatis mutandis*, that's the spirit down here – much intensified of course' – *One Rare Fair Woman: Thomas Hardy's Letters to Florence*

Henniker, 1893–1922, ed. Evelyn Hardy and F. B. Pinion (London: Macmillan, 1972) p. 60.

18. *Life*, p. 101; typescript of *Early Life*, p. 128 (Dorset County Museum).

19. See Gittings, *Young Thomas Hardy*, pp. 128–9.

20. Dorset County Museum.

21. Ibid.

22. See the poem 'We Sat at the Window (Bournemouth, 1875)' (*CP*, pp. 428–9).

23. *Thomas Hardy: Distance and Desire* (Cambridge, Mass.: Harvard University Press, 1971) p. 73.

24. Jemima may have visited Hardy in London in the autumn of 1878, for Hardy wrote to his brother as follows on 13 September 1878: 'Tell mother she must make up her mind to come while the fine weather lasts. I will [meet] her at Clapham Junction' – *The Collected Letters of Thomas Hardy*, ed. R. L. Purdy and Michael Millgate, vol. 1 (Oxford: Clarendon Press, 1978) p. 60. Gittings (*Young Thomas Hardy*, p. 208) notes that, though Mary and Kate Hardy met Emma on a picnic excursion to Corfe Castle in September 1875, 'Bockhampton and Hardy's mother did not appear in any way, either in [*The Hand of Ethelberta*, on which Hardy was at work at the time] or in his wife's diary, but he can hardly have held off the meeting [between Emma and Jemima] at this time.' It is Gittings's view that Jemima never accepted Emma into the family.

25. F. B. Pinion, in '*The Return of the Native* in the Making', in *Thomas Hardy: Art and Thought* (London: Macmillan, 1977) pp. 177–9, suggests that Hardy gathered materials for *The Return* during the Christmas visit to Higher Bockhampton in 1876.

26. See Bailey, *The Poetry of Thomas Hardy*, p. 427; also the *Life* (p. 442), where Hardy's last visits to Higher Bockhampton and Stinsford Churchyard are described with great poignancy. Stinsford, the resting place of his parents, of Mary and of Emma, was 'to him, the most hallowed spot on earth'.

27. The phrase, as noted above (p. 10), is from Wordsworth's 'Elegiac Stanzas' (line 15). Hardy's interest in the poem was in part local, for Captain John Wordsworth went down with the *Abergavenny* off Portland Bill, a fact Hardy would not fail to mention in *The Dynasts*.

28. Gittings (*Young Thomas Hardy*, pp. 128ff.) corrects the view that Emma was a victim of a mild form of madness from about 1876 on; he believes her 'madness' better described as eccentricity.

29. *Poetical Works*, New Edition, revised by Ernest de Selincourt (New York: Oxford University Press, 1969) pp. 452–3.

30. Both 'Overlooking the River Stour' and 'On Sturminster Footbridge' are dated '1877' in manuscript; they were probably written though in 1916, when Hardy revisited Riverside Villa after an absence of forty years (see Bailey, *Poetry of Thomas Hardy*, pp. 382–4; also *Life*, p. 373).

31. See Gittings, *Thomas Hardy's Later Years*, esp. chs 11, 12 and 13.

32. See especially Harvey Curtis Webster, *On a Darkling Plain* (Chicago: University of Chicago Press, 1947) pp. 1–77; also June M. Tuttleton, 'Thomas Hardy and the Christian Religion', (unpublished dissertation, University of North Carolina at Chapel Hill, 1967).

33. *Pragmatism: A New Name for Some Old Ways of Thinking* (New York: Longman, Green, 1909) p. 61. (First published 1907.)

34. I am indebted to Professor Michael Millgate for informing me that this incident almost certainly occurred two years earlier, in 1863, a fact that strengthens the connection between it and Hardy's association with H. R. Bastow, discussed below.

35. *The Collected Letters of Thomas Hardy*, vol. i, p. 136.

36. See Tuttleton, 'Thomas Hardy and the Christian Religion', p. 43: 'In such a scheme Christ becomes the moral savior of mankind, justification by faith the peace of mind which comes with righteousness, regeneration "an awakening of the forces of the soul", resurrection "a spiritual quickening", salvation deliverance from evil, propitiation the recovery of peace after the loss of it through sin, the eternal what belongs to God as spirit, the fires of hell "distracted remorse", and Heaven "the fulfillment of the love of God" '. See also Basil Willey, *More Nineteenth Century Studies* (London: Chatto and Windus, 1963) pp. 137–85.

37. In *Tess* (ch. 2), Angel Clare's brothers are reading a book titled *A Counterblast to Agnosticism*. In the manuscript of the novel the Clares are reading *Answers to 'Essays and Reviews'*, a title much like that of the actual *Replies to 'Essays and Reviews'* (1862), one of the responses to the book that Hardy read at Moule's urging in 1860 – see P. N. Furbank (ed.), *Tess of the d'Urbervilles*, New Wessex Edition (London: Macmillan, 1974) p. 452.

38. Hardy acquired a copy of *John Keble's Christian Year: Thoughts in Verse for the Sundays and Holidays Throughout the Year* (first published in 1860) in February 1861, at about the time he was studying *Essays and Reviews*. In Keble he found a happy combination of the romantic belief in regenerative nature and the orthodox Christian belief in renewal through Christ. The dates in his hand in the volume show that he used the volume frequently from 1861 to 1863; and this corresponds to the frequent datings from the years 1861–3 in the Gospels, the Acts of the Apostles, and the epistles of Paul in his 1861 Bible. The hymns celebrating the Redemption that Hardy marked and annotated in his personal copy of *Hymns Ancient and Modern* (1889) are too numerous to list here, though the titles of a few are suggestive: 'Return, O Wanderer, to Thy Home' (by the Rev. A. G. Purchas and Thomas Hustings, to the tune of W. H. Monk); 'Redeemed, Restored, Forgiven' (by H. W. Baker, to Sir John Stainer); 'Thou Turnest Man, O Lord, to Dust' (to the tune of St Stephen); 'Awake, My Soul, and with the Sun' (by Bishop Thomas Ken); 'Forgive Them, O my Father' (by C. F. Alexander, to R. W. Statham); 'It Is Finish'd! Blessed Jesu' (by Bishop W. D. Maclagan, to W. H. Langster); 'Christ the Lord is Risen Today' (by Jane E. Leeson, to G. J. Elvey); 'I Was a Wandering Sheep' (by Horatius Bonar, to G. J. Gauntlett); 'Lead, Kindly Light' (by J. H. Newman, to the Rev. J. B. Dykes). Hardy's Bible, his *Christian Year* and his *Hymns* are in the Dorset County Museum. See also Kenneth Phelps, *Annotations by Thomas Hardy in His Bibles and Prayer Book* (Mount Durand, St Peter Port, Guernsey: Toucan Press, 1966) pp. 1–14; and Gittings, *Young Thomas Hardy*, pp. 44–55.

39. The nine letters from Bastow to Hardy, eight of them written between January 1861 and December 1865, and one in 1907, are in the Dorset County Museum.

40. 'Bonar' is probably Horatius Bonar (1808–69), author of the hymn 'I Was a Wandering Sheep' mentioned above (note 38) and a minister of the Established Church of Scotland. For Hardy's interest in Newman, see *Life*, p. 48; and *The Literary Notes of Thomas Hardy*, ed. Lennart A. Björk, vol. i

(Göteborg, Sweden: Acta Universitatis Gothenburgensis, 1974) pp. 4–6.

41. I have not been able to decipher the remainder of this sentence.

42. In the other letters, Bastow advised Hardy of architectural opportunities in London, gossiped about a mutual acquaintance at Hicks's who preferred rifle-shooting to religion, scolded Hardy for not writing more often ('for you know you are a bit of a pupil of mine, seeing I was your senior for so long in the old office'), inquired about his progress with the study of Greek (cf. *Life*, p. 31), and even teased him about romance ('I suppose you have scarcely . . . gone and lost your heart yet, young man. . . . You must let me know if it has come to that, and tell me who is the fair damsel – though I am still of the opinion that you are not of a highly inflammable nature'). Probably because he wished to play down Bastow's influence on him, Hardy quoted only from the letter of 20 May 1861 in the *Life* (p. 31), referred to Bastow there as 'the emigrant', mentioned Bastow's failure to keep an appointment on one occasion, and noted that after Bastow's departure he [Hardy] 'like St. Augustine, lapsed from the Greek New Testament back to pagan writers'. The last of Bastow's letters in the Dorset County Museum is dated 28 April 1907. In it Bastow writes from retirement (he ended his career as Chief Architect of Victoria, Australia) to introduce his son, Arthur, whom he was sending to visit 'the old house [in Dorchester] where we used to work together under our old friend and Master John Hicks'. The last mention of Bastow in the *Life* occurs in Florence Hardy's diary entry for 17 November 1927, incorporated into chapter 38. Before publication she deleted some revealing, even hilarious, evidence of Hardy's mixed regard for his old mentor and colleague. They are restored in brackets. 'Today T. H. was speaking, and evidently thinking a great deal, about a friend, a year or two older than himself, who was a fellow-pupil at Mr. Hicks' office. I felt, as he talked, that he would like to meet this man again more than anyone in the world. He is in Australia now, if alive, and must be nearly ninety. His name is Henry Robert Bastow; he was a Baptist and evidently a very religious youth, and [but] T. H. was [always] devoted to him. I suggested that we might find something about him by sending an advertisement to Australian newspapers, but T. H. [said no, and that Bastow might be led to think there was a legacy awaiting him] thought that would not be wise' (*Life*, p. 443).

43. See Lionel Stevenson, *Darwin Among the Poets* (Chicago: University of Chicago Press, 1932) p. 53: 'Being essentially a poet of fatalism, Hardy believed that progress was an illusion, and that the primal force was merely a ceaseless craving for change in manifestation, unconscious of direction'.

44. See J. Hillis Miller, *Thomas Hardy: Distance and Desire* (Cambridge, Mass.: Harvard University Press, 1971) p. 86: 'For Hardy there is neither a transcendent nor an immanent conscious force sweeping through nature and expressing itself there. In a number of early poems he laments his inability to see nature as a religious man or as a romantic poet would see it.'

45. Hardy himself never delivered the address; it was read for him in his absence by another member. See *Personal Writings*, pp. 203–18.

46. Hardy's touchstone is again Wordsworth. The phrase is from 'Inside King's College Chapel, Cambridge' (line 12).

47. For a discussion of Hardy's attempt to reconcile the expressive and the mimetic, see Lawrence O. Jones, 'Imitation and Expression in Thomas

Hardy's Theory of Fiction', *Studies in the Novel*, 7 (1975) 507–25.

NOTES FOR CHAPTER 2: 'THINKING O' PERFECTION'

1. See Gittings, *Young Thomas Hardy*, pp. 161, 224.
2. In September 1888, for example, upon a visit to Woolcombe for materials for *Tess of the d'Urbervilles*, Hardy remarked, 'The decline and fall of the Hardys much in evidence hereabout. . . . So we go down, down' (*Life*, pp. 214–15).
3. See *Life*, p. 116; also Carl J. Weber, *Hardy of Wessex* (New York: Columbia University Press, 1965) pp. 216–18.
4. In the poem 'The Lacking Sense' creative nature works with a 'too remorseful air upon her face / As of an angel fallen from grace'. She has declined from 'her fair beginnings' because she is infected by a 'primal doom', she looks to men, with little hope, for a possible cure (*CP*, pp. 116–18).
5. W. R. Rutland, *Thomas Hardy: A Study of His Writings and Their Background* (Oxford: Basil Blackwell, 1938) pp. 114–32, argues that the 'Indiscretion' is virtually an unaltered extract from 'The Poor Man'. My discussion is based on Carl J. Weber's edition of 'An Indiscretion' (Baltimore, Md.: Johns Hopkins University Press, 1935).
6. The episode foreshadows Clym and Eustacia's interlude at Alderworth, Giles and Grace's at One-Chimney Hut, Angel and Tess' at Bramshurst Court, and Jude and Sue's three years of untroubled wandering after leaving Aldbrickham.
7. Ecclesiastes was one of Hardy's favourite books of the Old Testament. In 1865 he tried, unsuccessfully, to turn it into a poem in Spenserian stanzas (*Life*, p. 47).
8. G. R. Elliott, 'Spectral Etchings in the Poetry of Thomas Hardy', *PMLA*, 43 (1938) 1189, has discerned a 'paradisaic tendency' in Hardy.
9. Echoed perhaps in the name 'Egdon' in *The Return of the Native*, 'Overcombe' in *The Trumpet-Major*, 'Norcombe' in *Far From the Madding Crowd* – all echoes perhaps of Bockhampton, Hardy's Dorset birthplace.
10. *Phoenix* (New York: Viking, 1972) p. 435 (first published 1936). The moral drama of the novel has usually been subordinated to what Joseph Warren Beach and others have described as an almost exclusive emphasis on mystery and disguise. See Beach, *The Technique of Thomas Hardy* (Chicago: University of Chicago Press, 1922) pp. 23–36; also George Wing, '*Edwin Drood* and *Desperate Remedies*: Prototypes of Detective Fiction in 1870', *Studies in English Literature*, 13 (1973) 667–87.
11. 'In justice to desponding men, it is well to remember that the brighter endurance of women at these epochs – invaluable, sweet, angelic, as it is – owes some of its origin to a narrower vision that shuts out many of the leaden-eyed despairs in the van, than to a hopefulness intense enough to quell them' (*DR*, III, ch. 2).
12. The passage recalls the poem 'Her Dilemma' (1866), in which a woman meets a dying lover in 'a sunless church / Whose mildewed walls, uneven stones / And wasted carvings passed antique research' (*CP*, pp. 13–14), and falsely declares her love, all the while 'shamed to prize / A world conditioned thus, or care for breath / Where Nature such dilemmas could devise'.

13. The phrase is from Robert G. Hunter, *Shakespeare and the Comedies of Forgiveness* (New York: Columbia University Press, 1965) p. 2.

14. Reprinted in *Thomas Hardy: The Critical Heritage*, ed. R. G. Cox (London: Routledge and Kegan Paul, 1970) p. 4.

15. Meyer H. Abrams, *Natural Supernaturalism: Tradition and Revolution in Romantic Literature* (New York: Norton, 1971) p. 12. Cf. J. Hillis Miller, *Thomas Hardy: Distance and Desire*, p. 74: 'Hardy's work is a good illustration of the connection between the development of fiction as a dominant literary form and the attenuation of belief in God. . . . When God comes to be seen as an illusion created by man . . . then each person is likely to turn to other people as the best possible source of value or meaning.'

16. William A. Madden, 'The Search for Forgiveness in Some Nineteenth-Century English Novels', *Comparative Literature Studies*, 2 (1966) 150. Madden finds *Tess* an illustration of 'Western man's compelling need to find, in society or in nature, or, latterly, in himself, a source of grace equivalent to that offered in the Christian conception of forgiveness'.

17. Weber (see note 5 above) surmises that three elements of 'The Poor Man' found their way into *Greenwood Tree*: Christmas scenes in a tranter's house, descriptions of country life among workingmen, and country scenes dealing with the tranter. See also Richard L. Purdy, *Thomas Hardy: A Bibliographical Study* (London: Oxford University Press, 1968) p. 7 (first published 1954); and Michael Millgate, *Thomas Hardy: His Career as a Novelist* (New York: Random House, 1971) p. 43.

18. John E. Danby, '*Under the Greenwood Tree*', *Critical Quarterly*, 1 (1959) 6.

19. See W. R. Rutland, *Thomas Hardy: A Study of His Writings and Their Background* (Oxford: Blackwell, 1938) pp. 159–60, for an account of the hymn's origin.

20. Cf. Millgate, *Hardy: His Career as a Novelist*, p. 54: 'If *Under the Greenwood Tree* is an idyll, it is one in which, at the end, many things are less than idyllic.'

21. Michael Squires, *The Pastoral Novel: Studies in George Eliot, Thomas Hardy, and D. H. Lawrence* (Charlottesville: University Press of Virginia, 1974) p. 107.

22. See Millgate, *Hardy: His Career as a Novelist*, pp. 42–54.

23. See Gittings, *Young Thomas Hardy*, p. 167: 'He demonstrated in the two characters two deeper aspects of himself. There is the emotional immaturity, which is part of the boyish charm of Smith. There is the advanced intellectual stature, which nevertheless sits uneasily on Knight, because he too is emotionally unsure. . . . These two sides, underlined physically by the boyish Smith, spring from Hardy's inner self, and are the making of the two men in the novel.'

24. See *Some Recollections*, ed. Robert Gittings and Evelyn Hardy (London: Oxford University Press, 1961) p. xv. Elsewhere Gittings writes, 'In her impulses, her foibles, her frequent angers and jealousies, but also in her enthusiasms, ideals, and gaieties, Emma remained all her life a perpetual adolescent. This was her charm. Her recklessness and wilfulness, though sometimes alarming, were equally fascinating for Hardy' (*Young Thomas Hardy*, p. 132). In 'Rain on a Grave' Hardy noted Emma's love of daisies 'With a child's pleasure' (*CP*, p. 341); and in 'I Found Her Out There' he envisioned Emma's spectral return to Cornwall, where she would 'joy in . . . [the] throbs' of the western sea 'With the heart of a child' (*CP*, p. 342).

25. For an account of Hardy's debt to Wordsworth, see Frank B. Pinion, *Thomas*

Hardy: Art and Thought (London: Macmillan, 1977) pp. 167–74; also Peter J. Casagrande, 'Hardy's Wordsworth: A Record and a Commentary', *English Literature in Transition*, 20 (1977) 210–37.

26. See Michael Steig, 'The Problem of Literary Values in Two Early Hardy Novels', *Texas Studies in Language and Literature*, 12 (1970) 55–62; also Ronald Blythe, Introduction to the New Wessex Edition of *A Pair of Blue Eyes* (London: Macmillan, 1975) pp. 15–29.

27. See Howard Babb, 'Setting and Theme in *Far from the Madding Crowd*', *Journal of English Literary History*, 30 (1963) 147–61; also Squires, *The Pastoral Novel*, pp. 125ff.

28. This view of nature is at least as old as Shakespeare's *The Winter's Tale*, where Perdita is scolded by Polixenes for scorning 'carnations and streak'd gillyvors' because there is, he says, in their piedness an art that belongs to 'great creating Nature' (iv. 82ff). It gained some currency in the nineteenth century through the writings of Lyell, Chambers, Tennyson, Arnold, Spencer, and Huxley, as well as of Mill (see note 34 below). See also Leo J. Henkin, *Darwinism in the English Novel, 1860–1910* (New York: Corporation Press, 1940) esp. chs 5–11.

29. See John Halperin, *Egoism and Self-Discovery in the Victorian Novel* (New York: Burt Franklin, 1974) p. 217; and Dale Kramer, *Thomas Hardy: The Forms of Tragedy* (Detroit: Wayne State University Press, 1975) p. 31. For a more complete version of the view of Bathsheba that follows, see Peter J. Casagrande, 'A New View of Bathsheba Everdene', in *Critical Approaches to the Fiction of Thomas Hardy*, ed. Dale Kramer (London: Macmillan, 1979) pp. 50–73.

30. Hardy's 'defence' of Troy here helps explain Troy's spurious claim, later, that Bathsheba, not he, is responsible for Fanny's plight: 'If Satan had not tempted me with that face of yours, and those cursed coquetries, I should have married her' (ch. 43). Both J. I. M. Stewart, in *Thomas Hardy* (London: Allen Lane, 1971) pp. 89–90, and Robert Gittings, in *Young Thomas Hardy*, p. 175, have noted sexual pessimism and an inclination to misogyny in the novel. In a letter of November 1874, to Katherine Macquoid, Hardy, with remarkable equivocation, denied any satire against women in the novel. Bathsheba, he suggested, was a woman 'true and simple' enough to satisfy 'any reasonable being' but unable to exhibit her nature 'truly and simply'. See *The Letters of Thomas Hardy*, ed. Richard L. Purdy and Michael Millgate, vol. 1 (London: Oxford University Press, 1978) p. 33.

31. The phrase is from Keats's 'Eve of St Agnes' (stanza 27).

32. Cf. Richard C. Carpenter, *Thomas Hardy* (New York: Twayne, 1960) p. 87: 'Although Hardy allows us the questionable sop to our feelings of a marriage with Oak as denouement, the novel does not really end "happily". The vibrant and proud girl we see at the beginning has been as thoroughly destroyed as Troy and Boldwood.' In his conclusion to *Madding Crowd* Hardy may have had in mind the conclusion of Thackeray's *Vanity Fair*, with its acid view of Amelia's belated turn to the loyal, patient Dobbin: 'Farewell, dear Amelia – Grow green again, tender little parasite, round the rugged old oak to which you cling!'

33. In *The Hand of Ethelberta*, that novel that Hardy wrote after *Madding Crowd*, the rise of Ethelberta Chickerel Petherwin from a family of servants is identified

with the greed of Milton's Mammon and a Mephistophelean restlessness. See pp. 119–20.

34. Alan Ryan, *John Stuart Mill* (London: Routledge and Kegan Paul, 1974) p. 239. References to Mill's 'Nature' are from the *Collected Works of John Stuart Mill*, ed. J. M. Robson, vol. x (Toronto: University of Toronto Press, 1963) pp. 373–402.

35. Mill also used the lightning rod to illustrate the victory of human ingenuity over nature: 'Everyone professes to approve and admire many great triumphs of art over nature: the junction of bridges of shores which nature has made separate, the draining of nature's marshes, the excavation of her wells, the dragging to light of what she has buried at immense depths in the earth; the turning away of her thunderbolts by lightning rods. . . . But to commend these and similar feats is to acknowledge that the ways of nature are to be conquered, not obeyed . . .' (ibid., p. 378).

36. In *The Will and the Way* (Kuala Lumpur: University of Malaya Press, 1965) pp. 63–4.

NOTES FOR CHAPTER 3: 'NOTHING BACKWARD CLIMBS'

1. See note 4 to Introduction.
2. By 'irony' is meant a primary concern with a realistic level of experience (see Northrop Frye, *Anatomy of Criticism* [Princeton: Princeton University Press, 1957] p. 316). The chart below suggests some of the kinships among the four novels of return.

Types	UGT	RN	W	WB
Returning Native	Fancy Day	Clym Yeobright	Grace Melbury	Jocelyn Pierston
Jealous Parent	Geoffrey Day	Mrs Yeobright	George Melbury	–
Native Lover	Dick Dewey	Thomasin Yeobright	Giles Winterborne	Avice Caro
Alien Lover	Maybold	Eustacia Vye	Edred Fitzpiers	Marcia Bencombe
2nd Alien Lover	–	Damon Wildeve	Felice Charmond	–
2nd Native Lover	–	Diggory Venn	Marty South	Avice Caro II
3rd Native Lover	–	Charlie	Suke Damson	Avice Caro III

This chapter is a revision and expansion of my 'Shifted "Centre of Altruism" in *The Woodlanders*: Thomas Hardy's Third "Return of a Native"', *Journal of English Literary History*, 38 (1971) 104–25. See also John Paterson, *The Making of 'The Return of the Native'*, University of California English Studies, no. 19 (Berkeley and Los Angeles, Calif., 1960) pp. 24–133.

3. Quoted in Millgate, *Hardy: His Career as a Novelist*, p. 293.
4. Though in substantial disagreement with him at several points, I am indebted in much of what follows to Robert Gittings, *Young Thomas Hardy*, pp. 198–212; also to Gittings's 'Introduction' to the New Wessex Edition of *The Hand of Ethelberta* (London: Macmillan, 1975) pp. 15–28.
5. Quoted in Gittings, *Young Thomas Hardy*, p. 209.
6. Hardy complained that in 1875 he was forced by the success of *Far from the Madding Crowd* to write another novel before he knew what was of value in the

previous one; but he could not refuse because he was 'having . . . to live by the pen' (*Life*, p. 102).

7. *The Country and the City* (London: Chatto and Windus, 1973) p. 200.

8. *The Rise of the Novel* (Berkeley, Calif.: University of California Press, 1965) pp. 63ff. Cf. Hardy's determination during the winter of 1871–2 'to stifle his constitutional tendency to care for life only as an emotion and not as a scientific game' and to 'stick to the profession [architecture] which had been the choice of his parents for him rather than his own; but with a faint dream at the back of his mind that he might perhaps write verses as an occasional hobby' (*Life*, pp. 87, 104).

9. Cf. Hardy's description of his early years 'in a lonely and silent spot between woodland and heathland' (*Life*, p. 3), and the description of Clym Yeobright's attachment to Egdon Heath: 'He was permeated with its scenes, with its substance, and with its odours. He might be said to be its product. His eyes had first opened thereon; with its appearance all the first images of his memory were mingled; his estimate of life had been coloured by it . . .' (*RN*, III, ch. 2).

10. The allusion to Wordsworth's poem heightens the novel's attack on society by calling for restoration of 'the ancient English dower / Of inward happiness' through the ministry of the poet prophet who is somehow both 'pure . . . and majestic, free' *and* a creature of the world. Cf. Hardy's use of Wordsworth's 'Written in London, Sept. 1802' in *The Return* (III, ch. 2): 'Yeobright's local peculiarity was that in striving at high thinking he still cleaved to plain living'.

11. Cf. Humphry's remark in *The Return* (II, ch. 1) that both Clym and Eustacia 'are always thinking high doctrine'.

12. See, for example, F. B. Pinion, *Thomas Hardy: Art and Thought* (London: Macmillan, 1977) pp. 55–6.

13. The translation is Henry Francis Cary's (1805), the one that Hardy read at Higher Bockhampton, where the *Divine Comedy* ranked as Jemima Hardy's favourite book. Hardy's much-marked copy of John A. Carlyle's prose translation of the *Comedy* (London: George Bell, 1882) can be seen at the Dorset County Museum.

14. Cf. *The Return* (III, ch. 2), where Clym Yeobright expresses a wish to be 'a schoolmaster to the poor and ignorant, to teach them what nobody else will'.

15. From *Lycidas* (line 71), where the phrase describes the love of Fame that drives the 'clear' poetic spirit to scorn the delights of the world.

16. Gittings, *Young Thomas Hardy*, p. 199.

17. Ibid.

18. *The Country and the City*, pp. 347–8.

19. *Young Thomas Hardy*, p. 205; also Gittings, *Thomas Hardy's Later Years*, pp. 7–12.

20. Eleanor McCann, 'Blind Will or Blind Hero: Philosophy and Myth in Hardy's *The Return of the Native*', *Criticism*, 3 (1961) 140–67. McCann views *The Return* as the story of Clym's failure to achieve knowledge of his 'instinctual motivations' – that is, of the influence on him of his natural mother and his archetypal mother, nature, embodied in the heath: 'Psychologically speaking, Clym is a sick man who projects unto his environment a solace for the halfway solution to an oedipal conflict' (p. 157).

21. See Karl Young, *The Drama of the Medieval Church*, vol. I (London: Oxford University Press, 1933) pp. 10–11; quoted in Herbert Weisinger, *Tragedy and the Paradox of the Fortunate Fall* (Great Britain: Michigan State College Press,

1953) p. 212. See also J. Stevens Cox (ed.), *Mumming and the Mummers' Play of St. George: Three Versions Including that of Thomas Hardy* (Guernsey: Toucan Press, 1970) p. 426ff.

22. Clym's studies in Paris acquainted him with 'ethical systems popular at the time' (III, ch. 2). His age numbers 'less than thirty-three' (VI, ch. 4); he arrives at Egdon on Christmas Eve; while watching his suffering after his mother's death, Eustacia is likened to Judas Iscariot at the trial of Christ (V, ch. 1).

23. Quoted in Weisinger, *Tragedy and the Paradox of the Fortunate Fall*, p. 212.

24. See ibid., p. 65: '[Rebirth] is the most significant and far-reaching [element of the myth and ritual pattern] both in its function and effects. For, without the absolutely indispensable element of resurrection, the pattern would have no useful meaning, the well-being of the community could not be secured, and only chaos and despair would reign supreme.'

25. McCann, in *Criticism*, 3, p. 155.

26. See the Song of Solomon, 3:11: 'Behold King Solomon with the crown wherewith his mother crowned him in the day of his espousals, and in the day of the gladness of his heart.'

27. The passage is from 1 Kings 2:19.

28. John Paterson, in '*The Return of the Native* as Anti-Christian Document', *Nineteenth Century Fiction*, 14 (1959) 111–27, views Christian wholly as an expression of the novel's attack on Christianity.

29. See Gittings, *Young Thomas Hardy*, p. 29: 'Hardy's own analysis of his sexual "virility" . . . does seem to indicate that he developed sexually very late, if indeed he developed at all.' See note 12 to ch. 1.

30. Hardy added the following note in 1912: 'The original conception of the story did not design a marriage between Thomasin and Venn. He was to have retained his isolated and weird character to the last, and to have disappeared mysteriously from the heath, nobody knowing whither – Thomasin remaining a widow. But certain circumstances of serial publication led to a change of intent. Readers can therefore choose between the endings, and those with an austere artistic code can assume the more consistent conclusion to be the true one' (*RN*, VI, ch. 3).

31. The phrase is from a letter of 1915 in which Hardy expressed his dislike for Henri Bergson's concept of the *élan vital*. In another letter of the same year he dismissed Bergson's philosophy as 'only our old friend Dualism in a new set of clothes' (*Life*, p. 450).

32. 'Apology' to *Late Lyrics and Earlier* (1922), in *Personal Writings*, p. 58.

33. Hardy's use of the pathetic fallacy in *The Woodlanders* is an example of what Josephine Miles has called 'a reverse method of attribution' whereby all 'the structures of human feeling . . . are dealt with in terms of the color, form, and motion of the outer world . . . [and] are objectified thus' – *Pathetic Fallacy in the Nineteenth Century* (Berkeley, Calif.: University of California Press, 1942) p. 44.

34. 'The Ethical Structure of Hardy's *The Woodlanders*', *Archiv*, 211 (1974) 36.

35. The phrase is from a letter of 1908 from Hardy to an American lady on the question of vivisection: 'The discovery of the law of evolution, which revealed that all organic creatures are of one family, shifted the centre of altruism from humanity to the whole conscious world collectively' (*Life*, p. 346).

36. *Personal Writings*, pp. 215–16; cf. *Life*, p. 120.

37. *Young Thomas Hardy*, pp. 216–17, 64; and Alma Priestley, 'Hardy's *Well-*

Beloved: A Study in Failure', *The Thomas Hardy Society Review*, 1 (1976) 55–6.
38. Cf. Edmund Gosse's letter to Hardy (16 March 1897): '"The tragedy of a nympholept" – that is what your book is. And so delicate, and sculptural, and uplifted' (Dorset County Museum). Gosse, the author of a life of Swinburne, may have had Swinburne's 'A Nympholept' (1891) in mind. Hardy acknowledged Swinburne's influence in a letter of 1897 (*Life*, p. 287).
39. Priestley, in *The Thomas Hardy Society Review*, 1976, p. 51.
40. *One Rare Fair Woman*, p. 163. Cf. Priestley, 'Hardy's *Well-Beloved*', p. 57: 'If further proof were needed that Hardy is Jocelyn, forever pursuing "an image of his own creating", such proof can surely be found in the spate of beautiful love poems which Hardy wrote for a dead woman he had not loved for thirty years. He did not write them for the woman she had become, nor for the girl she had been, but for the image he had retained of that girl and of what he had made of that image, for those elements of himself which he had added. . . .'
41. The remarks that follow are indebted in part to *Hardy's Love Poems*, ed. Carl J. Weber (London: Macmillan, 1963), pp. 1–103.
42. Cf. Dryden's translation (IV, p. 26ff):

> Since Sichaeus was untimely slain
> This only man is able to subvert
> The fix'd foundations of my stubborn heart
> And to confess my frailty, to my shame
> Somewhat I find within, if not the same
> Too like the sparkles of my former flame.

Hardy echoes the last phrase in *Jude the Obscure* (II, ch. 11), where Jude, on the rebound from Arabella, seeks and finds the words 'Thither J. F.' he had engraved years before on a milestone between Marygreen and Christminster and feels his soul ignited by 'a spark of the old fire'. See p. 208.
43. The phrase is from a letter from Hardy to Florence Henniker on 17 December 1912 (*One Rare Fair Woman*, p. 155); see also the letter to Mrs Henniker of 3 June 1914, where Hardy speaks of Emma's 'latter years, when her mind was a little unhinged at times, and she showed unreasonable dislikes' (p. 160). Robert Gittings's *Thomas Hardy's Later Years*, which appeared after this chapter was written, confirms a failure of sympathy on Hardy's part, not only toward Emma but toward Florence as well. See esp. pp. 137–214.

NOTES FOR CHAPTER 4: 'TWICE-OVER CANNOT BE'

1. Millgate, *Hardy: His Career as a Novelist*, p. 23. The discussion that follows is indebted to Millgate's fine study, as well as to Kramer's *Thomas Hardy: The Forms of Tragedy*, esp. Chs 1, 4, 6, and 7; also to Herbert J. Muller, *The Spirit of Modern Tragedy* (New York: Knopf, 1956) pp. 3, 17, 26–9, 244–66, 211–35.
2. See Millgate, *Hardy: His Career as a Novelist*, p. 114: 'It was in *The Hand of Ethelberta*, with its multiplicity of settings and social levels, that [Hardy] apparently attempted for the first time to incorporate architecture more or less systematically as an element in an overall value-system.'

3. *Thomas Hardy* (London: Longman, 1961) p. 10. See also C. J. P. Beatty, 'The Part Played by Architecture in the Life and Work of Thomas Hardy (with Particular Reference to the Novels)' (unpublished dissertation, University of London, 1963).

4. The phrase is from Shelley's *Revolt of Islam*, VIII, 6.

5. The title of the first English edition of the novel – *A Laodicean; or The Castle of the de Stancys. A Story of Today* – suggests an equal prominence for heroine and building.

6. The same shift occurs between *Under the Greenwood Tree*, in which the 'modern' Fancy Day is reinstated within her traditional community, and *The Return* and *The Woodlanders*, in both of which the homecomer is left alienated from family and old friends.

7. See pp. 41ff. for a discussion of Hardy's interest in the sacrament of Baptism.

8. Though Hardy does not actually use the words of the service here, he seems to have them in mind, just as earlier (ch. 2) he used the denunciatory 53rd Psalm to comment on Swithin's neglect of choir practice in order to work on his sidereal calculations. The stanza from which Hardy quoted (his quotation is underlined) is as follows:

The wicked fools must sure suppose that God is but a name
This gross mistake their practice shows, since virtue all disclaim
The Lord look'd down from heaven's high tow'r, the sons of men to view
To see if any own'd his pow'r, or truth or justice knew
But all, he saw, were backwards gone, degen'rate grown, and base
None for religion car'd not one of all the sinful race.

9. Cf. Hardy's note of November 1880 (*Life*, p. 146): 'If Comte had introduced Christ among the worthies in his calendar it would have made Positivism tolerable to thousands who, from position, family connection, or early education, now decry what in their heart of hearts they hold to contain the germs of a true system.'

10. *Personal Writings*, pp. 216–17; see pp. 55ff. above.

11. For a useful summary, see Robert Schweik, 'Character and Fate in Hardy's *Mayor of Casterbridge*', *Nineteenth Century Fiction*, 21 (1966) 249. Among more recent critics, J. Hillis Miller (*Thomas Hardy: Distance and Desire*) has argued that in general Hardy's characters lack free will, Roy Morrell (*Thomas Hardy: The Will and the Way*) that they are responsible for their actions.

12. See Miller, *Hardy: Distance and Desire*, pp. 162, 259–60; Beatty, 'The Part Played by Architecture', pp. 442–92. The discussion that follows is a revision and extension of Peter J. Casagrande and Charles Lock, 'The Name "Henchard"', *Thomas Hardy Society Review*, 1 (1978) pp. 115–18.

13. The phrase is used throughout the novel to describe the demise of both persons and buildings: for example, in Henchard's description of the effects of his illness (ch. 12); in Henchard's account of the effect of his threats on Lucetta's health (ch. 35); by Hardy in his notes of 1912 on the fate of some of the old buildings of Dorchester (ch. 4).

14. See Purdy, *Hardy: A Bibliographical Study*, p. 53. In *The Mayor*, High Place Hall is located at the centre of Casterbridge.

15. Titled 'Reception of L. M. Andors at Dorchester by J. S. W. S. E. Drux Esq.,

High Sheriff of Dorset. 1840'. Vertical File no. 1: 'Dorchester Before 1900'.
16. See John Hutchins, *The History and Antiquities of the County of Dorset*, 3rd edn (London, 1861–73) vol. II, p. 546.
17. The exact date of demolition is not certain, though 1849 seems the most likely. See Casagrande and Lock, in *Thomas Hardy Society Review*, 1, (1978) 118, note 5.
18. See Hutchins, *History and Antiquities of Dorset*, vol. II, p. 353. I have been unable to determine William Lewis Hennings's lineage.
19. Beth Bohling, in 'Why "Michael Henchard"?', *English Journal*, 55 (1966) 203–7, suggests that 'Henchard' derives from '"hencher", someone who throws in an underhand motion, jerking the arm against the haunch.' This seems appropriate, according to Bohling, 'since Henchard, like a hencher, "throws" or acts without forethought, as in the impulsive sale of his wife'. Charles F. Hofling, in *Comprehensive Psychiatry*, 9 (1968) 428–39, noting that Henchard's given name had been James throughout the first draft of *The Mayor*, argues that since James Henchard is a masculinization of Jemima Hardy, the name of Hardy's mother, 'there seems a distinct possibility that the original name of the hero was influenced by [Hardy's] unconsciously associating to the names of his own family'. That Hardy probably went to his copy of Hutchins' *History and Antiquities of Dorset* (now in the Dorset County Museum) for the name of his hero is suggested by the fact that on the same page (vol. II, p. 353) on which is to be found the name 'William Lewis Henning' Hardy underlined the name 'Stansbie'. Farfrae's original name was Alan Stansbie (see Purdy, *Thomas Hardy: A Bibliographical Study*, p. 52).
20. 'A Man' was first published in *Poems of the Past and the Present* (1901). J. O. Bailey, in *The Poetry of Thomas Hardy*, pp. 169–70, suggests that the initials H. of M. refer to George Hand of Melbury Osmund, Hardy's maternal grandfather, or to his father or paternal grandfather, Hardy of Mellstock. The two letters also figure, of course, in the name Michael Henchard.
21. See fos 15, 17, 19, and 29 of the manuscript of *The Mayor* (in the Dorset County Museum). Though missing pages make it impossible to be sure, Hardy seems to have retained the identity of Henchard as a stonemason until the fourth chapter.
22. This is also the locale of the Trenchard Mansion; the Hangman's Cottage still stands north of the former sites of the Mansion and of Hardy's temporary residence on Glyde Path Road.
23. See Julian Moynahan, '*The Mayor of Casterbridge* and the Old Testament's First Book of Samuel: A Study in Some Literary Relationships', *PMLA*, 71 (1956) 118–30.
24. Schweik, in *Nineteenth Century Fiction*, 21, p. 249.
25. It is another aspect of the 'local' and yet universal quality of *The Mayor* that the name Abel Whittle, which most readers probably regard as mainly Biblical in origin, actually belonged to a man who died in October 1885, and whose tomb still stands, beside the tomb of his father, also named Abel Whittle (d. Oct 1863), near the entrance to Sherborne Abbey, Dorset. The inscription on the tomb is from the 23rd Psalm: 'I will fear no evil for thou art with me.' I am indebted to my wife, Pamela, for this observation.
26. This oversight is most strikingly evident in discussions of the genesis and composition of *Jude*. See Purdy, *Hardy: A Bibliographical Study*, pp. 87–90; Robert C. Slack, 'The Text of Hardy's *Jude the Obscure*', *Nineteenth Century*

Fiction, XI (1957) 261–75; John Paterson, 'The Genesis of *Jude the Obscure*', *Studies in Philology*, (1960) 87–98; and Patricia Ingham, 'The Evolution of *Jude the Obscure*', *Review of English Studies*, n.s. 27 (1976) 27–37, 159–69. In none of these discussions is *Tess* mentioned as a possible model for or influence on *Jude*.

27. 'Study of Thomas Hardy', in *Phoenix*, ed. McDonald, p. 488.

28. *Thomas Hardy: The Novels and Stories* (Cambridge, Mass.: Harvard University Press, 1949) p. 142.

29. The quotation is from Lawrence's 'Study of Thomas Hardy', in *Phoenix*, p. 489. For a brief discussion of Gosse's dislike for *Jude*, see Gittings, *Thomas Hardy's Later Years*, p. 80. Gittings also notes (pp. 63–78) the common origins of the two novels, 'in a remote yet intimate past, of people, events, and family traits'.

30. Harold Child, *Thomas Hardy* (New York: Holt, 1916) p. 75. Child adds 'His mind is far above his station; his passions keep him from rising to the level of his mind.'

31. Ibid., p. 76.

32. *Thomas Hardy: A Critical Study* (London: Martin Secker, 1935) pp. 113–14.

33. In 'The Tree of Knowledge', where he urges instruction in sexual matters for the young of both sexes. Repr. in *Life and Art*, ed. Ernest Brennecke (New York: Greenberg, 1925) pp. 113–14.

34. The titles in brackets are made to imitate, with appropriate changes, the titles of the comparable segment of the other novel, so as to illustrate the similar geographical and psychic movements in the two novels.

35. The theme of regeneration in *Tess* has been discussed frequently. See Allen Brick, 'Paradise and Consciousness in Hardy's *Tess*', *Nineteenth Century Fiction*, 17 (1962) 115–34; Langdon Elsbree, 'Tess and the Local Cerelia', *Philological Quarterly*, 45 (1961) 606–8; and Henry Kozicki, 'Myths of Redemption in Hardy's *Tess of the d'Urbervilles*', *Papers on Language and Literature*, 10 (1974) 150–8.

36. Hardy borrowed from his favourite Intimations Ode to describe in significantly different ways both Tess's wise and Jude's foolish attitude to things past. Tess, appalled at her family's bad luck, is one for whom 'there was ghastly satire in the poet's lines – "Not in utter nakedness / But trailing clouds of glory do we come."' Jude, promised Latin grammars by the deceitful Vilbert, smiles 'with that singularly beautiful irradiation which is seen to spread on young faces at the inception of some glorious idea, as if a supernatural lamp were held inside their transparent natures, giving rise to the flattering fancy that *heaven lies about them* then' (*JO*, I, ch. 4; emphasis added). Later, when his Christminster dream is sullied by Arabella, the 'supernatural lamp' will have dimmed: 'He . . . confronted the outmost lamps of the town [Christminster] – some of those lamps which had sent into the sky *the gleam and the glory* that caught his strained gaze in his days of dreaming, so many years ago. They wink their yellow eyes at him dubiously, and though they had been awaiting him all these years in disappointment at his tarrying, they did not much want him now' (II, ch. 1; emphasis added).

37. The contrast between Jude and Tess is sharp here: Alec's newly found faith is utterly overthrown by Tess, with the result great distress to Alec; Jude enjoys no such revenge on Arabella. Hardy devoted a whole 'phase' of Tess's story ('The Convert') to Alex's conversion and relapse, and less than a page to Arabella's.

Select Bibliography

See Note on the Texts, pp. x–xi, for titles of works by Hardy most frequently cited in my text.

Abrams, Meyer H., *Natural Supernaturalism: Tradition and Revolution in Romantic Literature* (New York: W. W. Norton, 1971).

Babb, Howard, 'Setting and Theme in *Far from the Madding Crowd*', *Journal of English Literary History*, 30 (1963) 147–61.

Bailey, J. O., *Poetry of Thomas Hardy: A Handbook and Commentary* (Chapel Hill, NC: University of North Carolina Press, 1970).

Beach, Joseph Warren, *The Technique of Thomas Hardy* (Chicago: University of Chicago Press, 1922).

Beatty, C. J. P., 'The Part Played by Architecture in the Life and Work of Thomas Hardy (with Particular Reference to the Novels)' (unpublished dissertation, University of London, 1963).

Brick, Allen, 'Paradise and Consciousness in Hardy's *Tess*', *Nineteenth Century Fiction*, 17 (1962) 115–34.

Casagrande, Peter J., 'Hardy's Wordsworth: A Record and a Commentary', *English Literature in Transition*, 20 (1977) 210–37.

—— and Charles Lock, 'The Name "Henchard"', *Thomas Hardy Society Review*, 1 (1978) 115–18.

Child, Harold, *Thomas Hardy* (New York: Holt, 1916).

Cox, R. G. (ed.), *Thomas Hardy: The Critical Heritage* (London: Routledge & Kegan Paul, 1970).

Danby, John E., '*Under the Greenwood Tree*', *Critical Quarterly*, 1 (1959) 5–13.

Elliott, G. R., 'Spectral Etchings in the Poetry of Thomas Hardy', *PMLA*, 43 (1938) 1185–95.

Elsbree, Langdon, 'Tess and the Local Cerelia', *Philological Quarterly*, 45 (1961) 606–8.

Frye, Northrop, *Anatomy of Criticism: Four Essays* (Princeton, NJ: Princeton University Press, 1957).

Gittings, Robert, *Young Thomas Hardy* (Boston, Mass.: Little, Brown, 1975; London: Heinemann, 1975).

——, *Thomas Hardy's Later Years* (Boston, Mass.: Little, Brown, 1978).

Guerard, Albert J., *Thomas Hardy: The Novels and Stories* (Cambridge, Mass.: Harvard University Press, 1949).

Halperin, John, *Egoism and Self-Discovery in the Victorian Novel* (New York: Burt Franklin, 1974).

Hardy, Thomas, *One Rare Fair Woman: Thomas Hardy's Letters to Florence Henniker, 1893–1922*, ed. Evelyn Hardy and F. B. Pinion (London: Macmillan, 1972).

——, *The Collected Letters of Thomas Hardy*, vol. 1: *1840–1892*, ed. Richard L. Purdy and Michael Millgate (Oxford: Clarendon Press, 1978).

——, *The Literary Notes of Thomas Hardy*, vol. 1, ed. Lennart Björk (Göteborg: Acta Universitatis Gothenburgensis, 1974).

Hardy's Love Poems, ed. Carl J. Weber (London: Macmillan, 1963).

Henkin, Leo J., *Darwinism in the English Novel, 1860–1910* (New York: Corporation Press, 1940).

Hofling, Charles F., 'Thomas Hardy and the Mayor of Casterbridge', *Comprehensive Psychiatry*, 9 (1968) 428–39.

Hunter, Robert G., *Shakespeare and the Comedies of Forgiveness* (New York: Columbia University Press, 1965).

Ingham, Patricia, 'The Evolution of *Jude the Obscure*', *Review of English Studies*, n.s., 27 (1976) 27–37, 159–69.

Jones, Lawrence O., 'Imitation and Expression in Thomas Hardy's Theory of Fiction', *Studies in the Novel*, 2 (1975) 507–25.

Kawin, Bruce F., *Telling It Again and Again: Repetition in Literature and Film* (Ithaca, NY: Cornell University Press, 1972).

Kierkegaard, Søren, *Repetition: An Essay in Experimental Psychology*, trs. Walter Lowrie (Princeton, NJ: Princeton University Press, 1946).

Kozicki, Henry, 'Myths of Redemption in Hardy's *Tess of the d'Urbervilles*', *Papers on Language and Literature*, 10 (1974) 150–8.

Kramer, Dale, *Thomas Hardy: The Forms of Tragedy* (Detroit: Wayne State University Press, 1975; London: Macmillan, 1975).

Lawrence, D. H., 'Study of Thomas Hardy', in *Phoenix*, ed. Edward D. McDonald (New York: Viking, 1936).

McCann, Eleanor, 'Blind Will or Blind Hero: Philosophy and Myth in Hardy's *The Return of the Native*', *Criticism*, 3 (1961) 140–67.

Madden, William A., 'The Search for Forgiveness in some Nineteenth-Century Novels', *Comparative Literature Studies*, 2 (1966) 139–53.

Miles, Josephine, *Pathetic Fallacy in the Nineteenth Century* (Berkeley, Calif.: University of California Press, 1942).

Miller, J. Hillis, *Thomas Hardy: Distance and Desire* (Cambridge, Mass.: Harvard University Press, 1971).

Millgate, Michael, *Thomas Hardy: His Career as a Novelist* (New York: Random House, 1971; London: The Bodley Head, 1971).

Morrell, Roy, *The Will and the Way* (Kuala Lumpur: University of Malaya Press, 1965).

Moynahan, Julian, '*The Mayor of Casterbridge* and the Old Testament's First Book of Samuel: A Study in Some Literary Relationships', *PMLA*, 71 (1956) 118–30.

Muller, Herbert J., *The Spirit of Modern Tragedy* (New York: Alfred A. Knopf, 1965).

Paterson, John, '*The Return of the Native* as Anti-Christian Document', *Nineteenth Century Fiction*, 14 (1959) 111–27.

——, *The Making of 'The Return of the Native'*, University of California English Studies, no. 19 (Berkeley and Los Angeles, Calif., 1960).

——, 'The Genesis of *Jude the Obscure*', *Studies in Philology*, 57 (1960) 87–98.

Pinion, Frank B., *Thomas Hardy: Art and Thought* (London: Macmillan, 1977).

Priestley, Alma, 'Hardy's *Well-Beloved*: A Study in Failure', *Thomas Hardy Society Review* (1976) pp. 55–6.

Purdy, Richard L., *Thomas Hardy: A Bibliographical Study* (London: Oxford University Press, 1968). (First published 1954.)

Reed, John R., *Victorian Conventions* (Athens, Ohio: Ohio University Press, 1975).

Rutland, W. R., *Thomas Hardy: A Study of his Writings and their Background* (Oxford: Blackwell, 1938).

Schweik, Robert, 'The Ethical Structure of Hardy's *The Woodlanders*', *Archiv für das Studium der neueren Sprachen und Literaturen*, 211 (1974) 31–45.

——, 'Character and Fate in Hardy's *Mayor of Casterbridge*', *Nineteenth Century Fiction*, 21 (1966) 249–62.

Slack, Robert C., 'The Text of Hardy's *Jude the Obscure*', *Nineteenth Century Fiction*, 11 (1957) 261–75.

Southerington, F. R., *Hardy's Vision of Man* (London: Chatto and Windus, 1971).

Squires, Michael, *The Pastoral Novel: Studies in George Eliot, Thomas Hardy, and D. H. Lawrence* (Charlottesville: University Press of Virginia, 1974).

Steig, Michael, 'The Problems of Literary Values in Two Early Hardy Novels', *Texas Studies in Language and Literature*, 12 (1970) 55–62.

Stevenson, Lionel, *Darwin Among the Poets* (Chicago: University of Chicago Press, 1932).

Stewart, J. I. M., *Thomas Hardy* (London: Allen Lane, 1971).

Trilling, Lionel, 'On the Modern Element in Modern Literature' (1961), in Irving Howe (ed.), *The Idea of the Modern* (New York: Horizon Press, 1967).

Watt, Ian, *The Rise of the Novel* (Berkeley, Calif.: University of California Press, 1965).

Weber, Carl J., *Hardy of Wessex*, rev. edn (New York: Columbia University Press, 1965).

Webster, Harvey Curtis, *On a Darkling Plain* (Chicago: University of Chicago Press, 1947).

Weisinger, Herbert, *Tragedy and the Paradox of the Fortunate Fall* (East Lansing: Michigan State University Press, 1953).

Willey, Basil, *More Nineteenth Century Studies* (London: Chatto and Windus, 1963).

Williams, Raymond, *The Country and the City* (London: Chatto and Windus, 1973).

Wing, George, '*Edwin Drood* and *Desperate Remedies*: Prototypes of Detective Fiction in 1870', *Studies in English Literature*, 13 (1973) 667–87.

Young, Karl, *The Drama of the Medieval Church* (London: Oxford University Press, 1933).

Index

Hardy's prose works are indexed under their titles; his poems are grouped together under the heading 'Poems'.

Abercrombie, Lascelles, 201
Architecture
  Hardy's interests while writing *The Mayor of Casterbridge*, 184
  in *Tess* and *Jude*, 203–5
  preservation versus restoration, 57, 59
  providing symbolic settings, 175
  recurring importance, 172
  symbolism in *The Mayor of Casterbridge*, 183, 186–7
  theme of restoration, 3, 5
  see also Restoration, architectural

Baptism
  discussion in *A Laodicean*, 178
  Hardy's beliefs, 13, 44–5
Bastow, Henry Robert, 44–7
Beatty, C. J. P., 185
Beauty, Hardy's perception in ugliness, 38
Bernardin de St Pierre: *Paul and Virginia*, 18
Brown, Douglas, 173
Bunsen, C. J., 42

Character types, 116–18, 233 (n.2)
  'nostalgic idealists', 5
  repeated use, 170–1
Children in Hardy's novels, 114
Christian belief, *see* Religious beliefs
Christmas party theme, 129
Church restoration work, *see* 'Memories of Church Restoration'; Restoration, architectural
Coleridge, Hartley, 35

Comedy, increasingly uncongenial to Hardy, 34
Community values, in *Under the Greenwood Tree*, 82
Crickmay, G. R., 25

Dante, derivation in *The Hand of Ethelberta*, 122
Defoe, Daniel, 120, 124
Desperate Remedies, 74–81, 155
  autobiographical aspects, 86–7
  publication, 62
  review in *Spectator*, 62, 80
  written at Higher Bockhampton, 30
Deteriorism in Hardy's work, 12–60
  evidence from 1870s notes, 34
  formed by Hardy's experience, 220
  in *The Mayor of Casterbridge*, 184–5
  in the poems, 63–9
  roots, 7
  theme in poems and novels 1867–74, 62
Dorchester
  destruction of Trenchard Mansion, 186–7, 190
  Hardy's education in, 19, 20
  Hardy's return to, 5
  occupancy of Max Gate, 33
Dryden, John: *Virgil*, 18
Dugdale, Florence (*later* Florence Hardy), 22
Dynasts, The, 50

Experience, bearing on literary development, 12, 220

Far from the Madding Crowd, 97–114
  architectural theme, 173
  aversion to women, 30
  Boldwood's deterioration, 105–6
  character of Gabriel Oak, 97
  development of Bathsheba, 99–105
  effect on Hardy's social status, 27–8
  emergence of 'Wessex', 13–14
  portrayal of women's 'infirmity', 101
  publication, 62
  rationality of Gabriel Oak, 106–8,
    110
  remedies for defects in human
    nature, 96
  restoration theme, 2
  Troy's ambiguous rationality, 112
  work of a 'house decorator', 124
Frye, Northrop, 6

Gifford, Emma (*later* Emma Hardy),
  22, 27, 61
  appeal of naivety, 90
  Hardy's attitude toward 'Poems of
    1912–13', 160–1
  Hardy's hopes of renewal through
    marriage to, 88–9
  influence of courtship and marriage
    on Hardy's work, 86
  introduction to Hardy's family, 126
  need for lenient judgement of, 41
Gittings, Robert, 22, 41, 155
Gothic artistry, 56–7
Grove, Agnes, 22
Guerard, Albert, 200

Hand of Ethelberta, The, 28, 115, 118–25
  apparent departure from previous
    themes, 118
  architectural allusions, 173
  character of Ethelberta, 119–20
  seen as attempt to hide Hardy's
    origins, 123–4
  uprooted native theme, 30
  written at Swanage, 31
Harding, Louisa, 40
Hardy, Jemima, 16, 18
  family background, 124
  model for Mrs Yeobright, 126
  visits after Hardy's marriage, 32

Hardy, Thomas
  abandons architectural career, 52
  as church restorer, 13
    see also 'Memories of Church
      Restoration'
  assistant to Crickmay, 25
  attitude to Emma in 'Poems of 1912–
    13', 160–1
  break with background, 28–9
  childhood, 16–20
  childlessness, 35, 62
  choice of vocation, 61–2, 90
  commuting between Dorset and
    London (1867–70), 25
  considering ordination, 41, 47–8
  decline of family, 16–17
  defence of his work, 219
  departure from and return to Dorset,
    12, 13
  encounters with loss, 7
  failure of first marriage, 7, 13, 27–41
  frequent changes of home (1874–85),
    33
  influence of personality on novels, 12
  involvement with Dorchester's
    buildings, 187–9
  late physical maturity, 21
  marriage to
    (1) Emma Gifford, 16, 27
    (2) Florence Dugdale, 22
  moves from romantic comedy to
    tragic realism, 170
  need for Dorset when writing, 24–5,
    30–1
  reliance on native surroundings, 6
  repeated use of character types,
    170–1
  social ambiguities, 124–5
  'truth and beauty' ideal, 23–4
  unwillingness to grow up, 17–21
Hatfield (Herts.), Hardy's visits to, 18,
  24
Henniker, Florence, 22, 160, 162
Henning, William Lewis, 187
Hicks, John, 25
Higher Bockhampton, 5, 7, 13
  Hardy's grandmother's recollections
    of, 15
  model for Egdon, 126

Higher Bockhampton (*contd*)
  sense of obliteration of childhood,
    14–15
  visits after first marriage, 32
Homecoming, *see* Return motif
Humanism, evidences of, in *Two on a
  Tower*, 181

Indiscretion in the Life of an Heiress, An, 70
  see also 'The Poor Man and the Lady'

Jersey, home of Hardy's ancestors, 25
Johnson, Samuel, *Rasselas*, 18
Jowett, Benjamin, 42
Jude the Obscure, 115, 199–218
  character of Phillotson, 214
    its deterioration, 197
  compared with *Tess*, 199, 222
  complex secondary characters, 211
  D. H. Lawrence's criticism of theme, 1
  pronounced element of suffering, 201
  religious aspects, 178
  restoration motif, 2
  satirical writing, 70

Laodicean, A, 115
  architectural aspects, 173
  as forerunner of *The Return*, 2
  importance of Stancy Castle, 177
  regeneration-through-baptism
    theme, 178
  restoration theme, 2, 176
  secularized faith, 43
  solution to creation–preservation
    problem, 177
Last, Isaac, 20
Lawrence, D. H., 1, 74, 200
Life, The, 14–15
  written as self-justification, 63
London, Hardy's years in, 13, 61
  his dislike of, 22–3

Martin, Lady Augusta, 16, 18–19
Mayor of Casterbridge, The, 115, 183–99
  architectural symbolism, 183, 186–7
  atonement theme, 193–4
  Hardy's concurrent architectural
    interests, 184

Henchard and Farfrae compared, 9
Henchard foreshadowed in *Desperate
  Remedies*, 79
importance of Trenchard Mansion,
  Dorchester, 186–7
redemption theme, 195
religious aspects, 178
restoration motif, 2, 176
turn from nature to architecture,
  173–4
'Memories of Church Restoration', 56,
  153, 175, 184–5
Mill, John Stuart, 108, 112
Miller, J. Hillis, 30, 185
Milton, John, 121–2
Morality play, *Desperate Remedies* as,
  74–5, 80
Morley, Lord, 42
Morrell, Roy, 8, 113
Moule, Horace, 42, 46, 90

Nature
  imagery in *Tess*, 203, 205
  in novels of return, 5
  in *The Woodlanders*, 143–4, 151
  J. S. Mill's essay, 108–9
  ruin of, 63
  three aspects in *Far from the Madding
    Crowd*, 98, 110–11
Newman, John Henry, Cardinal, 46, 47
Nostalgia, power over Hardy's actions,
  40

Pair of Blue Eyes, A, 85–95
  architectural theme, 53, 173
  as forerunner of *Madding Crowd* and
    Tess, 2
  autobiographical aspects, 86–7, 91
  aversion to women, 30
  publication, 62
  return to Dorset to complete, 30–1
  struggle against defective natures,
    96–7
Paterson, Helen, 22
Poems
  link with novels of 1867–74, 62
  of 1860s, 63–9
  'Poems of 1912–13', 160–9
  Wessex Poems, 64

'After the Journey', 165

'Afternoon Service at Mellstock', 41

'Amabel', 64

'As 'Twere Tonight', 89

'At a Bridal', 48

'At Castle Boterel', 166

'At Waking', 26

'Beeny Cliff', 167

'Childhood Among the Ferns', 17, 26

'Concerning his Old Home', 31–2

'A Death-Day Recalled', 167

'Discouragement', 48, 50, 63

'Ditty (E. L. G.)', 88

'Domicilium', 14–15, 17

'Dream of the City Shopwoman', 48, 66–7

'A Dream or No', 162, 163–4

'A Drizzling Easter Morning', 49

'For Life I Had Never Cared Greatly', 89

'The Going', 161, 162, 166

'Hap', 48, 65

'The Haunter', 162

'Heiress and Architect',.48, 55, 65, 173

'Her Dilemma', 173

'Her Initials', 67

'His Visitor', 162, 163

'I Found Her Out There', 162

'I Was the Midmost', 86, 90

'The Impercipient (at a Cathedral Service)', 48

'In a Wood', 50

'A January Night, 1879', 32, 36, 163

'The Lacking Sense', 50

'Lizbie Browne', 21

'Louie', 22

'Louisa in the Lane', 22

'A Man (In Memory of H. of M.)', 190–1

'The Mother Mourns', 50

'The Musical Box', 37

'Neutral Tones', 68

'Night in the Old Home', 49

'Old Excursions', 161

'Old Furniture', 58–9

'On Sturminster Footbridge', 37

'Overlooking the River Stour', 37

'The Oxen', 41

'The Phantom Horsewoman', 166

'Places', 162, 166

'Postponement', 68

'Rain on a Grave', 162

'Ruined Maid', 64

'St Launce's Revisited', 167

'The Self-Unseeing', 17, 26

'The Seven Times', 89

'She Opened the Door', 22, 88

'She, to Him: I', 68

'She, to Him: II', 68

'She, to Him: III', 58, 68

'A Sign-Seeker', 49

'The Sleep-Worker', 50

'The Spell of the Rose', 162, 167

'The Temporary the All', 64

'To Meet, or Otherwise', 101

'To Outer Nature', 50–1

'To Sincerity', 49

'The Two Men', 67, 69

'Unkept Good Fridays', 49, 183

'The Voice', 162, 163, 164

'The Walk', 162

'Welcome Home', 26

'Wessex Heights', 63

'When Oats are Reaped', 22

'Where the Picnic Was', 162, 167, 168

'A Young Man's Exhortation', 69, 72

'Your Last Drive', 162

'Yuletide in a Younger World', 41

'Poor Man and the Lady, The', 61, 62, 69–74, 81

   autobiographical aspects, 86–7

   based on Defoe, 120

   dramatic satire, 69

   written at Higher Bockhampton, 30

   see also An Indiscretion in the Life of an Heiress

Proust, Marcel, 1

Redemption motif

   as spiritual homecoming, 48–9

   defined, 3

   Hardy's loss of faith, 43

   in *Desperate Remedies*, 80

   in *Mayor of Casterbridge*, 195

   in *Under the Greenwood Tree*, 81

Redemption motif (*contd*)
  non-theological, in *Two on a Tower*,
    182–3
Regeneration motif
  development through *Under the Green-
    wood Tree*, 81
  form in later novels, 115
  in *An Indiscretion*, 73
  in *Desperate Remedies*, 74
  secular belief in, 7
  Tess and *Jude* compared, 199–218
Religious beliefs, 7
  atonement theme in *The Mayor of
    Casterbridge*, 193–4
  attacked in *Two on a Tower*, 181
  baptism discussion in *A Laodicean*,
    178
  confirmation debate in *Two on a
    Tower*, 178, 181–2
  early church involvements of Hardy,
    41
  Hardy's rejection, 7, 13
  in *Tess* and *Jude*, 210–11
  primitive forms, 130
Remedy motif, definition of, 3
Restoration, architectural
  analogy with spiritual renewal, 87
  dichotomy of ideals, 175
  Hardy's scepticism, 52
  Hardy's work, 8, 52–60
  see also 'Memories of Church Resto-
    ration'
Restoration motif, 2
  architectural and moral, 2–3
  in novels of return, 4
  sequence of novels, 3–4
Return motif, 1, 2
  basic elements, 116–17
  contrasts in *The Return of the Native,
    Under the Greenwood Tree* and *The
    Woodlanders*, 144
  defined, 2
  development, 116
  in *The Hand of Ethelberta*, 118–25
  in *Jude*, 209
  in the 'Poems of 1912–13', 160–9
  in *Under the Greenwood Tree*, 81
  in *The Well-Beloved*, 155–9
  in *The Woodlanders*, 143–53

'looped orbit' image, 144
related to Hardy's break with
  background, 5
related to restoration motif, 170
sequence of novels, 3–4
symbolic of thwarted regeneration, 4
Return of the Native, The, 115, 126–43
  autobiographical aspects, 126, 127
  character of Johnny Nunsuch, 134–7
  Clym's mother-obsession, 131–4
  conflict of loyalties, 127
  evidence of resentment of mother,
    20
  Hardy's new idea of beauty, 38
  material collected on visit to
    Bockhampton, 32
  return motif, 1
  revised ending, 8–9, 157, 158
  role of Thomasin, 141–2
  significance of Mrs Yeobright's
    death, 131
  uprooted native theme, 30
  use of character of Christian Cantle,
    137–9

St George mummers' play, 129
St Juliot's Church, Cornwall, 52–3, 61,
  161, 164
Sequence of novels, 3–4
Sexuality
  examples in *Return of the Native*, 138–
    40
  Hardy's development, 22
  in *Jude* and *Tess*, 201–2
  of Sue in *Jude*, 211–12
Social satire, 118
Sparks, Rebecca, 22
Sparks, Tryphena, 61
Stephen, Leslie, 28, 29

Tess of the d'Urbervilles, 199–218
  irrecoverable innocence, 10
  relationship to *Jude* theme, 1, 199,
    222
  religious aspects, 43, 178
  restoration motif, 2
Trilling, Lionel, 6
Trumpet-Major, The, 115
  architectural aspects, 173

importance of Overcombe Mill, 176–7
restoration motif, 2, 175, 176
Turner, J. M. W., 54
Two on a Tower, 115, 179–83
  architectural aspects, 173
  confirmation debate, 178, 181–2
  influence seen of Lady Martin, 19
  non-theological redemption, 182–3
  religious attitude, 43
  restoration motif, 2, 176–7
  symbolism of Ring's Hill Speer, 178–9

Under the Greenwood Tree, 29, 81–5
  autobiographical aspects, 86–7
  aversion to women indicated, 30
  choir connections, 41
  inclusion of ancient hymn, 82–3
  models from personal experience, 85–6
  publication, 62
  replacement of religious values, 43
  return motif, 1
  similarity of conclusion to *The Trumpet-Major*, 176
  view of nature, 143
  written at High Bockhampton, 30

Watt, Ian, 120, 121
Well-Beloved, The, 115, 153–60

as sketch of Hardy's temperament, 22
  autobiographical aspects, 155
  influence seen of Lady Martin, 19–20
  Jocelyn Pierston's role, 155–60
  relationship to other 'return' novels, 117
  revised ending, 157
'Wessex', 11
  as enduring image of old order, 60
  emergence in *Far from the Madding Crowd*, 13–14
Wessex Poems, 64
Williams, Roland, 42
Women, Hardy's attitudes to, 22, 30, 41
Woodlanders, The, 29, 115, 143–53
  evidence of resentment of father, 20
  'Intrusive Parent' figure, 145
  Marty South and Grace Melbury compared, 9
  return motif, 1
    compared with *Return of the Native*, 128
  revised ending, 157–8
  uprooted native theme, 30
  views of nature, 143–4, 151
Wordsworth, William, 10–11, 36–7, 91, 93, 113–14, 231–2 (n. 25), 239 (n. 36)

Young, Karl, 130